District of Columbia Ancestors

A Guide to Records of the District of Columbia

District Court-House (Formerly City Hall)

Wesley E. Pippenger

HERITAGE BOOKS
2008

HERITAGE BOOKS
AN IMPRINT OF HERITAGE BOOKS, INC.

Books, CDs, and more—Worldwide

For our listing of thousands of titles see our website
at
www.HeritageBooks.com

Published 2008 by
HERITAGE BOOKS, INC.
Publishing Division
100 Railroad Ave. #104
Westminster, Maryland 21157

Copyright © 1997, 2000 Wesley E. Pippenger

All rights reserved. No part of this book may be reproduced or transmitted in any form or by any means, electronic or mechanical, including photocopying, recording or by any information storage and retrieval system without written permission from the author, except for the inclusion of brief quotations in a review.

International Standard Book Numbers
Paperbound: 978-1-58549-432-3
Clothbound: 978-0-7884-7539-9

DISTRICT OF COLUMBIA ANCESTORS

A Guide to Records of the District of Columbia

Table of Contents

List of Illustrations vii

Preface ix

Introduction xi
    GEOGRAPHIC HISTORY xi
    RECORDS HISTORY xiii
    GOVERNMENT HISTORY xiii
        Mayors of the City of Washington xvi

Census Schedules and City Directories 1
    CENSUS SCHEDULES 1
        1790 Census 1
        1800 Through 1870 Census 1
        1880 Census 1
        1890 Census 2
        1900 Census 2
        1910 and 1920 Census 2
        Census Enumeration Districts Descriptions 2
        Mortality Schedules 2
        Industrial Census Schedules 3
        Agriculture Census Schedules 3
        Other Census Schedules 3
        Finding Aids and Sources 4
    CITY DIRECTORIES 4

Probate, Guardianships & Apprenticeships 6
        Records of the District Court of the U.S., District of Columbia 6
        Will Records 6
        Guardianship Records 7
        Estate Administration Records 7
        Finding Aids and Sources 8
    APPRENTICESHIP INDENTURES 8

Real and Personal Property Records 11
    LAND RECORDS 11
        Original Proprietors 12
        Office of Public Buildings and Grounds 13
    REAL AND PERSONAL PROPERTY ASSESSMENTS 13
        Georgetown Assessments of 1783, 1793, 1798 13
        Federal Assessment of 1798 for the District of Columbia 13
        Georgetown Tax Assessments, 1800-1879 14
        Internal Revenue Assessments 14
    BUILDING PERMITS 14
    RECORDS OF HOUSES 15
    COMMISSIONERS AND PUBLIC BUILDINGS 15
    GEORGETOWN RECORDS 15
        Journals of Proceedings 16
        Officials and Employees 16
        Ordinances 16
        Tax Records 16

A Guide to Records of the District of Columbia

Marriage and Divorce Records 17
   MARRIAGE RECORDS 17
      Marriage Registers 17
      Canceled Marriage Licenses 17
      Minister Applications 18
   Miscellaneous Administrative Records 18
      Minister Licenses 18
   DIVORCE RECORDS 18
      Finding Aids and Sources 18

Birth and Death Records 23
   BIRTH RECORDS 23
      Return of a Still Birth 23
   DEATH RECORDS 24
      Foreign Deaths 24

Church Records 29
   BAPTIST 29
      First Baptist Church 29
      First Baptist Church 29
      Second Baptist Church 30
      E Street Baptist Church 30
   CATHOLIC 30
      St. Francis DeSales Catholic Church 30
      St. Mary's Catholic Church 30
      St. Matthew's Catholic Church 30
      St. Patrick's Catholic Church 30
      St. Peter's Roman Catholic Church 30
      [Holy] Trinity Catholic Church, Georgetown 31
   EPISCOPAL 31
      Church of the Ascension 31
      Church of the Epiphany 31
      Christ Protestant Episcopal Church, Washington Parish 32
      Christ Episcopal Church, Georgetown 32
      Grace Episcopal Church 32
      St. Alban's Protestant Episcopal Church 32
      St. John's Protestant Episcopal Church 32
      St. John's Protestant Episcopal Church, Washington 33
      St. Paul's Episcopal Church, Rock Creek Parish 33
      Trinity Protestant Episcopal Church 33
   LUTHERAN 34
      German Evangelical Lutheran Church 34
      St. Paul's English Lutheran Church 34
      Trinity German Evangelical Lutheran Church 34
   METHODIST EPISCOPAL 34
      Anacostia Methodist Episcopal Church 34
      Asbury Methodist Episcopal Church 34
      Dumbarton Avenue Methodist Episcopal Church, Georgetown 34
      Emory Methodist Church 35
      Foundry Methodist Episcopal Church 35
      Fourth Street Methodist Episcopal Church 35
      Israel Bethel African Methodist Episcopal Church 36

Table of Contents

John Wesley Church	36
Little Ebenezer Church	36
McKendree Chapel of the Methodist Episcopal Church	36
Mount Zion Church	36
Ryland Chapel of the Methodist Episcopal Church	37
Second Colored Wesleyan Church	37
Trinity Methodist Church	37
Union Bethel African Methodist Episcopal Church	37
Union Chapel Methodist Episcopal Church	37
Wesley Chapel of the Methodist Episcopal Church	38
METHODIST PROTESTANT	38
Congress Street Methodist Protestant Church	38
Central Methodist Protestant Church	38
First Methodist Protestant Church	38
PRESBYTERIAN	38
Central Presbyterian Church	38
Eastern Presbyterian Church	38
Eckington Presbyterian Church	39
F Street Presbyterian Church	39
Fifteenth Street Presbyterian Church	39
First Presbyterian Church	39
Fourth Presbyterian Church	39
Georgetown Presbyterian Church	40
Metropolitan Presbyterian Church	40
New York Avenue Presbyterian Church	40
Second Presbyterian Church	40
Seventh Street Presbyterian Church of Washington	40
Sixth Street Presbyterian Church	41
SOCIETY OF FRIENDS (QUAKER)	41
Friends Meeting House	41
UNITARIAN	41
First Unitarian Church	41
Other Church Finding Aids and Sources	41
Cemetery Records	43
CEMETERIES AND BURIAL GROUNDS	43
Adas Israel Cemetery	43
Baptist Cemetery	43
Battleground National Cemetery	43
Beckett's Burial Ground	43
Belts [Family] Burial Ground	44
Brightwood Cemetery	44
Cephas [Family] Burial Ground	44
Chapel's [Private] Burial Ground	44
[Georgetown] College Burial Ground	44
Columbian Harmony Cemetery	44
Congressional Cemetery	44
Convent Burial Ground	45
Dangerfield [Family] Burial Ground	45
Dean's [Private] Burial Ground	45
[Eastern] Methodist Cemetery	45
Ebenezer Cemetery	45

A Guide to Records of the District of Columbia

      Francis DeSales Cemetery 45
      Garden's [Private] Burial Ground 45
      Glenwood Cemetery 45
      Good Hope Burial Ground 46
      Graceland Cemetery 46
      Hebbon's [Family] Burial Ground 46
      Hillsdale Burial Ground 46
      Holmead's Burial Ground 46
      Holy Rood Cemetery 46
      Methodist Burial Ground 47
      Howard's [Private] Burial Ground 47
      Jenkins' [Private] Burial Ground 47
      Jones' Chapel Burial Ground 47
      McPhearson's [Private] Burial Ground 47
      Macedonia Burial Ground 47
      Methodist Cemetery 47
      Moore's [Family] Burial Ground 47
      Mount Olivet Cemetery 47
      Mount Pleasant Plain Cemetery 47
      Mount Zion Cemetery 47
      Oak Hill Cemetery 48
      Payne's Burial Ground 48
      Presbyterian Cemetery 48
      Prospect Hill Cemetery 49
      Quaker Burial Ground 49
      Rock Creek Cemetery 49
      Rosemont Cemetery 50
      St. Elizabeth's Hospital Cemeteries 50
      St. Mary's [German] Catholic Cemetery 50
      St. Matthew's Catholic Cemetery 50
      St. Patrick's Catholic Cemetery 51
      St. Peter's Catholic Cemetery 51
      Scaggs' [Family] Burial Ground 51
      Shoemaker's Farm [Family] Burial Ground 51
      Smith's [Family] Burial Ground 51
      Soldiers' Home Cemetery 51
      Washington Asylum Burial Ground 51
      Washington Hebrew Congregation Cemetery 51
      Western Burial Ground 51
      Woodlawn Cemetery 51
      Other Finding Aids and Sources 52
   DISINTERMENT PERMITS 52

Court Records - Record Group 21 53
   UNITED STATES CIRCUIT COURT FOR THE DISTRICT OF COLUMBIA 53
      Law, Appellate and Criminal Records 53
      Chancery Records 54
      Bankruptcy Records 54
      Habeas Corpus Records 55
      Slavery Records 55
      Lien Law Records 55
      Marriage Records 56

Table of Contents

    UNITED STATES DISTRICT COURT FOR THE DISTRICT OF COLUMBIA 56
        General Records 56
        Admiralty Records 56
        Copyright Records 57
    UNITED STATES CRIMINAL COURT FOR THE DISTRICT OF COLUMBIA 57
        General Records 57
    UNITED STATES SUPREME COURT FOR THE DISTRICT OF COLUMBIA 57
        General Records 58
        Law Records 58
        Equity Records 58
        Criminal Records 59
        Habeas Corpus and Extradition Records 59
        District Court Cases 59
        Lien Law Records 60
        Bankruptcy Records 60
        Appointments 60
        Licenses 60
        Naturalization Records 60
                Abbreviations Used 61
        Justice of the Peace Records 62
        Probate Records 62
        Appellate Jurisdiction 62

Newspapers 63
    Finding Aids and Sources 64

Miscellaneous Records 65
    GENERAL GOVERNMENT 65
        Appointments 65
        Architectural Drawings 65
        Articles of Incorporation 65
        Bawdy Houses 65
        Board of Architects 65
        Board of Health 65
        Children 65
        Docket Book 66
        Employment 66
        Engineer Department 66
        Habeas Corpus 66
        Jail and Prison Records 66
        Licenses 66
        Manufactured Goods 66
        Police Records 67
        Register of Licensed Physicians and Midwives 67
        Tax Assessments 67
    MILITARY 67
                Pension and Bounty Land 68
        REVOLUTIONARY WAR 69
                Pension Application Files and Bounty Land Warrants 69
        WAR OF 1812 69
            1812 War Militia 69
            1812 Bounty Land Warrants 69

v

# A Guide to Records of the District of Columbia

```
            1812 Pension Application Files ................................. 69
        CIVIL WAR .................................................. 69
            Civil War Pension Application Files ........................... 69
            Other Civil War Topics ..................................... 70
            Soldiers' Home ........................................... 70
            Washington Light Infantry Battalion of Volunteers ................ 70
            Veterans' Census Schedules ................................. 70
        WORLD WAR I ................................................ 71
        OTHER MILITARY ............................................. 71
            District of Columbia Militia .................................. 71
            Register of Militia ......................................... 71
            Registers of Cadet Admissions, 1800-1953 ..................... 71
    Military Finding Aids and Sources ..................................... 72
    EMANCIPATION AND MANUMISSION ................................... 72
        Freedmen's Records ............................................ 74
    EDUCATION ....................................................... 74
        George Town Academy .......................................... 74
        Columbian College ............................................. 74
        Howard University ............................................. 75
    BUSINESSES ...................................................... 75
        Freedman's Savings and Trust Company ........................... 75
```

Collections 76
    MANUSCRIPT COLLECTIONS 76
        Library of Congress 76
        Maryland Historical Society 76
        D.A.R. Library 76
        Historical Society of Washington, D.C. 77
    GENEALOGIES 77
    MAPS AND PLAT BOOKS 77
    Finding Aids and Sources 78

Research Locations 84

Index 91

List of Illustrations

Figure 1 - "Plan of Hamburgh," drawn by E.F.M. Faehtz (1874). xvii
Figure 2 - "Plan of Carrollsburg," drawn by E.F.M. Faehtz (1874). xviii
Figure 3 - "Sketch of Washington in Embryo," by E.F.M. Faehtz and F.W. Pratt (1874),
  Showing the Division of Land on the Site of the National Capitol in 1791. xix
Figure 4 - "Map of Georgetown," Taken From Endpapers of A Portrait of Old Georgetown.
  Shows Additions and Both Old and New Street Names. xx
Figure 5 - "A Map of George Town With The Additions, 1814." Original in the Library
  of Congress, Geography and Maps Division. xxi
Figure 6 - "Map of the City of Washington, 1892." Shows Square Number For Use in
  Researching Land Records. xxii
Figure 7 - "Map of Washington City, District of Columbia, 1876." xxiv
Figure 8 - Sample Page from Guardianship Case File, No. 43, Maria C. Sutphin, 1879 9
Figure 9 - Apprenticeship Indenture for Sarah Ann Fletcher to Joseph LaFontane, 1840,
  Book H.C.N. No. 5, folio 261. 10
Figure 10 - Canceled Marriage License Issued to Herman W. Herndon and
  Sarah F. Van Gender, 1927 16
Figure 11 - Minister License for Charles J.S. Mayo, 1896, Licenses Book 2, Page 24. 19
Figure 12 - Record of Marriage, Matthew O'Callaghn to Mary C. Cleary, 1889,
  Marriage Record Book 26, Page 237. 19
Figure 13 - Return of a Marriage (Front Side), From Marriage Returns, Book 1, Number 112. 20
Figure 14 - Return of a Marriage (Back Side), From Marriage Returns, Book 1, Number 112. 21
Figure 15 - Minister Application of Isaac Clark, of the Congregational Church, 1896,
  Loose Ministers Applications 22
Figure 16 - Certificate of Death for William Tell Steiger, 1889, Foreign Death Certificates,
  Book 1, Number 49. 25
Figure 17 - Birth Certificate for Frank Monnier Richard, 1901, Loose Returns of a Birth,
  Number 108245. 26
Figure 18 - Addendum to Birth Certificate for Frank Monnier Richard, 1901. Note the
  Form Provides No Space for Entry of Child's Name and a Supplement Report
  Was Necessary. 27
Figure 19 - Return of a Still Birth, Infant Shepherd, 1874, Book 1. 28
Figure 20 - David C. Catlett, Disinterment Permit Within Payne's Burial Ground, 1914. 42
Figure 21 - Central Portion of the Ellicott Plan of Washington, 1792. 79
Figure 22 - "View of the City of Washington in 1792." 80
Figure 23 - "Defenses of Washington: Extract of Military Map of N.E. Virginia," 1865,
  by War Department, Engineer Bureau. 82
Figure 24 - Street Map of the City of Washington. Courtesy of A. Zenta,
  National Capitol Planning Commission. 86

Preface

Welcome to the Nation's Capitol! With use of this guide it is hoped you will soon see that the District of Columbia has experienced an exciting history. It's a history that started in the 1790's with a bunch of wishful speculators, financiers, political figureheads, and common folk, and can be extracted from the many extant public and private records that are spread amongst a number of records repositories throughout the Washington, D.C. metropolitan area.

People that founded the city came from many places and walks of life, and represented divergent cultural upbringing. Much evidence of this can be learned from studying the records left behind. While efforts were underway to establish the new Federal city, the rest of the world was whirring with activity. For instance, in 1800, Congress divided the Northwest Territory to form Ohio and Indiana; Rembrant Peale painted a portrait of Thomas Jefferson; Napoleon conquered Italy; Beethoven composed Symphony No. 1 in C Major; fireboats were first used in New York Harbor; and a yellow fever epidemic killed about 80,000 people in Spain. Events of the time that might be closer to our hearts include: the 4-tined fork came into common use in American homes (replacing 2- or 3-tined ones); John Chapman, "Johnny Appleseed," distributed religious material and apple seeds in the Ohio Valley; and the postal service for letters was introduced in Berlin. Needless to say, the city of Washington is a new kid on the block when compared to the age of other population centers along the eastern seaboard and abroad.

This guide focuses on the area that we now know as the District of Columbia. If you believe that your ancestors lived in Alexandria County during the time it was part of the District of Columbia (1801-1846), you may wish to check Virginia records. In 1920, the name of Alexandria County, Virginia, was changed to Arlington County. Records of the period when it was part of the District of Columbia are primarily found at the Arlington County Courthouse, the Alexandria City Courthouse and The Library of Virginia. The Virginiana Room of the Arlington County Library has many of these records on microfilm.

Some of the content in this guide is based upon a former publication by Eleanor Mildred Vaughan Cook, entitled Guide to the Records of Your District of Columbia Ancestors (Westminster, Md.: Family Line Publications, 1987). Any use of the text and makeup of Ms. Cook's work is done at the express permission of the publisher. For Maryland records before the District of Columbia was established, check Eleanor Cook's Guide to the Records of Montgomery County, Maryland: Genealogical and Historical (Westminster, Md.: Family Line Publications, 1989), which covers not only that county but general Maryland records such as patents, provincial court deeds, chancery cases and tax lists.

I am indebted to the works, expertise and enthusiasm of Dorothy S. Provine, of the Office of Public Records, who helped make this guide as comprehensive as possible.

Wesley E. Pippenger
Arlington, Virginia
October 2000

x

Introduction

Effective genealogical research in the District of Columbia can result only after first knowing something of the area history. To this regard, three aspects are presented: geographic history, records history, and government history.

GEOGRAPHIC HISTORY

The area now known as the District of Columbia was originally divided between a handful of early landowners. Patent records for these may describe faraway locations, and often use rivers, creeks and bays as landmarks. Names of some of the first settlers frequently appear in the early land records.

The most defined reference points in early land records are the large water bodies, i.e., the Potowmack River (with spelling changed) and Rock Creek, as well as the Anacostian and Anacostine River. The latter was known as the Eastern Branch of the Potowmack River, and today as the Anacostia River. A creek of considerable size, originally called Goose Creek, ran through the area. Francis Pope, after facetiously naming his land grant "Rome," contended that since there was a Pope in Rome, his residence should be on the Tiber. Goose Creek thus became Tiber Creek. St. James Creek lay east and south and at its mouth was St. Thomas Bay.

By 1696, there were enough settlers that a new county, Prince George's, was formed from Charles and Calvert counties. It was of great size, encompassing all the land from present-day District of Columbia and Prince George's to the northwest border of provincial Maryland. It was in Prince George's County in 1703 that Colonel Ninian Beall patented his "Rock of Dumbarton" tract for 795 acres on the Potowmack River at the mouth of Rock Creek. This is where Georgetown is today. In the following decades, Maryland continued to populate as vacant land was surveyed and patented. As homes were built, deeds began to describe "dwelling plantations." Early land grants were divided and re-patented with new names.

In 1748, Frederick County was formed from part of Prince George's County. It encompassed all the lands westward and northward of a line beginning at the lower side of the mouth of Rock Creek and running straight to the Patuxent River, then following the Patuxent River to the lines of Baltimore County, and going with the lines of Baltimore County to the extent of the province of Maryland. The lands northwest of the boundary line became the new county, named after Frederick, Lord Baltimore, and the lands southeast remained part of Prince George's County.

George Town was established in 1751. In response to a petition of the people of Frederick County which stated there was a convenient site for a town at the mouth of Rock Creek adjacent to George Gordon's tobacco inspection house, the legislation of 15 May 1751 authorized five commissioners to purchase 60 acres and survey it into 80 lots to be erected into a town to be called George Town (see Figure 5).

Another borough called Hamburgh was laid out by 1770 within the current District of Columbia (see Figure 1). Jacob Funk divided land he purchased between Rock and Tiber creeks in the area later known as Foggy Bottom, into 287 lots. Hamburgh, or Funkstown as it was sometimes called, did not prosper and few lots were sold. A third town, Carrollsburg, was in 1770 laid out by Charles Carroll between St. James Creek and the Eastern Branch (see Figure 2). The geographic relation of these localities can be seen in a "Sketch of Washington in Embryo." See Figure 3.

In 1776, Frederick County was divided. The lower part, from the Monocacy River to the mouth of Rock Creek became Montgomery County. This included George Town. George Town had grown beyond its original boundaries,

A Guide to Records of the District of Columbia

with new streets and lots laid out in several additions. George Town was incorporated as a city by Maryland legislature in 1789 (see map showing town additions at Figure 4).

A law of December 23, 1788, directed Maryland to offer Congress a 10-mile square in any district of the state. A similar offer was made by Virginia. The offers were accepted by an act approved July 16, 1790 (1 Stat. 130) which directed that a district be located on the Potowmack River between the mouths of the Eastern Branch (Anacostia River) and the Connogocheque. It was extended below the Eastern Branch by a change approved March 3, 1791 (1 Stat. 214). The boundary lines encircled parts of Montgomery and Prince George's counties in Maryland, and extended across the Potowmack to take in part of Fairfax County in Virginia, including the town of Alexandria.

Stipulations were made that the offices of the Federal Government were to be moved from New York to Philadelphia before the first Monday in December 1790, and to remain there until the first Monday in December 1800, when the seat of government was to be transferred to the new Federal district.

The plan for the City drawn by Pierre Charles L'Enfant (1754-1825) did not include George Town nor the land outside Boundary Avenue (now Florida Avenue) or any of the land on the Virginia side of the Potowmack. This restricted area had few settlers compared to George Town and Alexandria, and consisted principally of large tracts of farm and woodland. Map 2, below, shows the city of Washington in 1792. Jenkins Hill, on the east side of Tiber (Goose) Creek, was chosen as the site for the Capitol.

Although no official act of Congress or the President specifically named the area the "District of Columbia," it became to be called that and was so referred to in the title of an act approved May 6, 1797 (1 Stat. 461).

Several local governments were already operating in the area when the Federal Government moved to its new location in 1800.

The town of Alexandria was located in that part ceded by Virginia, and the town of George Town in the area donated by Maryland. The areas outside the boundaries of the two towns were governed by the levy court in the case of the Maryland cession and a county court in the case of the Virginia grant. In addition, the three Commissioners appointed by President Washington (Thomas Johnson, David Stuart and Daniel Carroll) had been granted certain governmental powers in the territory seat of the Potowmack River by the State of Maryland. These powers included granting liquor licenses, making building regulations, and appointing a clerk for the recording of deeds. Records of the early activities of these Commissioners, 1791-1802, can be found in Record Group 42 at the National Archives, Entries 21 to 23 and 104.

The District was divided into two counties by an act of February 27, 1801 (2 Stat. 103). The part that had been ceded by Maryland was to be called Washington County, and the part that had been ceded by Virginia was to be called Alexandria County. The laws of Virginia as they then existed were continued in Alexandria County, and the laws of Maryland in Washington County. After the incorporation of the city of Washington in 1802, the 10-mile square territory was subject to a variety of legislation: laws of Congress, laws of Maryland and Virginia as they existed in 1801, the ordinances of the Corporations of Georgetown and Washington City, and the enactments of the levy court of the county of Washington and the county court of the county of Alexandria. After Alexandria was retroceded to Virginia in accordance with an act dated July 9, 1846 (9 Stat. 35), Maryland law and custom as modified or supplemented by Congress predominated in the District.

No unified government was provided for the District until an act of February 21, 1871 (16 Stat. 419) abolished the corporations of Washington and Georgetown and the levy court of Washington County. The act provided for a single municipal government similar to that provided for territories of the U.S. This territorial government was replaced by a temporary government of three presidentially-appointed

Introduction

Commissioners in accordance with an act approved June 20, 1874 (18 Stat. 116). These commissioners were William Dennison, Henry T. Blow and John H. Ketcham. The commission form of government was declared permanent by an act of June 11, 1878 (20 Stat. 102). In 1967, in accordance with Presidential Reorganization Plan No. 3 (81 Stat. 948), the Board of Commissioners was replaced by a presidentially-appointed mayor-council form of government.

RECORDS HISTORY

Many records described in this guide are those of the government of the District of Columbia that were in the United States National Archives and Records Administration (referred hereafter as the National Archives) as of 1974. This large mass of records amounts to just over 1,000 cubit feet and is designated as Records of the Government of the District of Columbia, Record Group 21. A detailed guide for this record group was prepared in 1976 by Dorothy S. Provine, called Preliminary Inventory of the Records of the Government of the District of Columbia (Washington, D.C.: National Archives and Records Service, 1976). Introductory remarks and data from this inventory are used by the compiler of this guide with permission from Ms. Provine.

The records of the city of Georgetown in the National Archives relate mainly to fiscal activities. The Manuscript Division of the Library of Congress has the Journals of Proceedings of the Corporation of Georgetown, 1801-1805, and 1871; Journals of the Proceedings of the Board of Aldermen, 1805-1870 (with some gaps); and Journals of the Proceedings of the Common Council, 1807-1861 (with some gaps). Also in the Manuscript Division are Journals of Expenditures, 1826-1836; Tax Lists, 1814-1817 and 1819; and Corporation Ordinances, 1820-1831 and 1844-1855.

There is related material in several record groups in the National Archives. Reference to these is made throughout this guide. A number of inventories and discussions of records holdings appeared in different articles published in Records of the Columbia Historical Society. These are outlined in the Bibliography of this guide.

GOVERNMENT HISTORY

The city of Washington was incorporated by an act of May 3, 1802 (2 Stat. 195), which established a mayor-council form of government. The mayor was appointed annually by the President. He served as executive head of the government, appointed all officers under the corporation, and had veto power over legislation passed by the City Council, although his veto could be overridden by a three-fourths vote of both houses and the council. The City Council was divided into two branches: a council of 12 members and a second chamber of 7 members. The council was elected annually by the adult free white males who had resided in the city a year and who had paid taxes in the year preceding the elections. The second chamber was composed of five members of the council elected by the entire council. The corporation was empowered to lay and collect taxes; pass health regulations; establish night watches; repair bridges, streets, drains, and sewers; erect lamps; license auctions, taverns, hackney carriages, and carts; impose fines and penalties; and, in general, pass all by-laws and ordinances.

The 1802 charter was amended by an act of February 24, 1804 (2 Stat. 254), which recognized the City Council so that each chamber would consist of nine members elected annually on separate tickets by qualified voters. The amended charter was to run 15 years, but substantial changes were made in the system by an act of May 4, 1812 (2 Stat. 721). Henceforth, the government was to consist of a mayor, a board of aldermen, and a board of common council.

The Board of Aldermen was composed of eight members elected for a term of 2 years, two from each of the four wards into which the city was divided. The Board of Common Council consisted of 12 members, three from each ward, elected annually. The mayor was elected annually by the combined votes of the Common Council and the Aldermen. In addition to the powers granted by the 1802 charter, the corporation was empowered to provide for the relief of the poor, aged, and infirm; erect hospitals, workhouses, house of correction, and other public buildings for the use of the corporation; provide for the establishment of schools; hold lotteries with the approval of the President; open streets, avenues, and alleys; provide for fire protection; and restrain and prohibit the nightly and other disorderly meetings of slaves, free Negroes and mulattoes.

The city was granted a new charter by an act of May 15, 1820 (3 Stat. 584), which also provided for a mayor, a board of common council, and a board of aldermen, all elected by the adult free white male taxpayers having a minimum of 1 year's residence in the city. The mayor was elected biennially and retained his broad appointment and veto powers. His appointments, however, had to be approved by the Board of Aldermen, and his veto could be overridden by a two-thirds vote of both houses of the council. In addition, the mayor was given all powers of justices of the peace of the county. The Board of Aldermen consisted of two members chosen from each of the six wards into which the city was divided; each member served for 2 years. The Board of Common Council consisted of three members from each ward who served 1 year. Several additional offices, including the Board of Assessors, Register, Collector, and Surveyor of the city, were made elective by an act dated May 7, 1848 (9 Stat. 223). But with minor modifications, however, the structure of government outlined in the 1820 charter remained basically unchanged until after the Civil War.

The corporations of Washington City and Georgetown and the levy court of the county of Washington were abolished by an act of February 21, 1871 (16 Stat. 419), and a single unified system of government akin to that provided for territories of the U.S. was established for the District of Columbia. The municipality was composed of the Governor, the Secretary, a bicameral legislature, the Board of Health, and the Board of Public Works. The Governor was appointed for a term of 4 years by the President with the advice and consent of the Senate and served as executive head of the new government. He was empowered to commission all officials elected or appointed to office under the new government, to execute the laws, to grant pardons, and to veto legislation, although his veto could be overridden by a two-thirds vote of both houses of the legislature. The Secretary, who was also appointed by the President to a 4-year term with the approval of the Senate, acted as Governor in the absence of that official and recorded all the acts and proceedings of the government. The legislative power was vested in a legislative assembly consisting of two houses: a council and a house of delegates. The council was composed of 11 members, of whom two were residents of Georgetown and two residents of Washington County. The councilmen were appointed by the President with the advice and consent of the Senate; five of the original appointees were chosen for 1 year and six for 2 years. Thereafter, the appointments were for 2 years. The District was divided into 11 districts for the purpose of appointing councilmen. The House of Delegates consisted of 22 members elected for 1 year, one from each of the 22 districts into which the District was divided. All adult male citizens who had resided in the District 3 months were declared qualified voters for the first election, although thereafter a minimum residence requirement of 1 year applied. The qualified voters were also empowered to elect for a 2-year term a territorial delegate to congress who had the same privileges as delegates from other US. territories.

The legislative authority of the assembly was restricted in several ways. The legislature was forbidden to limit the franchise in any manner. The annual amount of appropriations was not to be increased unless approved by two-thirds vote of the members of both houses and was not to exceed the revenue authorized to be raised within the same term. The debt could not

Introduction

exceed 5 percent of the assessed value of property in the District unless legislation that provided for such an excess included provisions for tax revenue to pay the amount and unless such legislation had been approved by a majority of the votes cast for members of the legislative assembly. A two-thirds vote of the assembly was necessary to borrow money or issue stocks and bonds. In addition, the rate of taxation was limited to 2 percent of the cash value of property.

The Board of Public Works was composed of the Governor, who served as president of the board, and four members appointed to 4-year terms by the President with approval of the Senate. At least one of the appointees was required to be a civil engineer, one a resident of Georgetown, and one a resident of the county of Washington. Control of all local public works, including repairs of streets, alleys, and sewers, was vested in the board, as well as any other work entrusted to it by the legislative assembly or Congress. Money appropriated for local improvements was disbursed by the board's own warrant, and special assessments, not to exceed one-third of the cost, could be levied by the board on property adjoining and benefitting from public works. There was one major limitation on the board: no contracts were to be made except in pursuance of appropriations made by law, and not until such appropriations shall have been made.

The last major division of the new government was a board of health, which was composed of five members appointed by the President with the approval of the Senate.

The offices of Governor and Secretary, the legislative assembly, and the Board of Public Works were abolished by Congress by an act dated June 20, 1874 (18 Stat. 116). The Board of Health was allowed to continue, and the territorial delegate to Congress was permitted to finish his term. A temporary government consisting of three Commissioners appointed by the President with the approval of the Senate was established. The Board of Commissioners was to have all the authority formerly vested in the Governor and the Board of Public Works except it was not allowed to incur any obligations other than such contracts and obligations as may be necessary to the faithful administration of the valid laws enacted for the government of said District, to the execution of existing legal obligations and contracts, and to the protection or preservation of improvements existing, or commenced and not completed. In addition, the Commissioners were authorized to abolish or consolidate office, reduce the number of employees, and make removals and appointments to any offices authorized by law. The act also provided that the President appoint an officer of the Army Corps of Engineers to supervise and direct public improvements and to exercise the same powers as the chief engineer of the old Board of Public Works.

The commission form of government was made permanent by an act dated June 11, 1878 (20 Stat. 102). The three commissioners continued to be appointed by the President with the approval of the Senate, and one of the three was required to be an officer of the Army Corps of Engineers above the rank of captain. Initially, one of the civilian commissioners was appointed for a 1-year term and the others for 2 years; thereafter their successors were chosen for a term of 3 years. The commissioners were granted all the rights and duties of the early commissioners but were prohibited from making any contract or incurring any obligation without the approval of Congress. It was specifically provided that there could be no increase in the indebtedness of the District. It was further stipulated that Congress would pay a part of the approved budget of the District, with the remainder to come from local tax revenues.

For purposes of administration, the commissioners divided their duties into three groups and assigned one commissioner to each. Each commissioner was responsible for overseeing the operations of his special area and for making recommendations to the whole board on matters affecting his jurisdiction.

Both the Board of Health and the Metropolitan Police Board were abolished by the 1878 act.

A Guide to Records of the District of Columbia

The Board of Health was replaced by a health officer appointed by the commissioners, and the powers of the Metropolitan Police Board were transferred to the commissioners.

Presidential Reorganization Plan No. 3 of 1967 (81 Stat. 948) abolished the board of commissioners and created in its stead a type of mayor-council government. The chief executive is a presidentially appointed commissioner (or mayor, as he has usually been called) who serves for 4 years unless removed by the President. The general executive powers of the old board of commissioners for organizing and administering the local government have been granted to the mayor-commissioner.

An act of September 22, 1970 (84 Stat. 848), allows the citizens of the District to elect to the House of Representatives a nonvoting delegate who serves for the duration of each Congress.

Mayors of the City of Washington

Robert Brent, June 1802-June 1812
Daniel Rapine, June 1812-June 1813
James H. Blake, June 1813-June 1817
Benjamin G. Orr, June 1817-June 1819
Samuel N. Smallwood, June 1819-June 1822
    and June 1824-Sept. 30, 1824
Thomas Carberry, June 1822-June 1824
Roger C. Weightman, Oct. 4, 1824-July 31, 1827
Joseph Gales, Jr., July 31, 1827-June 1830
John P. Van Ness, June 1830-June 1834
William A. Bradley, June 1834-June 1836
Peter Force, June 1836-June 1840
William Wilson Seaton, June 1840-June 1850
Walter Lenox, June 1850-June 1852
John W. Maury, June 1852-June 1854
John T. Towers, June 1854-June 1856
William B. Magruder, June 1856-June 1858
James G. Berret, June 1858-Aug. 24, 1861
Richard Wallach, Aug. 26, 1861-June 1868
Sayles J. Bowen, June 1868-June 1870
Matthew Gault Emery, June 1870-June 1871

Maps in the Following Illustrations

Figure 1 is a plan of the Town of Hamburgh, drawn by E.F.M. Faehtz in his Washington in Embryo, published in 1874. Hamburgh was laid out in 1768, but did not prosper. The few purchasers of lots in Hamburgh were offered exchange lots when the town was consumed by the city of Washington.

Figure 2 is a plan of the Town of Carrollsburg, drawn by E.F.M. Faehtz in his Washington in Embryo, published in 1874.

Figure 3, entitled "Sketch of Washington in Embryo," by E.F.M. Faehtz and F.W. Pratt (1874), displays the relationship of the "new" streets to the properties and towns of an earlier regime. From this one can develop an appreciation for some of the origins, actions and interests of folks like Notley Young, Daniel Carroll, David Burnes, James M. Lingan, Samuel Davidson, and Robert Peter.

Figure 4 reproduces a map used as endpapers in A Portrait of Old Georgetown by Grace Dunlop Peter. The boundaries of the various additions to Georgetown are given as well as both the old and new names of streets.

Figure 5 is entitled "A Map of George Town With the Additions," drawn in 1814. Beall's Second Addition to Georgetown is not reflected.

Figure 6 presents a "Map of the City of Washington," prepared in 1892 for use in Evans' Visitors Companion At Our National Capitol. Square numbers shown can be used for studying land transactions. When Georgetown fell under the jurisdiction of the city of Washington, square numbers for the District of Columbia c.1895 replaced former designations used by a separate Georgetown system.

Figure 7 shows some of the major buildings in the city of Washington in 1876.

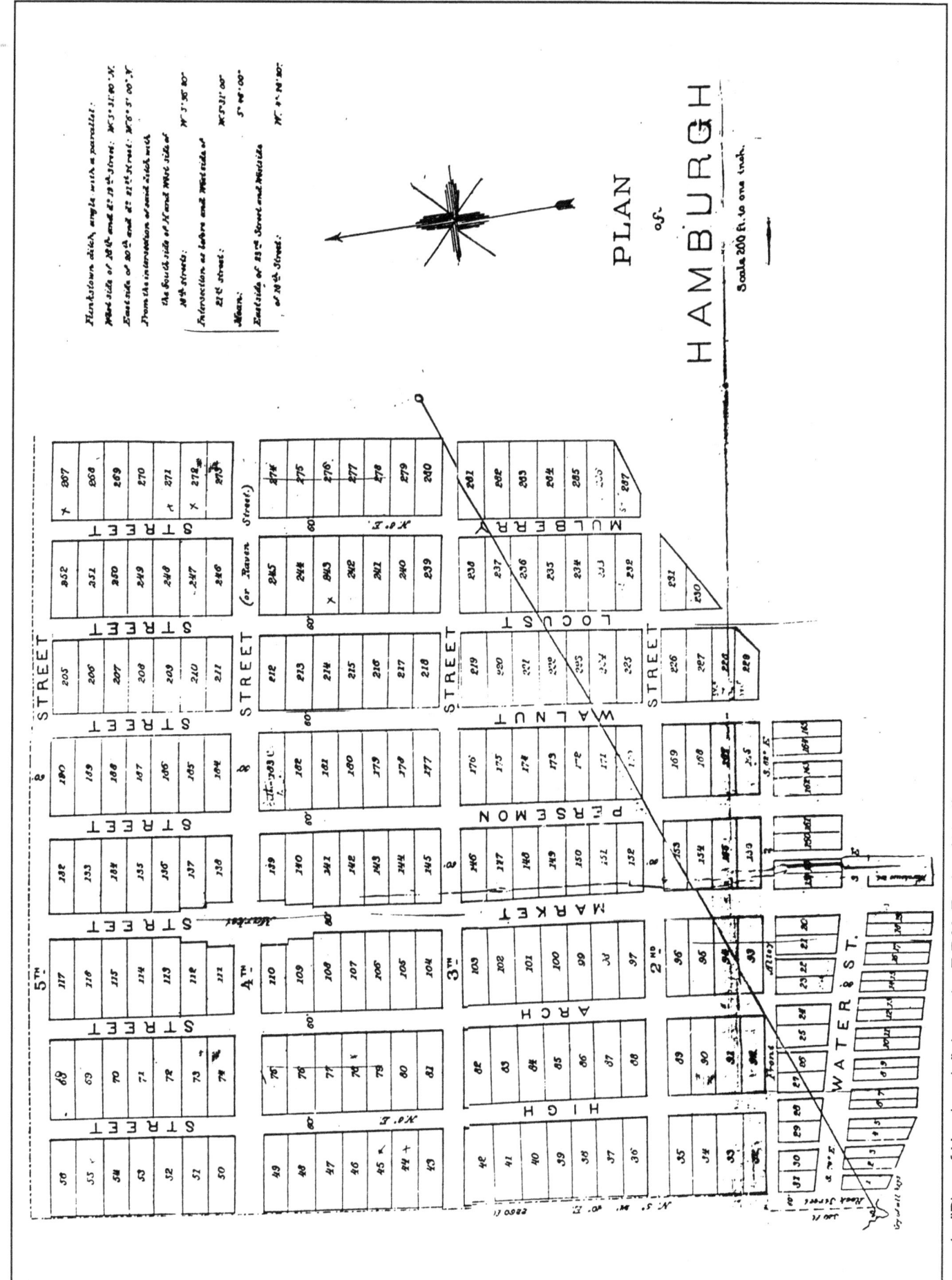

Figure 1 – "Plan of Hamburgh," drawn by E.F.M. Faehtz (1874).

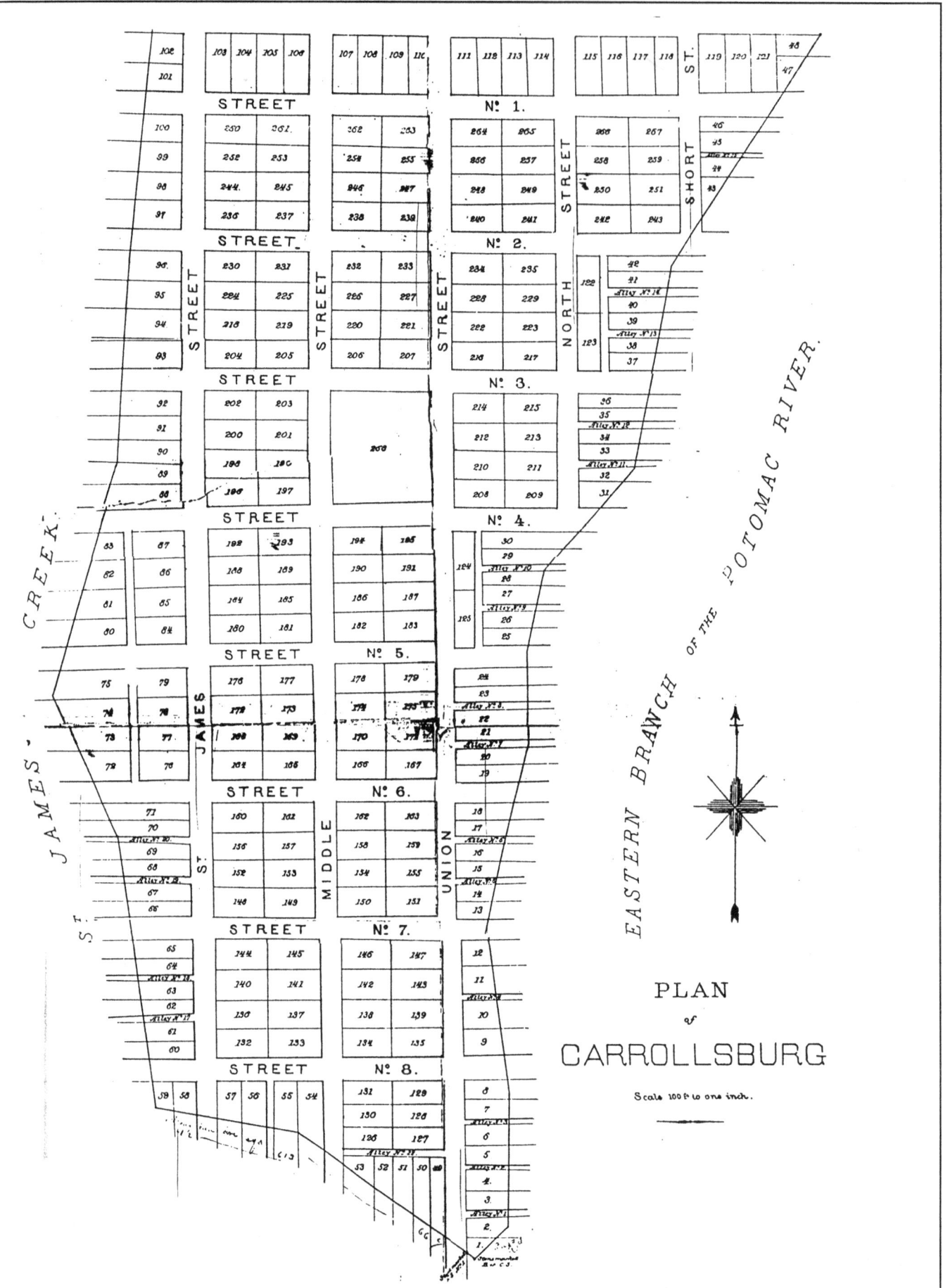

Figure 2 - "Plan of Carrollsburg," drawn by E.F.M. Faehtz (1874).

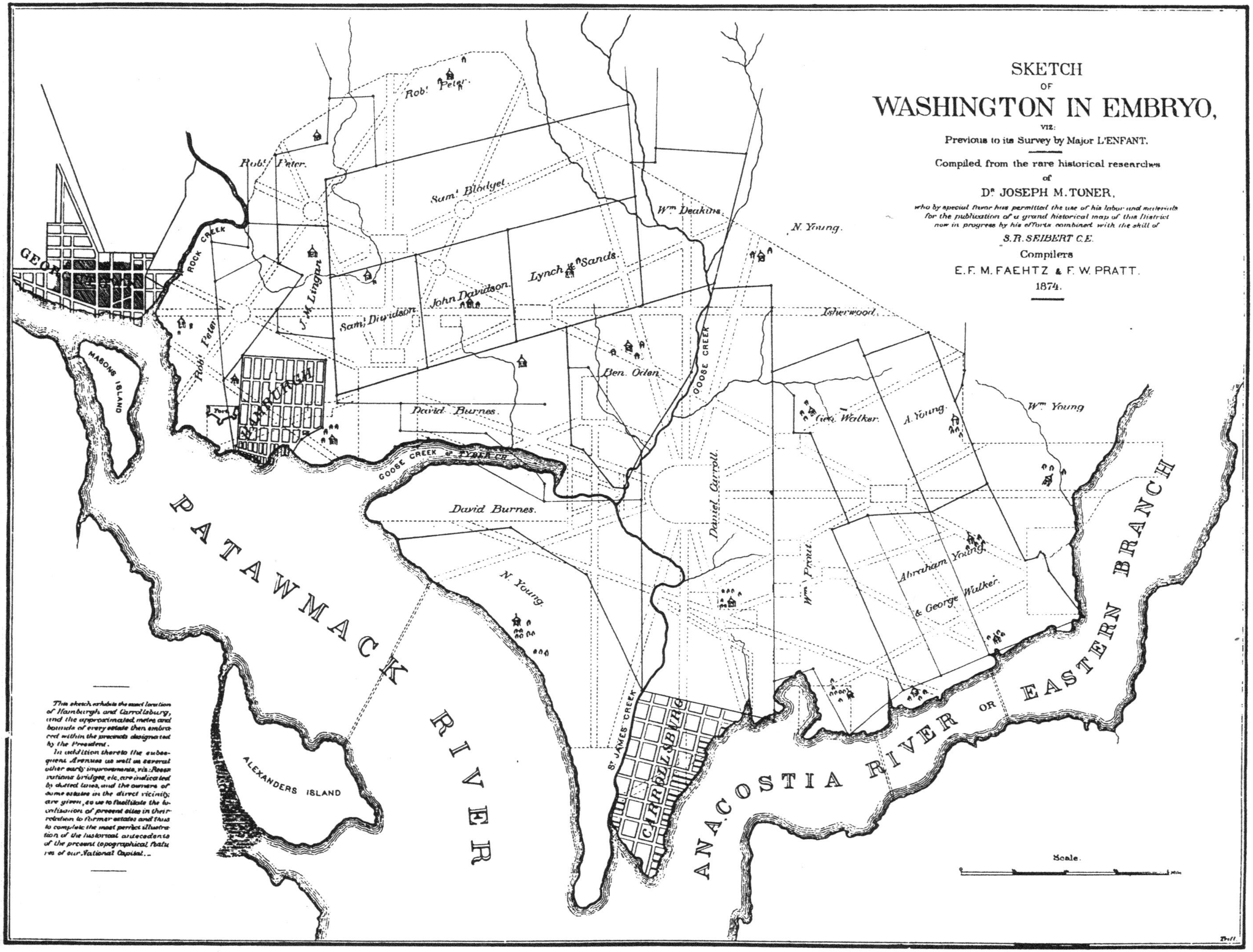

Figure 3. – "Sketch of Washington in Embryo," by F.F.M. Faehtz and F.W. Pratt (1874). Showing the Division of Land on the Site of the National Capitol in 1791

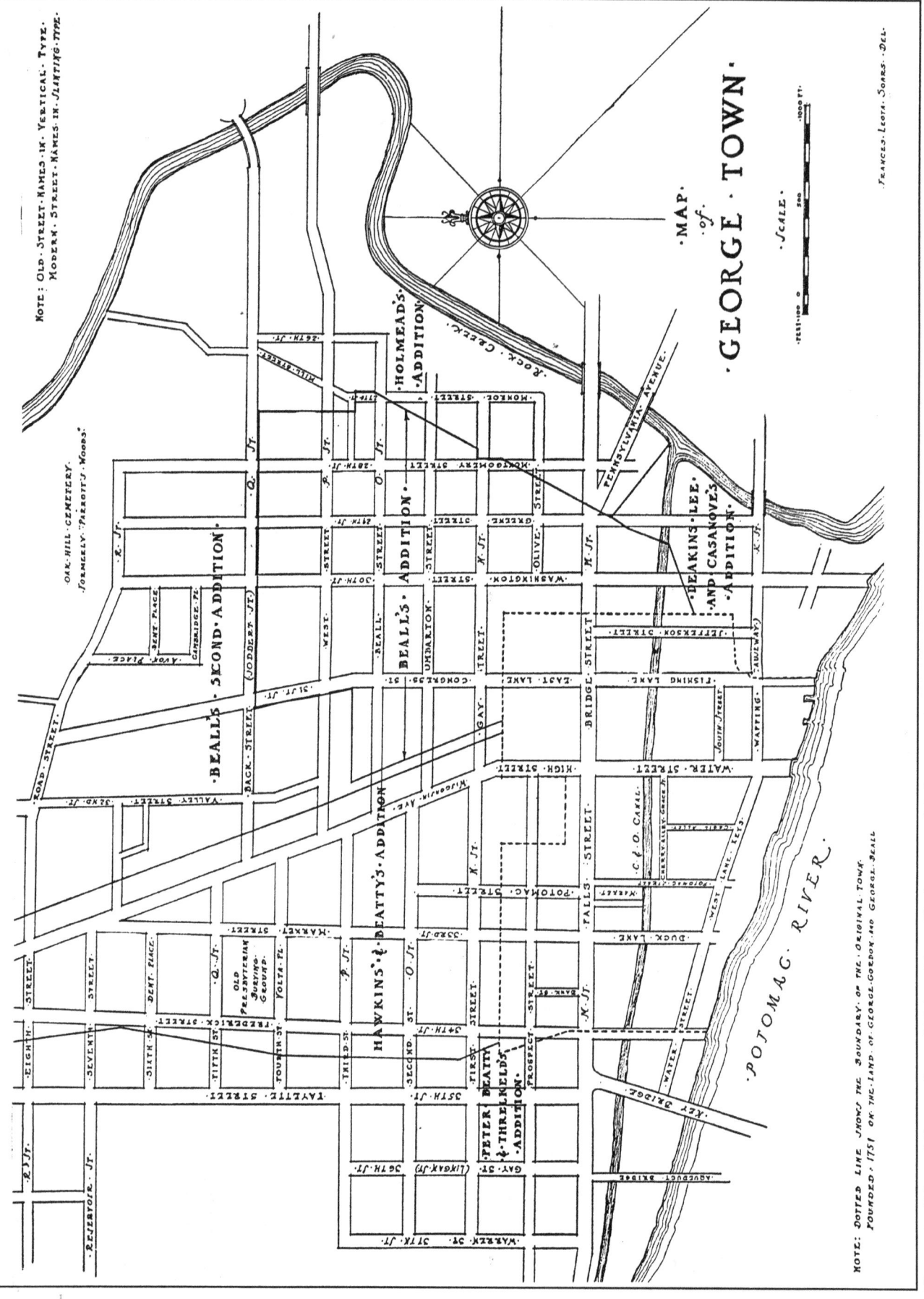

Figure 4 – "Map of Georgetown," Taken From Endpapers of A Portrait of Old Georgetown. Shows Additions and Both Old and New Street Names.

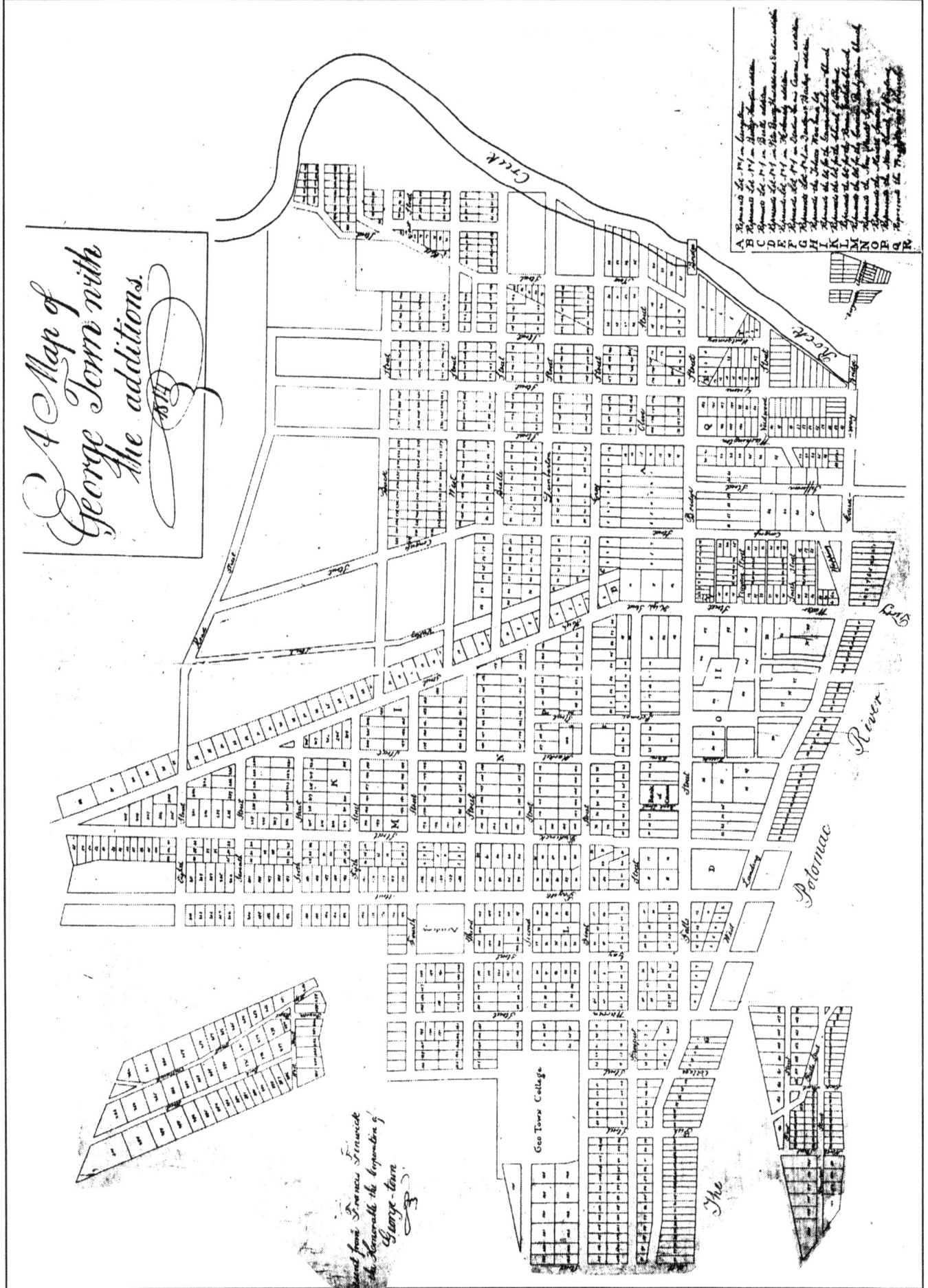

Figure 5 - "A Map of George Town With The Additions, 1814." Original in the Library of Congress, Geography and Maps Division.

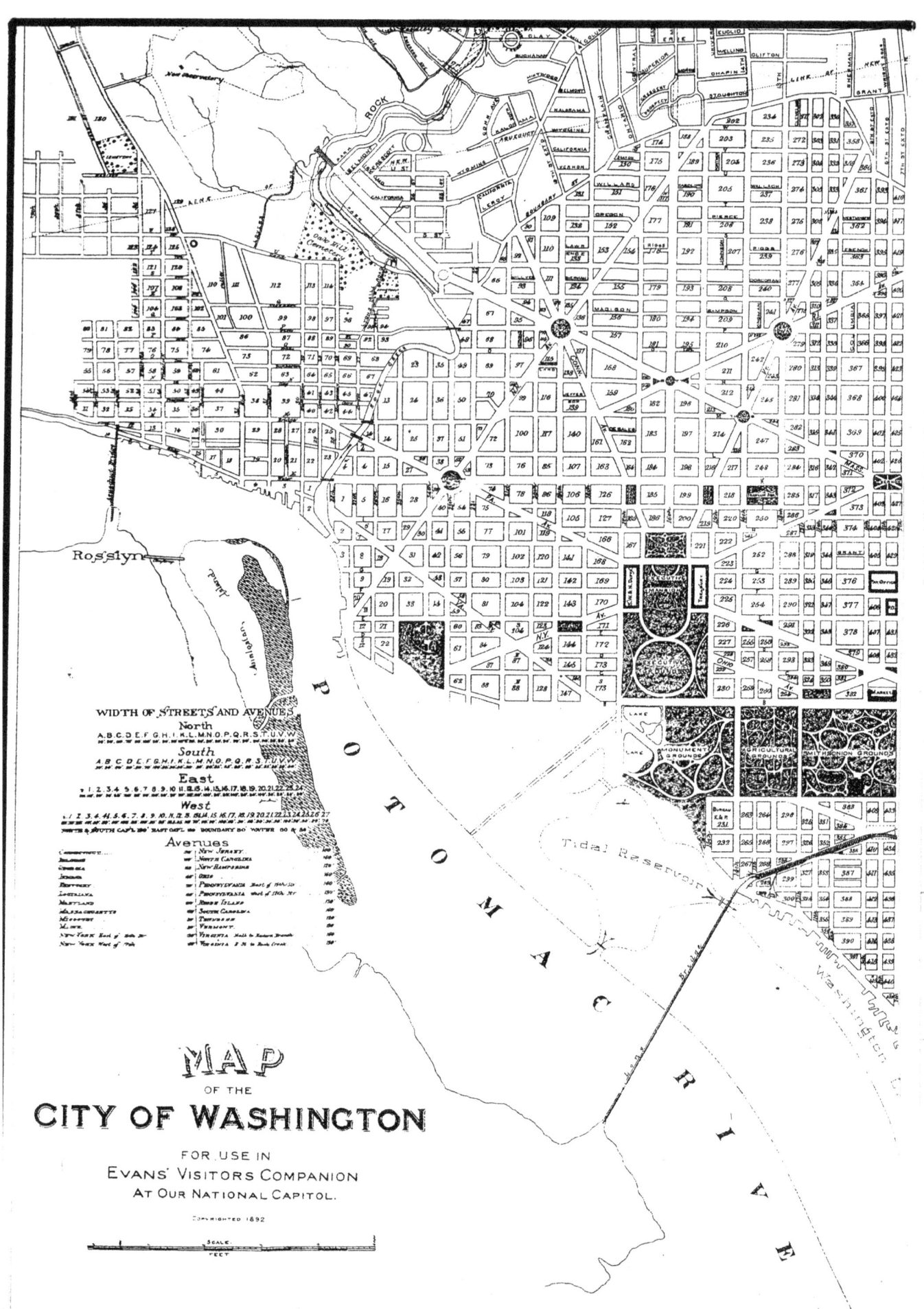

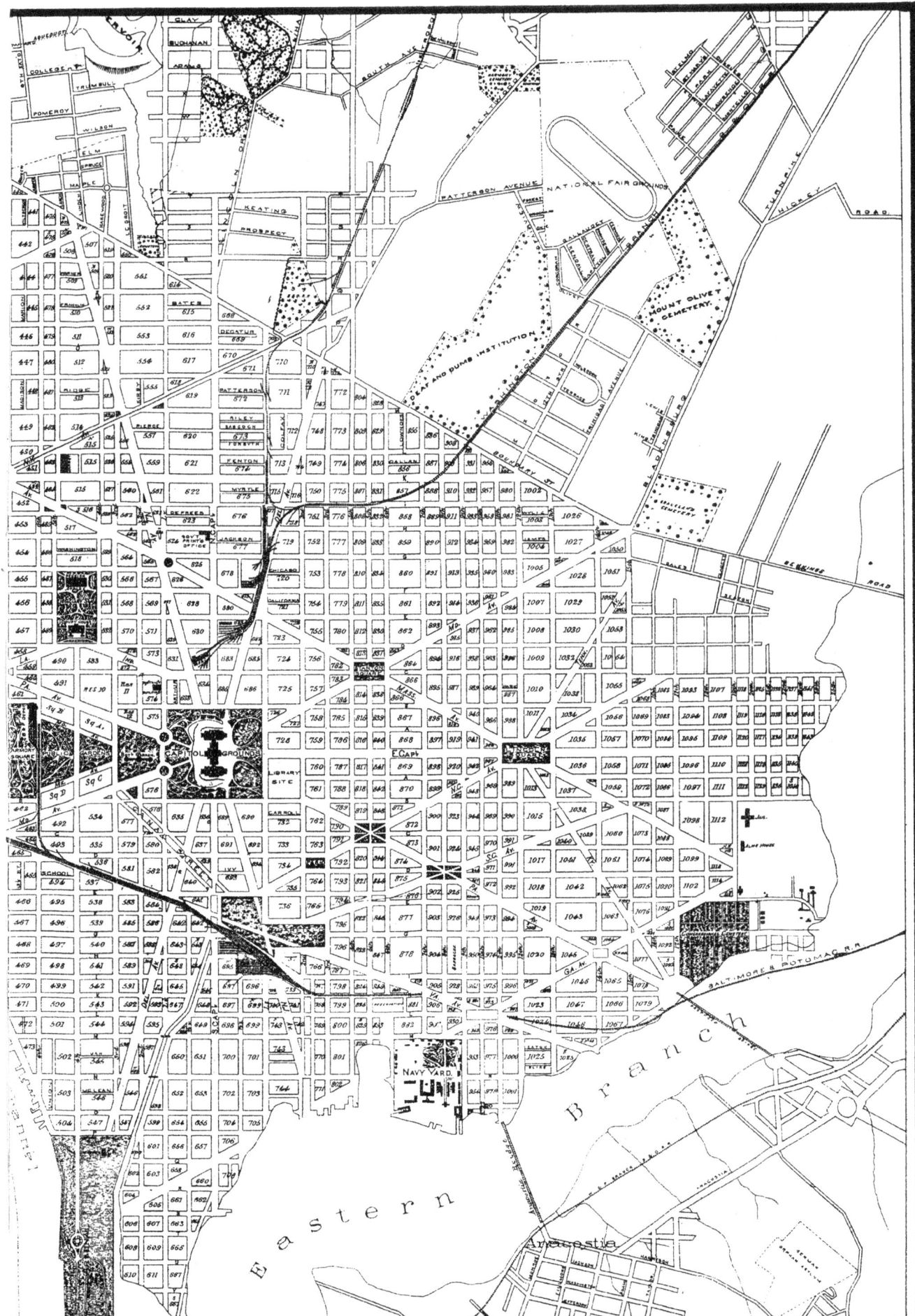

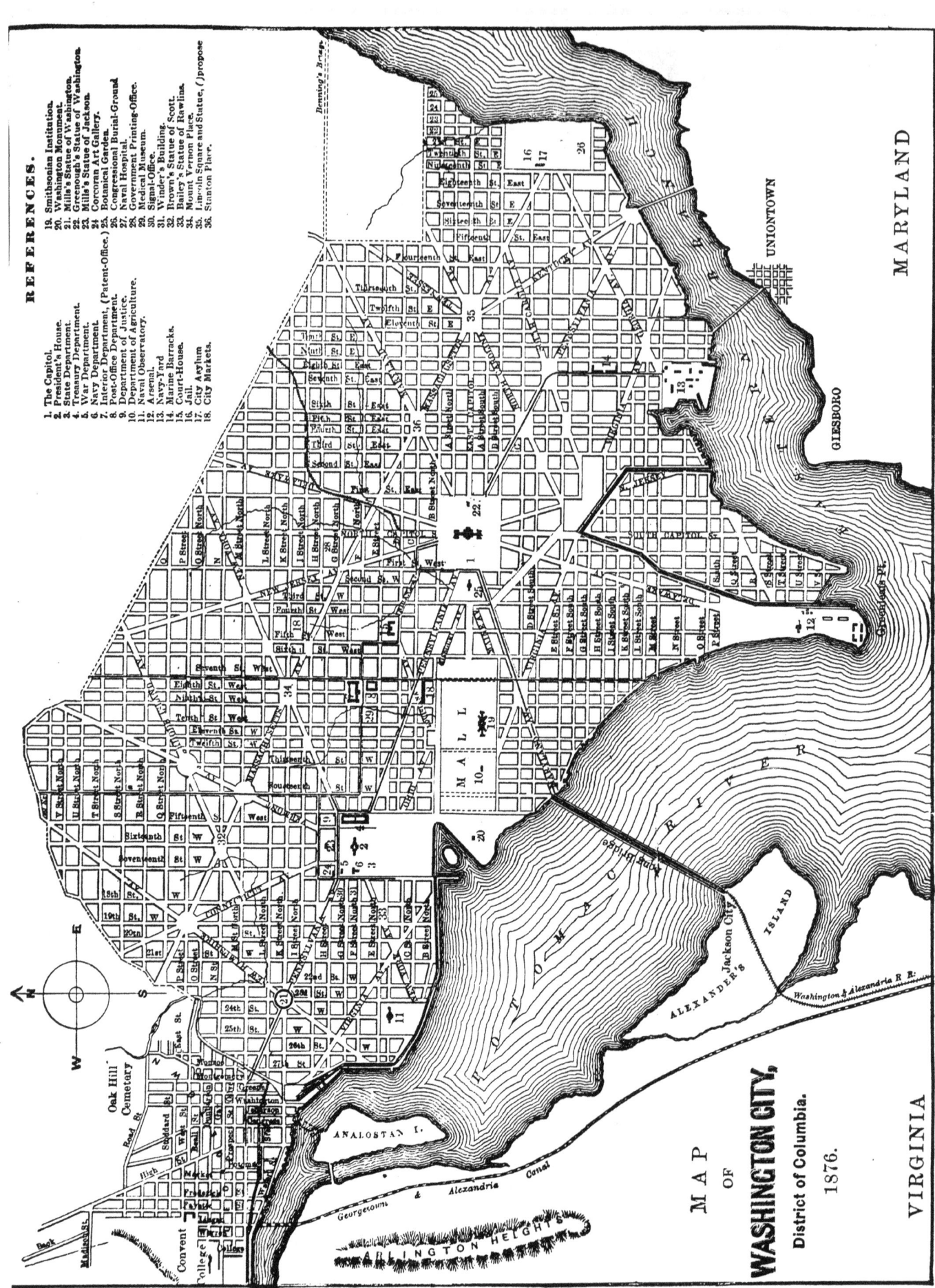

Census Schedules and City Directories

CENSUS SCHEDULES

Among the most basic of Federal records, census or population schedules are a natural place to begin. District of Columbia census schedules are available on microfilm at many locations, but the National Archives in Washington is the area's most convenient. It not only has the census records for all states, but also printed indexes, enumeration district records, and the original census books. If a microfilmed census schedule is difficult to read, you may request to view the original census book. Census material on microfilm can be copied.

◘ 1790 Census. The District of Columbia was included in the Federal census for Maryland. Households in the area that had been part of Prince George's County were included in that county's census, and households in Georgetown and the remainder of the area that had been part of Montgomery County were included in that county's census. A printed index to the Maryland 1790 census, is at the National Archives.

◘ 1800 Through 1870 Census. The District of Columbia census for each decade between 1800-1870 has been indexed by Ronald Vern Jackson, and that for 1860-1870 by Bryan Lee Dilts. These may be found in book form in numerous locations. For the 1810 census, only the Georgetown District is indexed. The 1850 and 1860 "Free Schedules" provide the name of each free household member. There are separate "Slave Schedules" for these years, which give the name of the slave owner and the age, sex and color of the slaves, but not their names.

Before 1850, the only name given in the census was the name of the head of the household. However, it is well worth taking the time to check the census record itself for clues to ages of family members, which can give some idea as to marriage date (i.e., one male and one female aged 16-25 and one child under 10 in 1810 hints at a marriage c.1805), and should help distinguish between father and son of the same name. Also, the occupational group was given in some years.

At the D.A.R. Library, there is a card index listing every person in the District of Columbia 1850 census, in addition to the head of the household.

Procedure for using the 1790-1870 Censuses: (1) Locate the name in the index and note information given. (2) In the Archives' booklet "Federal Population Censuses, 1790-1890," find the year desired, then county, ward or area given in the index. To the left is a column giving microfilm roll number. (3) On the numbered roll for that year, find the correct county, ward or area and then the correct page where the household will be listed.

◘ 1880 Census. A printed index was published by Ronald Vern Jackson, Wylma Winmill and Shirley P. Zachrison. Households in which there were children 10 years of age or younger were indexed, using a Soundex system intended to group together the various spellings of each name.

Procedure for using the 1880 Census: (1) From the Information Desk at the Archives, obtain a copy of the brochure explaining the Soundex system. (2) Determine the Soundex code for the desired surname. (3) In the "Federal Population Censuses" book covering 1880, the Soundex Index for the District of Columbia will give the microfilm roll number for that Soundex code. (4) After locating the household in the microfilmed Soundex index, copy all information, especially noting the Enumeration District (E.D.), sheet number in the upper right corner. (5) Going back to the "Federal Population Censuses" book, in the 1880 census section, find the District of Columbia and the microfilm roll that covers the E.D. (6) On this roll, locate the correct E.D. and sheet number, which will give you the complete census record.

A Guide to Records of the District of Columbia

◘ <u>1890 Census</u>. Most of the 1890 Federal population schedules were so badly damaged by fire in the Commerce Department Building in January 1921 that they were disposed of. For the District of Columbia, the only surviving population schedules cover: 13th, 14th, 15th, Q, R, S, and Riggs streets, and Johnson Avenue. These are included in a special index on Microfilm M496 at the National Archives, or on LDS Microfilm #0926498. See discussion of the special census of Union veterans under "Military" in this guide.

◘ <u>1900 Census</u>. All households were indexed using the Soundex system.

Procedure for the 1900 Census: same as for 1880 Census, except use "1900 Federal Population Census" booklet.

◘ <u>1910 and 1920 Census</u>. The "1910 Federal Population Census" booklet gives the microfilm roll numbers for the census, but the census is not indexed for the District of Columbia. Indexes that were prepared for the 1880 and 1900 censuses were done after the Social Security Act was passed in 1935. The 1910 census was not indexed for states whose vital records were considered sufficiently established and complete by 1910. Although there are no significant changes to the 1920 Census and its use over that of 1910, it contains additional information.

◘ <u>Census Enumeration Districts Descriptions</u>. When a census is not indexed or is only partly indexed, as in 1910, or you cannot find a person in the available index, it is very time consuming to go through the entire census schedule page by page. Also it is easy to overlook the name when it is there. If you know the person's address from a city directory or from personal knowledge, use of the microfilmed "Census Enumeration Districts Description" at the National Archives can be helpful. (The temporary numbers are T1210 for the 1900 census and T1224 for 1830-1950.)

For each census, the census takers were assigned given areas which were numbered and called enumeration districts. If you have a person's address, finding the enumeration district in which s/he lived in the District of Columbia for the year of a specific census will enable you to confine your search to the relatively few pages covering that enumeration district, rather than searching through the entire census.

Procedure: (1) In the enumeration district records for the desired year, find the number of the district for the address you have. For example, if the address in 1910 was 911 G Street, N.W., it was in the 4th Enumeration District, described as "H to F, 7th to 12th Streets." (2) In the Federal Population Census booklet for the appropriate year, locate the microfilm roll that contains that enumeration district. (3) The address should be easily found in that district.

Garlet, Charles B. <u>Washington, D.C. Enumeration Districts for the 1910 Census: A Genealogical Aid</u> (Rockville, Md.: By the Author, 1983). Contains maps which may be helpful in locating the correct district.

◘ <u>Mortality Schedules</u>. When the 1850, 1860, 1870 and 1880 Federal census were taken, a separate schedule was used to collect information about persons who had died during the 12 months preceding June 1 of the census year. The mortality census schedule for 1880, which was the most comprehensive, gives the name of the deceased, age at death, sex, color, marital status, birthplace of deceased and of his or her father and mother, cause of death, how long a resident of the District, and place disease contacted. The National Office of Vital Statistics estimates that only 60 per cent of actual deaths were reported.

Mortality census schedules for the District of Columbia are at various libraries. The LDS Library has on microfiche in one Accelerated Index Systems file, all mortality census schedules for each decade of the entire Federal census. These include names of the deceased in alphabetical order, followed by county and state of residence, age and sex of the individual,

Census Schedules and City Directories

month of death, place of birth, and cause of death.

Jackson, Ronald Vern. District of Columbia 1850 Mortality Schedule (Bountiful, Utah: Accelerated Indexing Systems, 1981). LC Call Number F193.J3364.

Jackson, Ronald Vern. District of Columbia 1860 Mortality Schedule (Bountiful, Utah: Accelerated Indexing Systems, 1981). LC Call Number F193.J338.

Jackson, Ronald Vern. District of Columbia 1870 Mortality Schedule (Bountiful, Utah: Accelerated Indexing Systems, 1981). LC Call Number F193.J339 1981.

Jackson, Ronald Vern. District of Columbia 1880 Mortality Schedule (Bountiful, Utah: Accelerated Indexing Systems, 1981). LC Call Number F193.J34.

◘ Industrial Census Schedules. There was a census of manufacturers in 1820 which listed persons who made items and their trade or the item made: tailor, tanner, miller, makers of shoes, bricks, carriages, etc. Included in the schedules were the number of persons employed, annual wages paid, capital investment, market value of annual production, cost of raw materials, amount of expenses, and quantity and kind of machinery. The "Records of the 1820 Census of Manufactures" are on Microfilm M279 at the National Archives. The schedule for the District, including Alexandria, is found on Roll 17 thereof.

Microfilm copies of the District of Columbia industrial census schedules, for 1850 to 1880, are at the National Archives as "Bureau of Census Non-Population Schedules, 1850-1880," Roll 1 and Roll 93. They are not stored in the Microfilm Research Room, but will be made available to you upon request at the information desk. The schedules contain basically the same information as those for 1820.

◘ Agriculture Census Schedules. There is an 1850 agriculture schedule for the District of Columbia on Roll 1 of the above-described non-population schedules, 1850-1880. The schedule gives the name of owner, agent or manager of the farm, acreage, cash value of farm and of farming equipment, number of horses, mules, milch cows, working oxen, sheep, swine and their value. Listing of almost every conceivable farm product (wheat, Indian corn, sweet potatoes, wine, butter, hops, hemp, flax, silk cocoons, beeswax and honey, to name a few), the schedule asks for annual production figures.

The 1880 agriculture census, on Roll 88 of the schedules, gives the same information and, in addition, gives the weeks of hired labor, if any, and amount of wages paid. The schedules are such that you will be able to tell whether your ancestor's farm was dairy farm or truck garden, a one-horse family operation, or one with many hired hands.

◘ Other Census Schedules. Other schedules concerning the District of Columbia in 1880 are on Roll 93 of the Non-Population Schedules. These are described as schedules of "Defectives, Dependents and Delinquents." They give the name, "residence when at home," and date of admission to institution. There are lists of homeless children in institutions, one list titled "Association of Relief for Destitute Colored Women and Children," and others of paupers and indigents in poor houses, blind persons, deaf-mutes. Most of the lists give "residence when at home" and those for the children have a column to indicate whether the parents are alive and ask whether the child has been rescued from criminal surroundings.

Finding Aids and Sources:

Dilts, Bryan Lee. 1860 District of Columbia Census Index (Salt Lake City, Utah: Index Publishing, 1983). Heads of households and other surnames in households index. LC Call Number Microfiche 88/280 F.

A Guide to Records of the District of Columbia

Dilts, Bryan Lee. 1870 District of Columbia Census Index (Salt Lake City, Utah: Index Publishing, 1983). Heads of households and other surnames in households index. LC Call Number Microfiche 97/2004 F.

Federal Population Censuses, 1790-1890 (Washington, D.C.: National Archives and Records Service, 1977).

Jackson, Ronald Vern and Richard Allen Moore. Washington, D.C. 1800 Census (Bountiful, Utah: Accelerated Indexing Systems, 1972). LC Call Number F193.J33 1975.

Jackson, Ronald Vern. District of Columbia 1810 Census Index (Accelerated Indexing Systems International, 1981). Georgetown District only. LC Call Number F193.D59 1981.

Jackson, Ronald Vern. District of Columbia 1820 Census Index (Bountiful, Utah: Accelerated Indexing Systems, 1976). LC Call Number F193.J333.

Jackson, Ronald Vern. District of Columbia 1840 Index Census (Bountiful, Utah: Accelerated Indexing Systems, 1977). LC Call Number F193.J335.

Jackson, Ronald Vern and Gary Ronald Teeples. District of Columbia 1830 Index Census (Bountiful, Utah: Accelerated Indexing Systems, Inc., c.1980). LC Call Number F193.J334.

Jackson, Ronald Vern and Gary Ronald Teeples. District of Columbia 1850 Census Index (Bountiful, Utah: Accelerated Indexing Systems, Inc., 1977). LC Call Number F193.J336.

Microfilm Resources for Research: A Comprehensive Catalog (Washington, D.C.: National Archives and Records Administration, 1996).

1900 Federal Population Census (Washington, D.C.: National Archives Trust Fund Board, 1996).

The 1910 Federal Population Census: Catalog of National Archives Microfilm (Washington, D.C.: National Archives Trust Fund Board, 1996).

The 1920 Federal Population Census: Catalog of National Archives Microfilm (Washington, D.C.: National Archives Trust Fund Board, 1991).

Parks, Gary W., comp. Index to the 1820 Census of Maryland and Washington, D.C. (Baltimore, Md.: Genealogical Publishing Co., Inc., 1986). LC Call Number F182.P37 1986.

Pippenger, Wesley E. Georgetown, District of Columbia 1850 Federal Population Census (Schedule 1) and 1853 Directory of Residents of Georgetown (Westminster, Md.: Willow Bend Books, 1999).

CITY DIRECTORIES

Washington directories are a valuable source of information, readily available and easily used, that should not be overlooked. Beginning in 1822, the directories were published every few years and, later, every year. The earliest directories covered only the city of Washington. By 1834, Georgetown and Alexandria were included. When the remainder of the District of Columbia became more populated, the entire area was covered.

In the city directories you may find not only the name and address of heads of families, but also such information as the occupation, business address, the name of a widow's deceased husband, and the name of another household member who was employed. Content of the city directory changed periodically. Issues may contain a business directory, lists of churches, cemeteries, newspapers, secret and benefit

Census Schedules and City Directories

societies, streets and alleys, public school trustees, clerks in government offices, salaries of government officials, members of Congress and even, in the early years, where the members of Congress resided.

The Local History and Genealogy Room, Jefferson Building, Library of Congress, has a complete collection of District of Columbia city directories. The books were taken apart for reproduction and not reassembled, but the directories have been reproduced on microfiche for 1822 to 1860, and on microfilm from 1861 to 1934, as listed below. No directories were published for years not given below.

Year	Description
1822	Washington City, by Judah Delano
1827	Washington City, by S.A. Elliot
1830	Washington City, by S.A. Elliot
1834	Washington City, Georgetown and Alexandria, by E.A. Cohen & Co.
1843	Washington, by Anthony Reintzel
1846	Washington, by Gaither & Addison
1850	Washington, by Edward Waite
1853	Washington and Georgetown, by Alfred Hunter
1855	Washington and Georgetown, by I. Ten Eyck
1858	Washington and Georgetown, by William H. Boyd
1860	Washington and Georgetown, by William H. Boyd
1862	Washington and Georgetown, by Thomas Hutchinson
1863	Washington and Georgetown, by Hutchinson & Brother
1864-1866	Washington and Georgetown, with business directory including Alexandria, Va., by Andrew Boyd
1867	Washington and Georgetown, with business directory including Alexandria, Va., by William H. Boyd
1868-1869	Washington and Georgetown, by William H. Boyd
1870-1871	Washington, Georgetown and Alexandria, by William H. Boyd
1872-1901	District of Columbia. That for 1875 includes a list of physicians and nurses, and the following year lists midwives and lawyers. The 1888 directory is compiled by Mrs. Wm. H. Boyd, but he continues on with that for 1889.

The 1830 Georgetown directory, printed by Benjamin Homans, is in the Rare Book and Special Collections Room, Jefferson Building, Library of Congress. In the Alfred W. Stern Collection there is an 1858 Washington business directory. A copy of the 1830 Georgetown directory is also at the Martin Luther King Memorial Library.

The Historical Society of Washington, D.C. and the Martin Luther King Memorial Library have more recent Washington city directories available on open shelves. There are directories after 1862 in the small library off the Microfilm Research Room at the National Archives. The George Washington University's Gelman Library has city directories on microfilm and microfiche. The 1822 and 1827 Washington city directories were reprinted by R.L. Polk. In the 1822 directory, there are over 1,700 entries giving occupation and residence of each family head and person in business.

Finding Aids and Sources:

City Directories of the United States, 1860-1901 (Woodbridge, Conn.: Research Publications, 1984). LC Call Number Z5771.2.C58 1984 E154.5.

Pippenger, Wesley E. Georgetown, District of Columbia 1850 Federal Population Census (Schedule 1) and 1853 Directory of Residents of Georgetown (Westminster, Md.: Willow Bend Books, 1999).

The Washington Directory, Showing the Name Occupation, and Residence of Each Head of a Family & Person in Businss Together With Other Useful Information (S.A. Elliott, 1827; reprinted Willow Bend Books and Family Line Publications, 1997). LC Call Number F192.5.A 1827-30.

Probate, Guardianships & Apprenticeships

Records of the District Court of the U.S., District of Columbia

In early 1996, the bulk of Record Group 21, formerly housed at the Washington National Records Center, Suitland, Maryland, was transferred to the downtown Archives facility. With this change, many of the oldest records for the District were made more readily accessible to researchers. Though Record Group 21 is discussed at length on page 53 of this guide, the items therein that relate to probate, guardianships and apprenticeships have been extracted from the inventory and placed below.

◘ Will Records. A combined index to wills, administration of estates and guardianships, for the period 1801-1927, is at the office of the Register of Wills. Source citations to wills are found on probate index cards, 1801-1930, at the D.C. Archives. The cards are also on microfilm there. The index cards give the number of each "administrative" case, data which is important in locating the records. Some case numbers contain the letters "O.S." (Old Series). All O.S. case files are housed in the National Archives.

If a will was filed, the card will show both the date of the will and the date it was admitted to probate. The card may note the appointment of an administrator *de bonis non* (d.b.n.), which was done when the executor or administrator died before all matters pertaining to the estate were completed. Also on the card are notations which may prove useful. These may concern petitions, orders, bonds, letters testamentary, inventories, accounts, and, if they were recorded, at what Liber and folio (i.e., book and page).

Original wills from 1801 through 1994 are at the D.C. Archives. The LDS Church has recently microfilmed the earliest records and will continue foreward as resources permit. Typescript copies of the wills for the District were made starting around the turn of this century. Bound typescript volumes exist at the D.C. Archives for Will Books 1 through 131. Beginning in 1926 with Will Book 132, bound photostat copies are at the D.C. Archives up through wills probated in 1965.

Original bound handwritten "court" copies of wills probated, which also contain a few apprenticeship indentures, for the period 1801-1888, are in Record Group 21, Entry 111.

Wills probated after 1994 are at the office of the Register of Wills at the D.C. Courthouse, 500 Indiana Avenue, Room 5006, Washington, D.C. Contact: (202) 879-1497 or (202) 879-4800.

The original bound indexes to wills filed, recorded and probated, 1801-1920, are in Record Group 21, Entry 110.

Wills in the District include those of non-residents whose wills were probated in the District, sometimes many years after death. This may be because the decedent owned property in the District and heirs were establishing claim to the property so it could be sold or partitioned.

◘ Abstracts of Wills. The District of Columbia Daughters of the American Revolution (D.A.R.) Genealogical Records Committee (G.R.C.) abstracted District wills probated between 1801 and 1845. These are to be found in D.C. G.R.C. Volumes 129 (1801 to 1808), 130 (1808 to 1815), 148 (1815-1829), 149 (1828-1837), and 159 (1837-1845) at the D.A.R. Library in Washington, D.C.

In 1996, this compiler made comprehensive abstracts of all District of Columbia wills through 1852, and devised a list of all O.S. administrative case files through 1852.

Abstracts can be invaluable in locating maiden names of female ancestors (as when the decedent names "my daughter Keziah, wife of Zadoc Wilson") and establishing other relationships. Also, abstracts may be

Probate, Guardianship & Apprenticeship Records

inaccurate or incomplete, and the original will should be checked if questions arise.

◘ Guardianship Records. Guardianship records relate to estates inherited usually by minors who have been made wards of the court. Typically, a creditor or heir filed a petition in the Chancery Court requesting sale or partition of property of the deceased. A guardian has been appointed to represent interests of minor heirs. A card index, 1801-1930, at the D.C. Archives lists the name of the ward, guardian, parent or decedent, the ward's date of birth, amount of bond required, and date of any orders for sale of real or personal property.

Early guardianship papers in the O.S. series are found in Record Group 21 at the National Archives. The index of guardianship records, 1801-1905, is in two volumes under Entry 122. The original O.S. guardianship case files, 1801-1878, are stored in approximately 48 boxes at Entry 125. Guardian Dockets, 1818-1892, are at Entry 123. Receipts from guardians, wards, administrators and others, 1841-1895, are at Entry 118. Loose original O.S. guardianship bonds, 1801-1878, are arranged numerically by O.S. number, and are at Entry 125. Transcripts of guardian bonds, 1802-1880, in eight volumes, are at Entry 124.

Guardianship case files at the D.C. Archives cover the period 1879 to 1934. Also at the Archives are guardianship bonds, 1902-1939, and later guardianship administration bonds.

At the D.C. Archives are foreign guardian and lunatics estate records, found in Liber Z.C.R. No. 1, November 15, 1862 to June 20, 1900. Records of guardians sales and orphans real estate are found in Liber Z.C.R. J.R.O'B., May 19, 1863 to December 18, 1871, Liber A.W. No. 1, March 16, 1869 to October 29, 1895, and Liber J.N. McG. No. 3, September 27, 1896 to June 7, 1900. See Figure 8.

◘ Estate Administration Records. An index to the O.S. administrative case files, 1801-1878, is in the National Archives at Record Group 21, Entry 112. The original estate administrative case files for the period 1801-1878, are stored in approximately 139 boxes in Record Group 21, Entry 115. Old Series administration docket books, 1801-1837 and 1853-1889, are in Record Group 21, Entry 113. The files for the period 1879 to 1994 are found in the D.C. Archives. To arrange access to more recent files, contact Register of Wills, District of Columbia Courthouse, 500 Indiana Avenue, N.W., Washington, D.C. 20001; telephone (202) 879-4800.

The administrative case files contain probate and estate papers filed by the executor or executrix of a will (or, if no will, the administrator appointed by the court), which may provide important genealogical information: waivers signed by heirs, funeral bills may name a cemetery, accounts may provide clues to business transactions or lawsuits, and inventories, which are usually fascinating in themselves, may offer details concerning possessions.

If an O.S. estate document is mutilated or missing, refer to the books at the National Archives in which they were recorded. For instance, another version of the record may be found in a bound volume noted on the probate index cards at the D.C. Archives, i.e. Liber J.H. Accounts 1, folio 73.

Administrative bonds for the period 1879 to 1939 are at the D.C. Archives. Administration docket books for this period are at the office of the Register of Wills. These are arranged chronologically by case number (which allows for locating the case number if it is not in the card index), and give the name of executor or administrator, amount of bond, and names of sureties. Sometimes there are notations about a decedent such as "of Prince George's County," "of Marine Corps." If the name you are researching is a common one, information in the Docket books may help you identify or eliminate a specific decedent as your ancestor.

Transcripts of bonds executed by administrators of estates, 1808-1879, are in Record Group 21,

A Guide to Records of the District of Columbia

Entry 114. Original administration bonds, 1801-1878, are at Entry 116.

◘ Estate Accounts and Inventories. Accounts submitted by administrators of estates, guardians and others, for the period 1802-1879, are in Record Group 21, Entry 117. As part of these 28 volumes, there are a few receipts for the period 1814-1849. Accounts of sales and records of goods sold from estates, 1801-1819, are found at Entry 120. Balances and distribution of assets showing how assets of estates have been distributed, for the period 1818-1857, are at Record Group 21, Entry 121. Inventories and sales, reports of appraisers on goods, chattels and personal estates, for 1799-1885, are catalogued at Entry 119.

Finding Aids and Sources:

Pippenger, Wesley E. District of Columbia Probate Records, Will Books 1 Through 6, 1801-1852 and Estate Files, 1801-1852 (Westminster, Md.: Willow Bend Books, 1996). LC Call Number F193.P57 1996.

Pippenger, Wesley E. District of Columbia Guardianship Index, 1802-1928 (Westminster, Md.: Willow Bend Books, 1998). LC Call Number F193.P557 1998.

Pippenger, Wesley E. Proceedings of the Orphans' Court, Washington County, District of Columbia, 1801-1808 (Westminster, Md.: Willow Bend Books, 1998).

Provine, Dorothy S. Index to District of Columbia Wills, 1801-1920 (Baltimore, Md.: Genealogical Publishing Co., 1992). LC Call Number F193.P76 1992.

Provine, Dorothy S. Index to District of Columbia Wills, 1921-1950 (Westminster, Md.: Willow Bend Books, 1996).

Walker, Homer A. Historical Court Records of Washington, District of Columbia, Death Records, 1801 to 1878. Names for some case numbers. LC Call Number F193.W26.

APPRENTICESHIP INDENTURES

An apprenticeship indenture is a contract by which an apprentice is bound to serve a master, generally for a specified period, terminable at the apprentice's majority or prior thereto, to learn the art or mystery of some trade, craft, profession, or business in which his/her master is bound to instruct. See Figure 9.

Indentures of apprenticeship cover the period 1801-1893, and are limited to Washington County. Alexandria County records were maintained in Virginia. The first volume is at the National Archives, and the others identified below are in the D.C. Archives. The bound records are indexed, and typically give the name and age of the apprentice, the name of one parent, the name and trade of master, and the terms of apprenticeship. Initials "J.H." below show that John Hewitt was the first Register of Wills. Records bound as below:

Liber J.H. No. 1, May 21, 1801 to December 17, 1811, at Entry 127 of Record Group 21 at the National Archives. This is also available on Microfilm M2011.
Liber J.H. No. 2, January 1, 1812 to May 30, 1822
Liber H.C.N. No. 3, May 30, 1822 to April 4, 1827
(Liber 4 has not been located)
Liber H.C.N. No. 5, November 21, 1835 to November 24, 1849
Liber E.N.R. No. 6, September 28, 1847 to August 4, 1893

An additional record system for indentures of apprenticeship, 1812-1893, is at Entry 128 of Record Group 21 in the National Archives. These are unbound, trifolded original indentures that were signed by the parties and presented for approval by the Orphans Court.

Finding Aids and Sources:

Provine, Dorothy S. District of Columbia Indentures of Apprenticeship, 1801-1893 (Westminster, Md.: Willow Bend Books, 1998). LC Call Number F193.P75 1998.

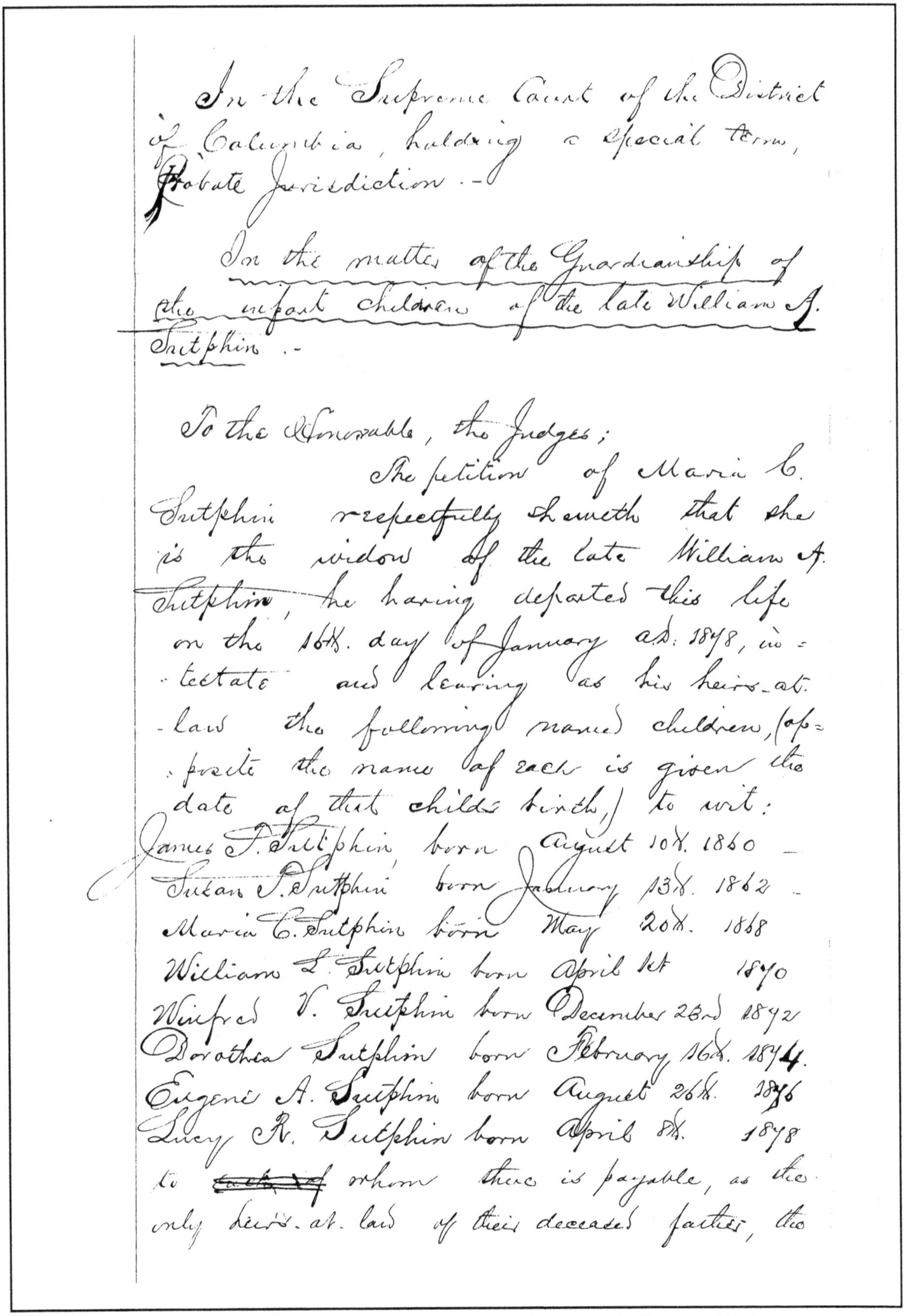

In the Supreme Court of the District of Columbia, holding a Special term, Probate Jurisdiction.—

In the matter of the Guardianship of the infant children of the late William A. Sutphin.—

To the Honorable, the Judges;

The petition of Maria C. Sutphin respectfully sheweth that she is the widow of the late William A. Sutphin, he having departed this life on the 16th day of January a.d. 1879, intestate and leaving as his heirs-at-law the following named children, (opposite the name of each is given the date of that child's birth,) to wit:

James F. Sutphin born August 10th. 1860
Susan F. Sutphin born January 13th. 1862
Maria C. Sutphin born May 20th. 1868
William L. Sutphin born April 1st 1870
Winifred V. Sutphin born December 22nd 1872
Dorothea Sutphin born February 16th. 1874
Eugene A. Sutphin born August 26th. 1876
Lucy R. Sutphin born April 8th. 1878

to whom there is payable, as the only heirs-at-law of their deceased father, the

Figure 8 - Sample Page from Guardianship Case File, No. 43, Maria C. Sutphin, 1879

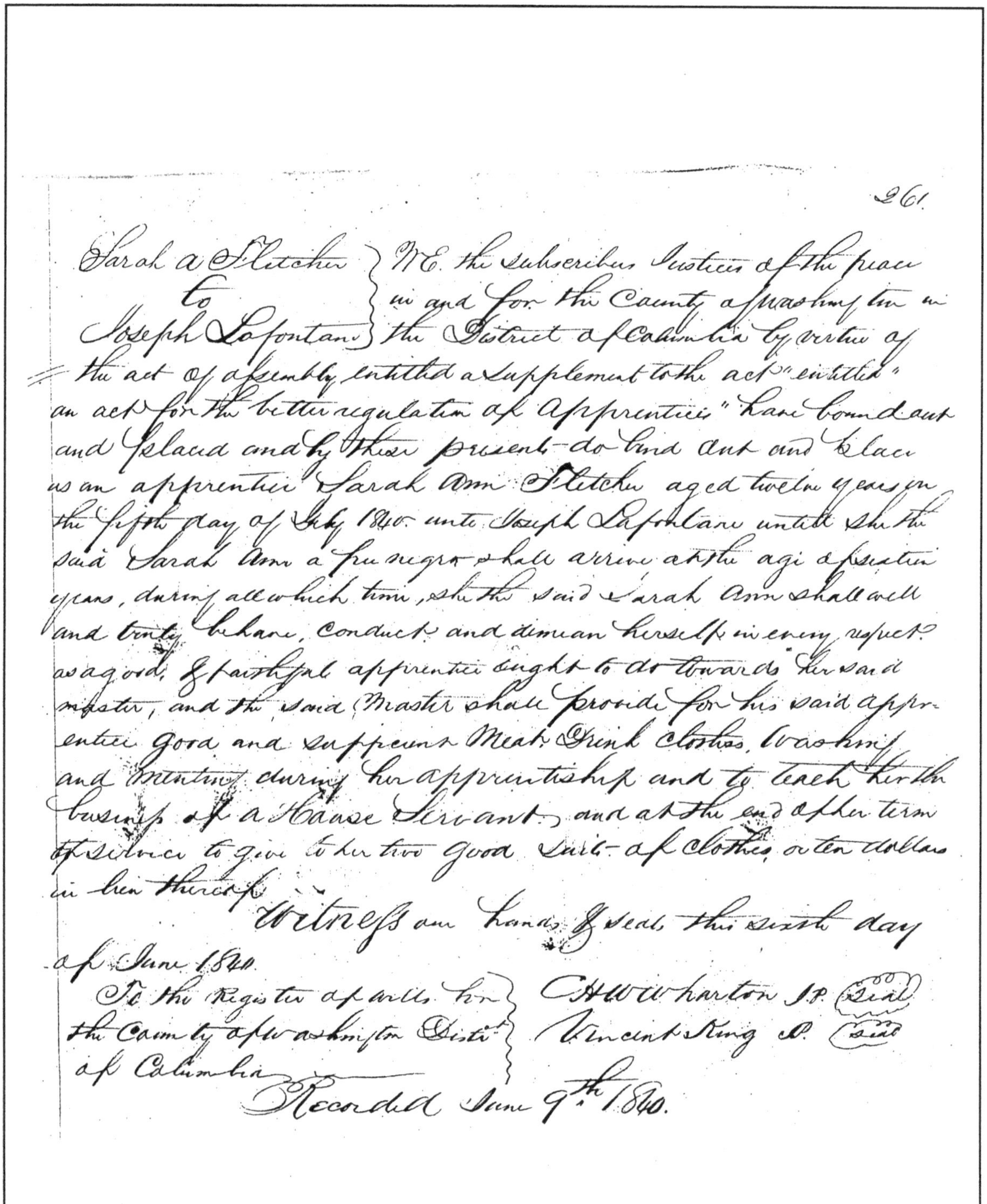

261.

Sarah A Fletcher to Joseph LaFontane } We the subscribers Justices of the peace in and for the County of Washington in the District of Columbia by virtue of the act of assembly entitled a Supplement to the act entitled "an act for the better regulation of Apprentices" have bound out and placed and by these present do bind out and place as an apprentice Sarah Ann Fletcher aged twelve years on the fifth day of July 1840, unto Joseph LaFontane until she the said Sarah Ann a free negro shall arrive at the age of sixteen years, during all which time, she the said Sarah Ann shall well and truly behave, conduct and demean herself in every respect as a good & faithful apprentice ought to do towards her said master, and the said Master shall provide for his said apprentice good and sufficient Meat, Drink, Clothes, Washing and Mending during her apprentiship and to teach her the business of a House Servant, and at the end of her term of service to give to her two good Suits of Clothes, or ten dollars in lieu thereof. Witness our hands & seals this sixth day of June 1840.

To the Register of wills for the County of Washington District of Columbia

H W Wharton J.P. (Seal)
Vincent King D. (Seal)

Recorded June 9th 1840.

Figure 9 - Apprenticeship Indenture for Sarah Ann Fletcher to Joseph LaFontane, 1840, Book H.C.N. No. 5, folio 261.

Real and Personal Property Records

LAND RECORDS

Land records for the District of Columbia contain not only deeds, leases, and mortgages, but bills of sale, agreements, manumissions and bonds posted for public office (such as tobacco inspector). They sometimes give a person's occupation, describe an equity or bankruptcy case, or list the heirs when the property owner died without executing or receiving a deed.

Records for District of Columbia lands originating in Maryland were recorded and indexed, beginning in 1792, at the office of the Recorder of Deeds in Washington, D.C. Each index volume separately covers a period, and there is no master index for 18th and 19th century deeds. As each deed was recorded, the names of grantor and grantee were listed in an index volume simply by the beginning letter of the last name. In 1882, use of a "vowel" system began, wherein last names starting with the same first letter were grouped according to their first vowel. Then, under each vowel grouping, names were indexed by the beginning letter of the first name.

The Historical Society of Washington, D.C. has a good collection of maps of Washington and Georgetown that may help you in determining the location of early properties as they give square numbers and early names of streets.

The typed index volumes are simple to use for the early period when the District has few residents, but locating transactions in later index volumes, when each index volume covers as little as 6 months, is very time-consuming. After about 1840, it will narrow a search considerably if you will first check the Georgetown and Washington assessment and tax books (see pages 13 and 13, 67 of this Guide). By checking each year's assessment records in sequence, you can determine the year an ancestor acquired a particular piece of land and the year it was sold. Then check the land records index for the period just preceding any transaction noted.

Beginning in the 1890's, early deed books were copied. These typed copies are available to researchers at the office of the Recorder of Deeds. Contact: (202) 727-5204. The indexes for this early period refer to both "old page number" (which is the page in the original handwritten deed book) and "new page number" (page in the typed copy). As you check the indexes, note the Liber number, Liber date, and folio of the entries that interest you and then ask to see the specific deed books involved. In 1900, the indices were separated by grantor and grantee.

Occasionally, the typed deed books will have an underscored word indicating that the typist had trouble deciphering the handwritten word in the original deed book. If the word is crucial to your research, you may wish to examine the original handwritten record.

Original deed books that were formerly with the Office of Recorder of Deeds, for the period 1792 to 1869, are in Record Group 351 at the National Archives (Entry 112). These are the handwritten court copies of deeds and comprise 551 volumes. The original deed books were microfilmed by the Genealogical Society of Utah. A complete list may be obtained from the LDS Church. The series of LDS Microfilm numbers are:
 #0895251-0895265 #0893983-0893995
 #0878258-0878269 #0878138-0878151
 #0893996-0894000

LDS Microfilm #0898001 is for the general indexes to deeds, 1792-1899. Only the first 50 volumes are listed below. Liber A1 series of land records for the single and double alphabetical series is found on 22 rolls of microfilm. Beginning in 1820, land records continue with Liber WB1 through WB148. In 1848, Liber JAS1 up to JAS134 in 1857. Liber JAS135 is missing. From 1857, Liber JAS136

A Guide to Records of the District of Columbia

continues the series to JAS230 for 1863. The next sequence is with Liber NCT1 for 1863, continuing to Liber NCT53 for 1865, continuing with RMH1 up to RHM31 in 1867. Series ECE begins with Liber ECE1A up through ECE32 in 1868. Series T&R begins with Liber T&R1 in 1868 up to T&R18 in 1869. There is a series Liber D1 to D14 in 1869. Afterward, the land record books begin with Liber 557 and are numbered sequentially to 566, and continue with 601 forward. To demonstrate the quantity of this record type, the last deed book for 1886 is Liber 1190.

Roll	Description
0895251	General Index to Deeds, vols. 1-4, 1792-1828
0898252	General Index to Deeds, vols. 5-8, 1828-1845
0895253	General Index to Deeds, vols. 9-12, 1846-1854
0895254	General Index to Deeds, vols. 13-16, 1854-1859
0895255	General Index to Deeds, vols. 17-19, 1859-1863
0895256	General Index to Deeds, vols. 20A-20B, 1863-1864
0895257	General Index to Deeds, vols. 21-24, 1864-1867
0895258	General Index to Deeds, vols. 25-28, 1867-1871
0895259	General Index to Deeds, vols. 29-31, 1871-1872
0895260	General Index to Deeds, vols. 32-34, 1872-1874
0895261	General Index to Deeds, vols. 35-37, 1874-1876
0895262	General Index to Deeds, vols. 38-40, 1876-1878
0895263	General Index to Deeds, vols. 41-43, 1878-1880
0895264	General Index to Deeds, vols. 44-46, 1880-1882
0895265	General Index to Deeds, vols. 47-48, 1882-1883
0893983	General Index to Deeds, vols. 49A-49B, 1883
0893984	General Index to Deeds, vol. 50, 1883
0899401	Land Records, Liber A1, Part 1, 1792-1793
"	Land Records, Liber A1, Part 2, 1793-1794
0899402	Land Records, Libers B2A-B2B, 1794-1797
0899403	Land Records, Liber D4, 1798-1799;
"	Land Records, Liber E5, 1799-1800; and
"	Land Records, Liber F6, 1800-1801
0912602	Land Records, Libers G7A-G7B, 1801
0912603	Land Records, Liber H8, 1802
0907816	Land Records, Libers I9A-I9B, 1802-1803
0907817	Land Records, Libers K10-M12, 1803-1805
0907818	Land Records, Libers N13-Q16, 1805-1807
0907819	Land Records, Libers R17-U20, 1807-1808
0907820	Land Records, Libers V21-X23, 1809-1810

◘ Original Proprietors. Deeds and other records, 1790-1889, relating to: (1) property of the original proprietors and those in Carrollsburg and Hamburgh; (2) the property of Greenleaf and Morris & Nicholson; and (3) property bought by or donated by the U.S., are in a volume in Record Group 42 in the National Archives (Entry 11). The volume is chiefly deeds, but also agreements, lists of property and proprietors, Maryland and District of Columbia court decrees, reports, and several letters.

Deeds of trust, c.1791 to 1823, to Beall and Gantt, trustees, from the proprietors in Carrollsburg and Hamburgh, with some from original proprietors of Washington City, can be found in a single bound volume in Record Group 42 at the National Archives (Entry 24). A plat book of city squares in the towns of Hamburgh and Carrollsburg after their redivision in 1794 is found in this record group (Entry 28). A plat for each square details dimensions and shape of the square, lots; includes "water property," street and water boundaries. Notations may be found for date of sale, to whom sold, and amount of sale. Plats and schedules are arranged numerically by Washington City square number.

Real and Personal Property Records

Schedules of sales of public lots, for the period 1791 to 1802 and 1817 to 1854, are in Record Group 42 of the National Archives (Entry 12). Arranged chronologically by date of sale and thereunder usually numerically by square and lot number. Also within this record group are several other systems of records showing sales of lots and squares, configuration, and division.

◘ Office of Public Buildings and Grounds. Among the several duties of the Officer in Charge of Public Buildings and Grounds were selling lots, maintaining land records, and making additions and corrections to existing records. In 1899, an act was passed which allowed the Secretary of War to correct titles to certain lots. Later, a commission to investigate the title of U.S. to lands in the District (sometimes known as the McMillan Commission after Senator James McMillan) was created by section 26 of the Public Buildings Act of May 30, 1908 (35 Stat. 543). Records are found in Record Group 42 at the National Archives.

As a result of the activity of this office and commission, a few records series provide useful information about land and water properties, 1871-1919. Entry 225 in Record Group 42, is "Case Files of Corrections to Land Records, 1899-1905." A typical file includes a case abstract showing lot and square numbers, to whom conveyed, date record was corrected, copies of deeds, and title correction certificates. Records of similar interest are found in the record group inventory. Records for the period 1899 to 1905 are arranged numerically by case number.

Finding Aids and Sources:

Dowd, Mary-Jane. Records of the Office of Public Buildings and Public Parks of the National Capital: Record Group 42, Inventory 16 (Washington, D.C.: National Archives and Records Administration, 1992). LC Call Number CD3035.O35 1992.

Gahn, Bessie Wilmarth (Brown). Original Patentees of Land at Washington, Prior to 1700 (Baltimore, Md.: Genealogical Publishing Co., 1969; reprinted 1998 by Clearfield Co.). LC Call Number F197.G25 1969.

Pippenger, Wesley E. District of Columbia, Original Land Owners, 1791-1800 (Westminster, Md.: Willow Bend Books, 1999).

Thomas, Milton P. The District of Columbia Liber Reference Book: A Cross Reference Guide to Instruments Filed in the Office of the Recorder of Deeds for the District of Columbia (Washington, D.C., By the Author, 1985). LC Call Number F193.T46 1985.

REAL AND PERSONAL PROPERTY ASSESSMENTS

◘ Georgetown Assessments of 1783, 1793, 1798. Typed copies of the assessments for Georgetown real property for the years 1783, 1793 and 1798 are at the Peabody Room of the Georgetown Regional Library. The 1783 assessment lists owner's name, lots owned and valuation. The 1793 and 1798 assessments list, in addition to this information, the improvements on the property.

◘ Federal Assessment of 1798 for the District of Columbia. Assessment records list dwellings and lands that are identified as being in the city of Washington, Georgetown, Prince George's County and Montgomery County. The lists have information on name of owner, name of "possessor" (tenant), number of dwelling houses and outhouses, quantity of land, valuation and a description of the buildings that gives size, number of stories, number and size of windows, and material of which each is constructed (log, plank, etc.). The writing is difficult to decipher, but the records are most interesting. There is also a "General List of Slaves," which is less informative, as it simply gives name of owner, name of superintendent and number of slaves.

A Guide to Records of the District of Columbia

The original of the Federal Assessment of 1798 record for Maryland and the District of Columbia is at the Maryland Historical Society in Baltimore (MS807), but is not available to researchers. Microfilm copies of the Federal assessment for the District of Columbia, 1798-1800, is available at the Maryland Historical Society (#605), the Peabody Room of the Georgetown Regional Library, and the Maryland State Archives, Hall of Records, Annapolis, Maryland (M862). The assessment was imposed for a number of Maryland counties, including neighboring Prince George's County. See LDS Microfilm #0499893-0499905.

◘ Georgetown Tax Assessments, 1800-1879. A microfilm copy of the tax assessment records for Georgetown, 1800-1879, are on Microfilm M605 at the National Archives. There are assessments of real and personal property for the years 1800 to 1819. Records are not always dated and appear incomplete for the early years. They list under each name the individual's property, its assessed value and, if the lot is improved or if the dwelling is frame or brick. See LDS Microfilm #1024464-1024465. Also included on the microfilm are assessments of real property, 1862 to 1879. See LDS Microfilm #1024475 (1862-1868), #1024466 (1865-1873), #1024471 (1871-1872), and #1024467-1024470 (1874-1879). Original records are in Record Group 605 in the National Archives.

In addition to records that are on microfilm, there are Georgetown assessment books for the years 1835 to 1865 found in the National Archives, Record Group 351, "Records of the Government of the District of Columbia" (Entry 184).

◘ Internal Revenue Assessments. Internal Revenue assessment lists for the District of Columbia, 1862-1866, are found on Microfilm M760 at the National Archives. A copy is at the Martin Luther King Memorial Library. The Internal Revenue Act of July 1, 1862, placed a tax on various products and manufactures, the sales of slaughtered cattle and hogs, interest on bonds, legacies, gross receipts from auction sales, newspaper advertisements and required annual licenses for trades, annual tax on income over $600 and annual duties on such items as carriages, billiard tables and gold plate. Monthly, annual and special lists are indexed. See LDS Microfilm #1578491-1578498. Original records are in the National Archives.

BUILDING PERMITS

Original building permits for February 17, 1877 to June 30, 1915, are found in Record Group 351 at the National Archives (Entry 96). They are arranged chronologically and numbered sequentially. Permits, 1877-1949, are on Microfilm M1116 at the National Archives. Square numbers appear in deeds and leases, or can be determined from a map showing squares. Part of the microfilm is a card index, 1877-1958, arranged by square number, name of street, or name of subdivision, gives square and lot numbers, house number and address, date, type of permit, and permit number. Plans that accompanied permit applications, July 1, 1915 to September 7, 1949, have been destroyed. Permits 1949-1990 are found at the D.C. Archives. Permits after 1990 are at Records Management Branch, Building and Land Regulations Administration, Department of Consumer and Regulatory Affairs, 614 H Street, N.W., Washington, D.C. 20001; telephone (202) 727-7512.

Permits and applications concern houses, stables, churches, theaters, stores, and other buildings. Some permits for repairs or alterations are interesting, with references like "to convert to blacksmith shop and set up forge," "to put in store front," or "to add a tower." Applications for permission to build give name of owner, architect and builder, size and location of lot, purpose of building, and note special features such as bay windows and tower projections. Many of the applications, such as the one in 1887 for a $16,000, 17 by 50 foot, three-story mansion on Rhode Island Avenue, were accompanied by plans.

Plans from permits, 1877-1915, are located at the Archives II, 8601 Adelphi Road, College

Real and Personal Property Records

Park, Maryland; telephone (301) 713-6800. These have not been microfilmed.

Finding Aids and Sources:

Hoagland, Kim. Guide to Resources for Researching Historic Buildings in Washington, D.C. (Washington, D.C.: Don't Tear It Down, Inc., 1982). LC Call Number F204.A1 H6 1982.

RECORDS OF HOUSES

There are two card file indexes at the Martin Luther King Memorial Library which have information concerning specific houses in the District of Columbia. "House Index" relates to clippings, indexed by owner, occupant, architect and the name of the house, if it has been given a name. "House Index by Quadrant" is arranged according to street address and consists of a few lines, cut from an unknown publication and dated 1922, giving the history of the house.

The Peabody Room of the Georgetown Regional Library has collected and organized information on specific properties and houses in Georgetown and is developing a "chain of title" index. Doorways and Dormers of Old Georgetown by Alice Coyle Torbert, published in 1930, contains a listing of Georgetown homes, street by street. The information as to when each of the old houses was built, its history and owners, past and present, may be helpful to genealogists.

COMMISSIONERS AND PUBLIC BUILDINGS

Record Group 371, "Records of the District of Columbia Commissioners and of the Offices Concerned With Public Buildings, 1791-1867," is found on 27 rolls of Microfilm M371 at the National Archives and at the Martin Luther King Memorial Library. The original three commissioners, appointed January 22, 1791 by George Washington, held their first meeting in George Town in April of that year. These are the records of the original commissioners and their successors, the Superintendent of the City of Washington and the Commissioner of Public Buildings.

This record group contains letters, agreements, accounts, directions, reports and contracts relating to surveying and planning the city, designating and dividing squares, selling lots, opening streets and constructing public buildings. The material is indexed. If your ancestor was in the District of Columbia during this period, he may have corresponded with the commissioners or been paid by them for work on public buildings, supplies or services. Also recorded are purchases of lots from the commissioners and sometimes the terms of sale, the commissioners agreeing to a lower price if the new owner erected a house within a set time.

GEORGETOWN RECORDS

Georgetown, which was founded in Maryland by an act passed May 15, 1751, was governed by its own mayor and council until February 1871 when Congress revoked its charter (16 Stat. 428). Georgetown retained its name as a topographical designation until 1895, when Congress abolished its title and existence as a separate city and it was consolidated with Washington, D.C. The bulk of the oldest surviving records of the city of Georgetown, D.C., 1800-1879, are found in Record Group 351 at the National Archives.

The "Records of the City of Georgetown, 1800-1879," are described in a pamphlet and are on 49 rolls of Microfilm M605 at the National Archives. The content is scattered with genealogical tidbits for a patient researcher. Included are journal and account books, general ledgers, daybooks, and employee and service accounts. Copies of this microfilm in the LDS collection are identified as rolls #1024458-1024463, #1024472-1024474, #1024476, and #1694980-1694993.

A Guide to Records of the District of Columbia

◘ Journals of Proceedings. Proceedings of the Corporation of Georgetown, for the period 1801-1805, 1847, and 1871; along with Journals of the Proceedings of the Board of Aldermen, 1805-1870 (with some gaps); and Journals of the Proceedings of the Common Council, 1807-1861 (with some gaps), are in the Manuscript Division of the Library of Congress.

◘ Officials and Employees. A list of employees at the pumphouse and elsewhere, 1878-1882, is found on LDS Microfilm #1024482.

◘ Ordinances. Printed ordinances of Georgetown, 1791-1870, comprise eight volumes in Record Group 351 at the National Archives (Entry 191). Copies of these are available on Microfilm M605 at the National Archives. The original index to ordinances and resolutions, 1791-1871, is described at Entry 189 of Record Group 351. LDS Microfilm for ordinances: 1791-1838, roll #1024478; 1803-1831 and 1837-1864, roll #1024479; and 1865-1870, roll #1024480. An index to ordinances, 1816-1869, can be found on roll #1024481.

◘ Tax Records. In the Manuscript Division of the Library of Congress is found Journals of Expenditures, 1826-1836; Tax Lists, 1814-1817 and 1819; and Corporation Ordinances, 1820-1831 and 1844-1855.

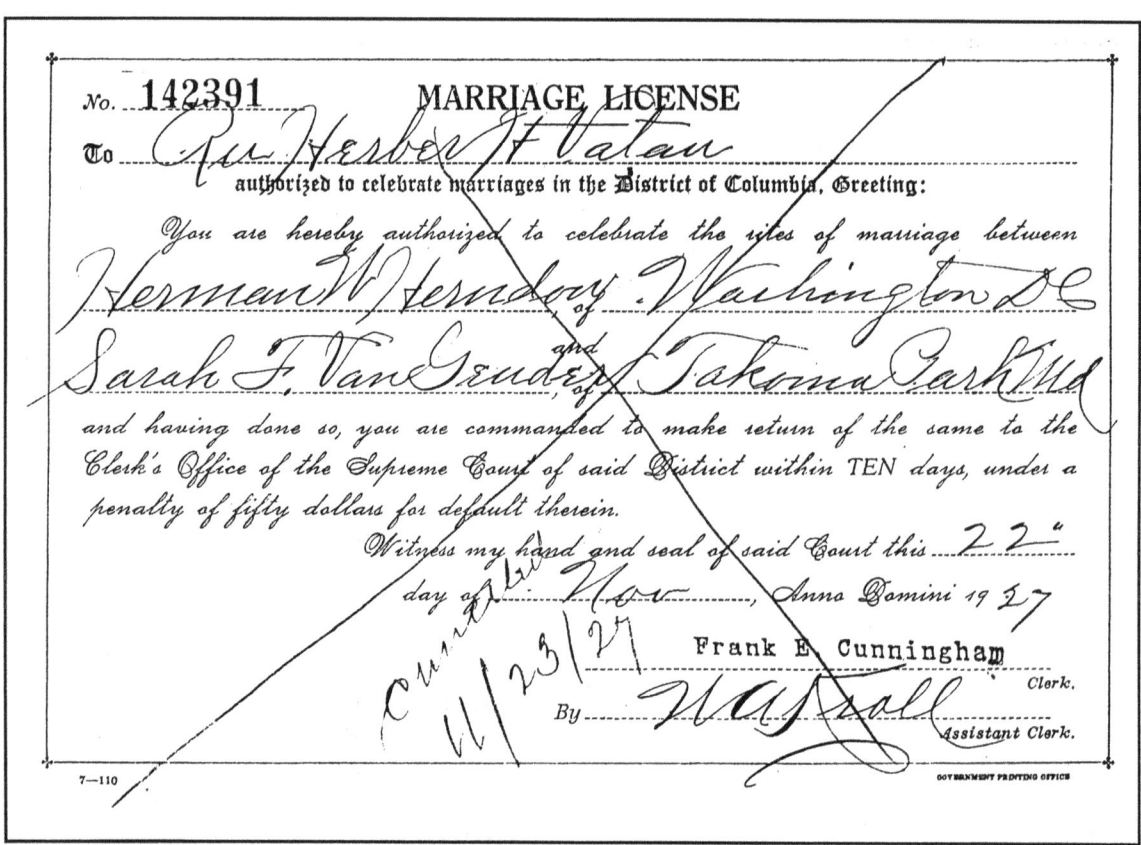

Figure 10 - Canceled Marriage License Issued to Herman W. Herndon and Sarah F. Van Gender, 1927

Marriage and Divorce Records

MARRIAGE RECORDS

The Marriage Bureau of the Superior Court of the District of Columbia maintains on location the marriage records after 1990. Write to the Bureau and give the name of both marriage partners (or either, if that is all you have), and approximate year of marriage. There is a $10.00 charge for a certified copy of a marriage record, no personal checks are accepted. Provide full name of bride and groom and the date of marriage, or the license number. An additional charge of $10.00 is assessed for requests to the Marriage Bureau for copies of marriage records previous to 1921. All charges can be circumvented by writing to the D.C. Archives where requests are filled as time permits. Contact: Marriage Bureau, 500 Indiana Avenue, N.W., Room 4485, Washington, D.C. 20001; telephone (202) 879-4848. Recorded information is on (202) 879-4840.

◘ Marriage Registers. Two "marriage" registers, beginning December 23, 1811, are found at the D.C. Archives. One register was made in chronological order as marriage licenses were issued, and the other is a later product that indexes names of the bride and groom together. Each of these registers gives the same information: name of groom, name of bride, and a date. That's it. The first register of marriage licenses issued, 1811-1858, can be found on LDS Microfilm #0845825 and #0845826. A few loose marriage licenses, 1837-1862, are found in Record Group 21 at the National Archives, Entry 35, and are listed on this compiler's Web page at:
   http://users.erols.com/pipp/dcmaradd.html

The second register is for the period September 1, 1858 to June 16, 1870. Another small index book is entitled "Index to Marriage Records, 1870-1986," and is a reference of what years of records are contained in the respective volumes.

Index books covering the period August 1, 1874 to January 9, 1902, give the name of the bride and groom and a certificate number. The certificates are sequentially numbered chronologically and are in bound volumes entitled "Marriage Returns." These certificates at the D.C. Archives are essentially a license which was sent out to the officiating minister. They provide names of the bride and groom, and also their age, residence, color, occupation, birthplace and number of marriages. On the back of the certificate is provided the date and place of actual marriage, and is signed by the officiating minister. A separate "Index to Marriage Returns" covers the period November 1, 1879 to July 1888. It is found at the D.C. Archives. See Figures 13 and 14. No index exists for 1902-1920.

For the period 1921 to 1991, there are indexes of marriages on microfiche. The microfiche gives full name of parties, date of certificate, and volume and page on which the written record appears.

The original bound Marriage Record volumes are at the D.C. Archives, and begin with Book 1 for June 1, 1870, and continue through Book 1,052 for November 1966. In this series, there are approximately 504,000 individual marriage records. At the later time, the sequence starts again at Book 1 and continues through Book 283 for August 1989. The second series covers approximately 14,280 individual marriage records. Each volume has an index at the front that gives the surnames of the parties, i.e. Thompson-Stewart for Elizabeth Thompson to John Stewart. See Figure 12.

◘ Canceled Marriage Licenses. On occasion parties were issued a license but didn't get married. In these cases a minister's return and a marriage certificate were never issued. A box of canceled marriage licenses for the period 1927 to 1935 is at the D.C. Archives, and is filed chronologically. See Figure 16.

A Guide to Records of the District of Columbia

◘ Minister Applications. An Act of May 13, 1896, required any minister who was appointed or ordained according to the rites and ceremonies of his church, shall, before the Supreme Court of the District of Columbia, produce proof that he is duly appointed or ordained as such. Loose minister applications are found at the D.C. Archives. These begin in 1896 and continue through 1961. Applications are filed by year then alphabetically. Applications for the period 1971-1986 were destroyed in 1993. See Figure 15.

◘ Minister Licenses. At the D.C. Archives are bound volumes of minister licenses, for the period June 1896 to July 1951. Information given is the name of minister, church affiliation, and date license was granted. Each volume has a separate index. Volume 1 (which is labeled 2 on the spine) covers June 1896 to May 1902; No. 2, May 1902 to October 1911; No. 3, October 1911 to August 1920; No. 4, August 1920 to June 1928; No. 5, June 1928 to December 1936; No. 6, December 1936 to January 1943; No. 7, January 1943 to December 1946; and No. 8, December 1946 to July 1951. See Figure 11.

◘ Miscellaneous Administrative Records. Relating to appointment of Registers, rules of the Probate Court, office forms, legislation affecting probate matters, payroll records, fees charged, etc., c.1886-1906, at the D.C. Archives.

Finding Aids and Sources:

Pippenger, Wesley E. District of Columbia Marriage Licenses, Register 1: 1811-1858 (Westminster, Md.: Willow Bend Books, 1994). LC Call Number F193.P56 1994.

Pippenger, Wesley E. District of Columbia Marriage Licenses, Register 2: 1858-1870 (Westminster, Md.: Willow Bend Books, 1996).

Pippenger, Wesley E. District of Columbia Marriage Records Index, June 28, 1877 to October 19, 1885 (Marriage Books 11 to 20) (Westminster, Md.: Willow Bend Books, 1997). LC Call Number F193.P563 1997.

Provine, Dorothy S. District of Columbia Marriage Records, 1870-1877 (Westminster, Md.: Willow Bend Books, 1997). LC Call Number DX145.P67 1997.

Sluby, Paul Edward, Sr. Blacks in the Marriage Records of the District of Columbia, Dec. 23, 1811-Jun. 16, 1870 (Washington, D.C.: Columbian Harmony Society, 1988), 2 vols. LC Call Number E185.93.D6.S58 1988.

Walker, Homer A. Historical Court Records of Washington, District of Columbia, Marriages, 1811-1858, at D.A.R. Library, D.C. G.R.C., Vols. 19-22. LC Call Number F193.W26.

Wright, F. Edward, Marriage Licenses of Washington, D.C., 1811-1830 (Silver Spring, Md.: Family Line Publications, 1988). LC Call Number F193.M37 1988.

DIVORCE RECORDS

Old divorce records are in Record Group 21 (Entries 16 and 23) at the National Archives (see Page 54 of this Guide). Records from September 16, 1956 to the present are maintained by Domestic Relations, 500 Indiana Avenue, N.W., Room 4230, Washington, D.C. 20001; telephone (202) 879-1421. Records previous to September 16, 1956 and after those in Record Group 21 (as above), are maintained at the Washington National Records Center, Suitland, Maryland. To access these one must know the divorce case number. An index on microfiche that gives the names of the parties involved and divorce case number, for the period previous to September 16, 1956, is kept with the U.S. District Court for the District of Columbia, Clerk's Office, 3rd Street and Constitution Avenue, N.W., Room 1225, Washington, D.C. 20001; telephone (202) 273-0520.

For additional information, call (202) 879-1261.

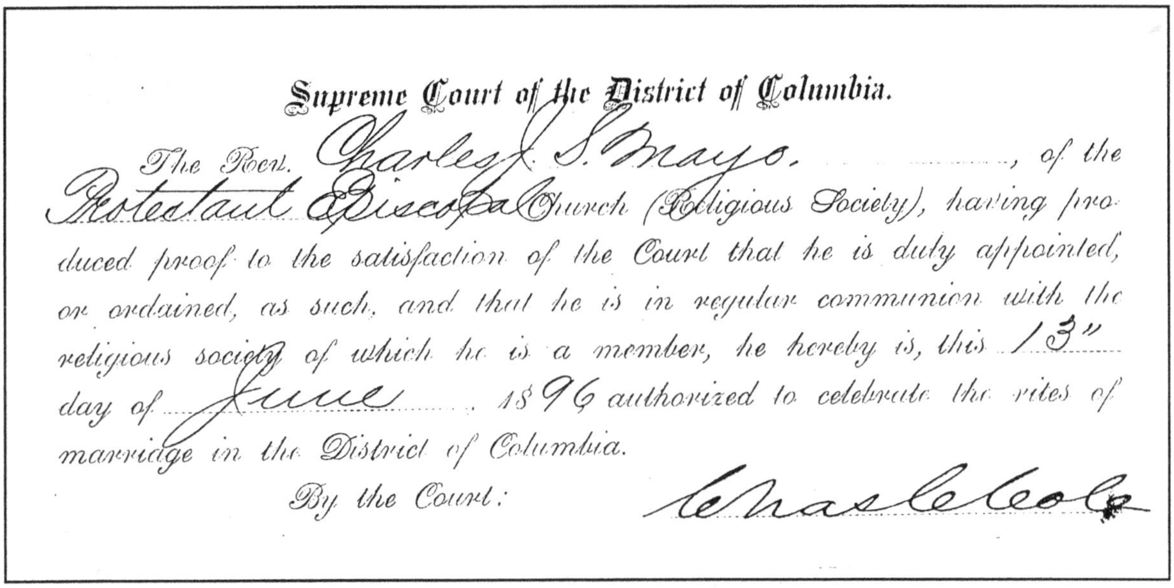

Supreme Court of the District of Columbia.

The Rev. Charles J. S. Mayo. , of the Protestant Episcopal Church (Religious Society), having produced proof to the satisfaction of the Court that he is duly appointed, or ordained, as such, and that he is in regular communion with the religious society of which he is a member, he hereby is, this 13" day of June 1896 authorized to celebrate the rites of marriage in the District of Columbia.

By the Court: Chas Cole

Figure 11 - Minister License for Charles J.S. Mayo, 1896, Licenses Book 2, Page 24.

To any Minister of the Gospel authorized to Celebrate Marriages in the District of Columbia, Greeting:

You are hereby LICENSED to solemnize the RITES OF MARRIAGE between Matthew O'Callaghn , of Washington DC AND Mary A. Cleary , of do if you find no lawful impediment thereto; and having so done, you are commanded to appear in the Clerk's Office of the Supreme Court of said District and certify the same.

Witness my hand and the seal of said Court this 5 day of June , 1889.

R. J. Meigs , Clerk.

By L. P. Williams , Asst. Clerk.

I, Jas F Mackin , Minister of St Matthews Church in Washington DC , hereby certify that, by authority of a License of the same tenor as the foregoing, I solemnized the marriage of the parties aforesaid on the 5 day of June , 1889, at St Matthews , in the District of Columbia.

Rev. Jas F. Mackin
Per H. S. H.

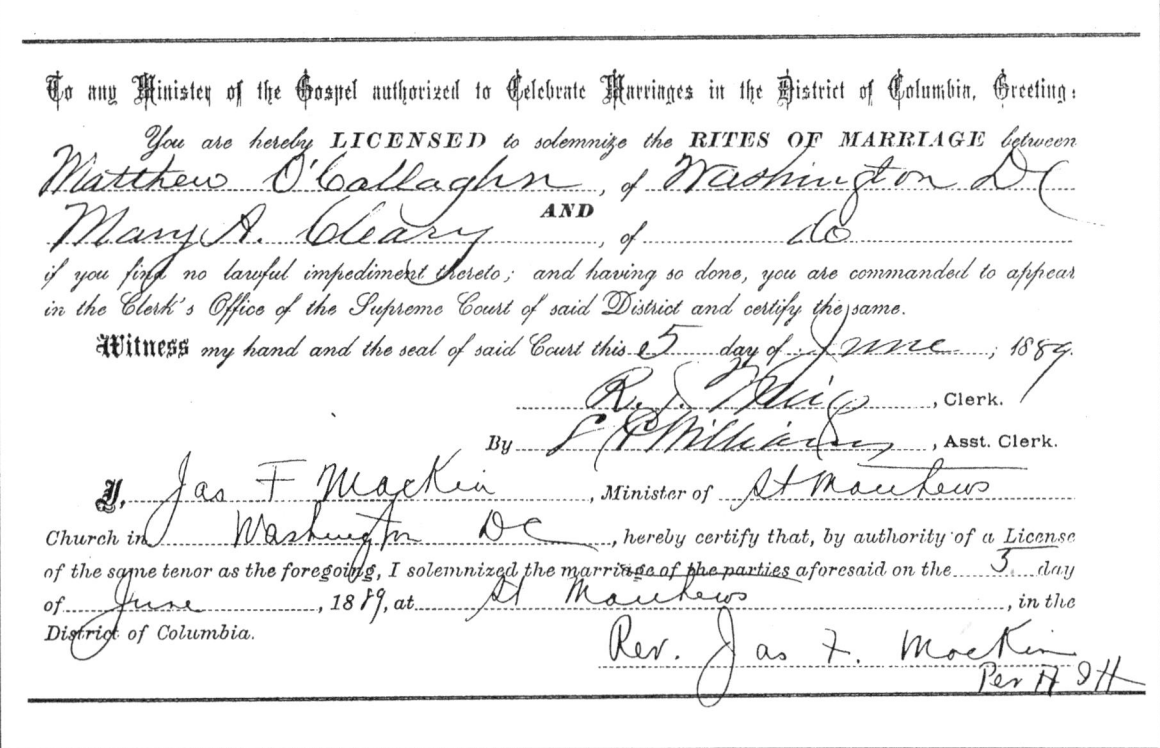

Figure 12 - Record of Marriage, Matthew O'Callaghn to Mary C. Cleary, 1889, Marriage Record Book 26, Page 237.

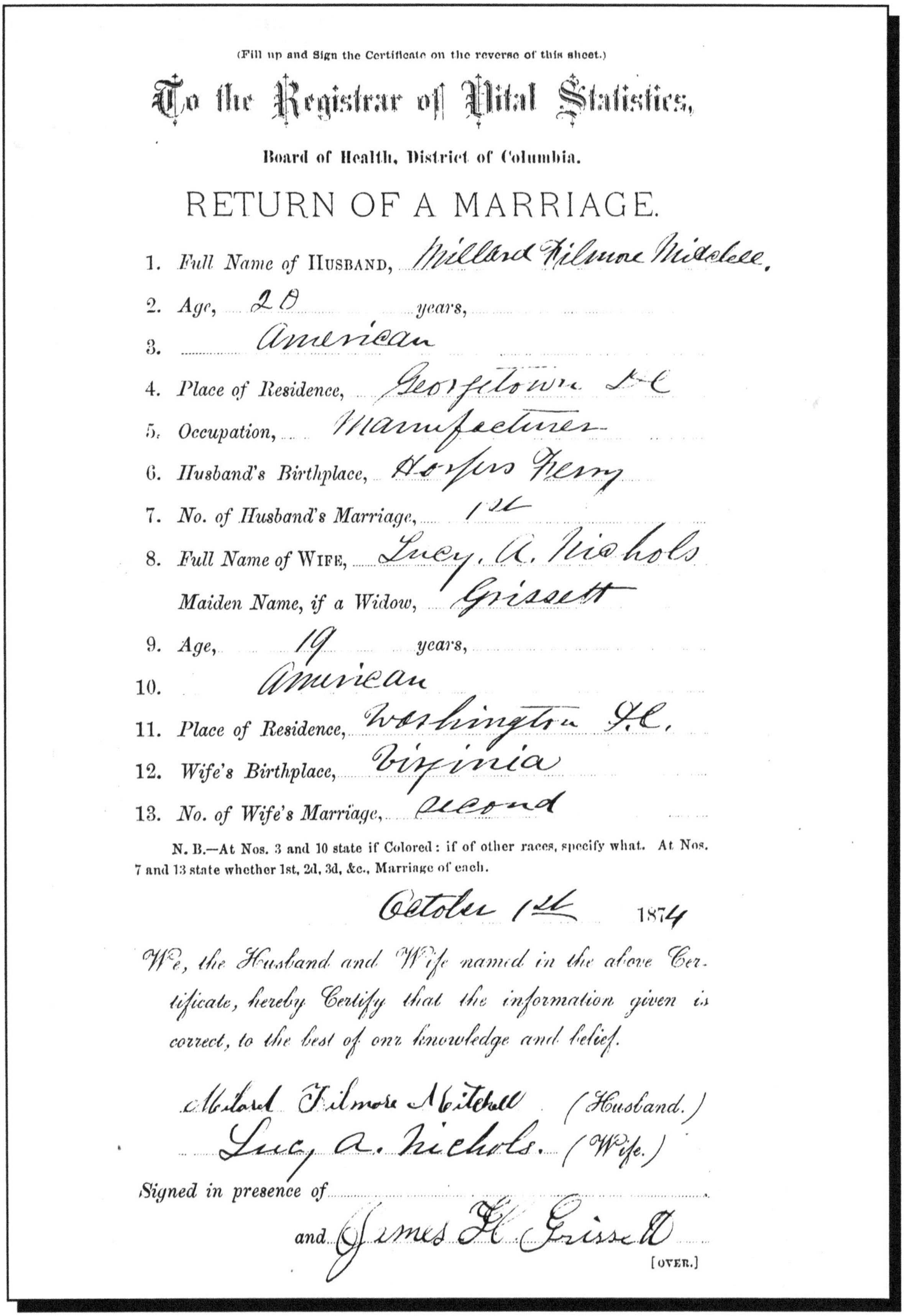

(Fill up and Sign the Certificate on the reverse of this sheet.)

To the Registrar of Vital Statistics,

Board of Health, District of Columbia.

RETURN OF A MARRIAGE.

1. Full Name of HUSBAND, Millard Filmore Mitchell
2. Age, 20 years,
3. American
4. Place of Residence, Georgetown DC
5. Occupation, Manufacturer
6. Husband's Birthplace, Harpers Ferry
7. No. of Husband's Marriage, 1st
8. Full Name of WIFE, Lucy A. Nichols
   Maiden Name, if a Widow, Grissett
9. Age, 19 years,
10. American
11. Place of Residence, Washington DC
12. Wife's Birthplace, Virginia
13. No. of Wife's Marriage, second

N. B.—At Nos. 3 and 10 state if Colored: if of other races, specify what. At Nos. 7 and 13 state whether 1st, 2d, 3d, &c., Marriage of each.

October 1st 1874

We, the Husband and Wife named in the above Certificate, hereby Certify that the information given is correct, to the best of our knowledge and belief.

Millard Filmore Mitchell (Husband.)
Lucy A. Nichols. (Wife.)

Signed in presence of
and James H. Grissett

[OVER.]

Figure 13 - Return of a Marriage (Front Side), From Marriage Returns, Book 1, Number 112.

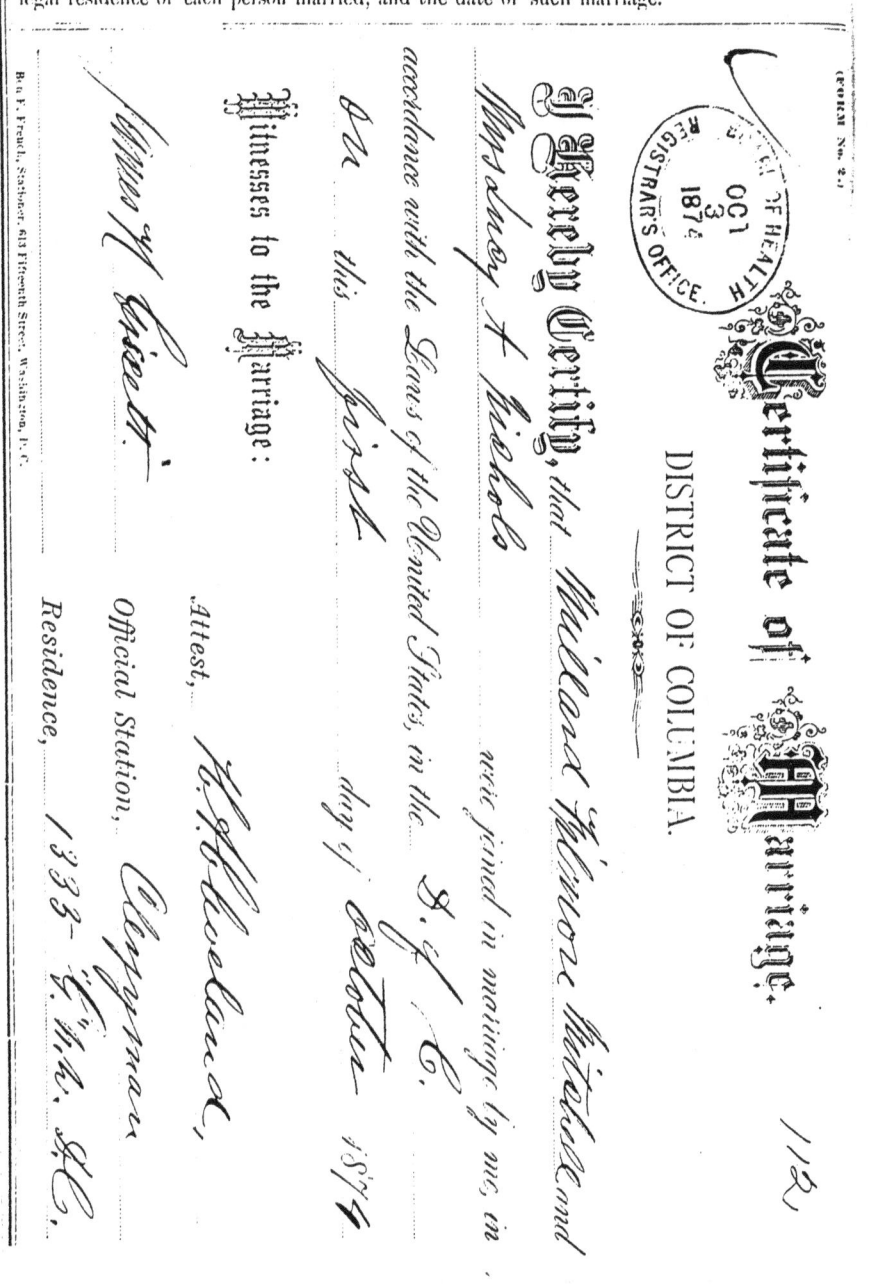

Figure 14 - Return of a Marriage (Back Side), From Marriage Returns, Book 1, Number 112.

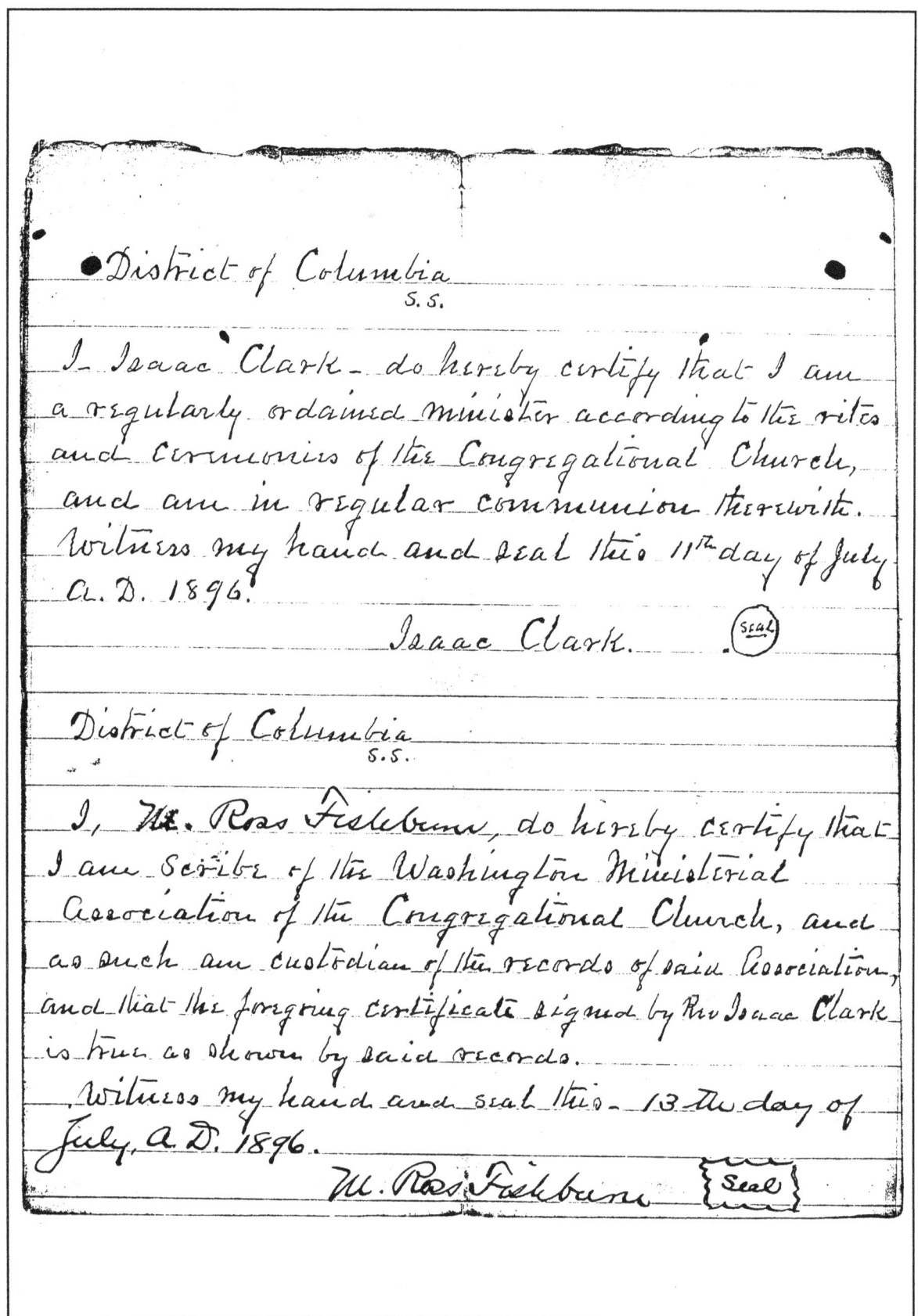

Figure 15 - Minister Application of Isaac Clark, of the Congregational Church, 1896, Loose Ministers Applications

Birth and Death Records

Records of births and deaths for the District of Columbia are held at two locations, the District of Columbia Archives and the Vital Records Division. The latter is one of three functions of the State Center for Health Statistics (SCHS), as part of the Commission of Public Health, Department of Human Services. To obtain birth or death records more recent than 1932, you may be asked to provide proof of your relationship to the deceased and purpose for requesting a copy. Birth and death records become public records after 100 years have elapsed from the date of birth and 50 years have elapsed from the date of death. Aunts, uncles, grandparents, etc. cannot obtain a birth or death certificate from Vital Records prior to the record becoming open to the public.

Requests for birth and death records may be made in writing to the address given below. For emergencies, a certificate may be ordered by telephone with use of a credit card, by calling 1-800-255-2414. When requesting an early birth record, be sure to include the names of the parents. This is especially true for early records from the D.C. Archives, as the name of the child often does not appear in the record.

The charge for death records is: $12.00 for a death certificate. The charge for birth records is $12.00 for a 'short' computerized version, and $18.00 for the 'long' certificate copy.

Contact: District of Columbia Department of Human Services, Vital Records Division, 825 North Capitol St., N.E., First Floor, Room 1312, Washington, D.C. 20002; telephone (202) 442-9009; walk up counter hours 8:00 a.m. to 3:30 p.m. Additional information is found on the Internet at:
   http://www.dchealth.com/vitalrecords.htm

Not all births and deaths in the District of Columbia were reported or recorded in the early years.

BIRTH RECORDS

The earliest register of births is at the Vital Records Division and covers the period January 20, 1872 to July 31, 1874. The register is arranged alphabetically by first letter of surname of parents, but is in poor condition, and the "A's" are missing. Recorded in the register are date of child's birth, names of parents and where they were born, sex, color and physical condition of child (healthy, stillborn, etc.), and name of physician or midwife. The name of the child, however, is not given.

Birth certificates, officially called "Return of a Birth," begin in August 1874. Original birth certificates are sequentially numbered and filed at the D.C. Archives. For the early years, the certificate had no place to record the name of the newborn child. Because of this, only the parents are given. Through the years, addenda have been made to the records by pasting something on the back of the certificate, making pencil notations, or typing a given name in a margin. Original birth certificates from 1874 to 1932 are at the D.C. Archives, with some gaps. There is no index to these at the Archives, so researchers must know the certificate number and/or the exact date of birth to facilitate a search. See Figures 16 and 17.

The index to birth records is on LDS Microfilm: 1874-1889, roll #2020343; and 1889-1897, roll #2020344.

◘ Return of a Still Birth. A system of records was kept to document still births. Extant records at the D.C. Archives cover the period 1874 to 1962. Returns provide for: name of mother, name of father, residence of mother, period of utero-gestation, date of birth, sex, color, nativity of mother and father, cause of dead-birth (if known), signature and residence of medical attendant, name and residence of other person making the return, date, undertaker, place of burial. No index. See Figure 19.

A Guide to Records of the District of Columbia

◘ Other Birth Records. Other birth records found at the D.C. Archives include: correction forms for births, 1952-1955; supplements for births, 1956-1957; legitimations, 1951-1965; and delayed births, 1957-1966.

DEATH RECORDS

Under the auspices of "death records," a journal of interments was begun February 1, 1855 and continued to July 30, 1874. The record is noted that there were no records kept from August 1, 1862 to January 1, 1866. The original register is kept at the Vital Records Division. See LDS Microfilm #1994618 for the index to interments, and #1994617 for the register. The register contents has been published by Pippenger as noted in the Finding Aids portion.

Certificates of death are extant from August 1874. On these is found the date of death, name of deceased, age, color, sex, occupation, place of birth, length of residence in Washington, primary and secondary disease, duration, marital status, and where buried. Certificates up to about 1932 are found at the D.C. Archives. The original index volumes for death records are with the Vital Records Division. The index is on LDS Microfilm, with a copy at the D.C. Archives:

1874-1882, roll #1994618
1882-1900, roll #1994619
1900-1916, roll #1994620
1916-1929, roll #1994621
1930-1943, roll #2020341
1944-1949, roll #2020342, missing the "A" portion.

Beginning with 1930, the index includes the date of death.

◘ Foreign Deaths. A separate system of records was kept for persons who died outside of, but were buried in, the District of Columbia. Also, a number of "foreign" deaths are documented in the series of death records above. Foreign death records at the D.C. Archives begin on December 1888 with certificate No. 1 and continue to No. 59,900 for 1959. The sequence then begins over for each calendar year and continues through 1965. The is no separate index for foreign deaths, as they are included in the regular index of death records and are identified by a different numbering system. See Figure 16.

Finding Aids and Sources:

Pippenger, Wesley E. District of Columbia Death Records, August 1, 1874 to July 31, 1879 (Westminster, Md.: Willow Bend Books, 1997).

Pippenger, Wesley E. District of Columbia Interments (Index to Deaths), January 1, 1855 to July 31, 1874 (Westminster, Md.: Willow Bend Books, 1999).

(ALWAYS WRITE WITH INK.)

Form No. 3.

No. 49

The Special Attention of Physicians is respectfully invited to the Remarks below, and to the List of Diseases on the back of this Certificate.

CERTIFICATE OF DEATH.

TO THE HEALTH OFFICER, DISTRICT OF COLUMBIA.

Permit No. 2643

Date of Death March 23 1889

Full Name of Deceased William Tell Steiger

Sex Male

Age 38 Years five Months 25 Days.

Color White

Married, Single, Widow, or Widower. Single

Occupation

Birthplace Washington, D.C.

Duration of Residence in the District of Columbia Seventeen years from birth

Nativity of Father _____ Nativity of Mother New York (Schenectady)

Place of Death, [Give Street and Number.] Laurel, Maryland (Howard County)

Cause of Death,
- First, (Primary) Consumption
- Duration
- Second, (immediate)

Duration of Last Sickness _____

All of the above information should be furnished by the Physician.
In case of death by zymotic disease, please state what, if any, local cause exists to produce the same.

Place of Burial Oak Hill - Georgetown D.C.

Date of Burial March 25" 1889

Undertaker William Millstead

Place of Business Laurel, Maryland

D. W. Snowden M.D.

Address Laurel, Md.
per WWS

Extract from Regulations to secure a Full and Correct Record of Vital Statistics in the District of Columbia.

SECTION 4. That whenever any person shall die within the District of Columbia it shall be the duty of the Physician attending such person during his or her last sickness, or of the Coroner of the District, when the case comes under his official notice, to furnish and deliver to the undertaker, or other person superintending the burial of said deceased person, a certificate, duly signed, setting forth, as far as the same may be ascertained, the name, age, color, sex, nativity (giving State or country), occupation, whether married or single, duration of residence in the District of Columbia, cause, date, and place of death (giving street and number), and duration of last sickness of such diseased person. And it shall be the duty of the undertaker, or other person in charge of the burial of such deceased person, to state in said certificate the date and place of burial, and, having signed the same, to forward it to the Registrar aforesaid within twenty-four hours after such death: *Provided*, That in case of death from any infectious or contagious disease, said certificate shall be so made and forwarded within eight hours thereafter. [OVER.]

Figure 16 - Certificate of Death for William Tell Steiger, 1889, Foreign Death Certificates, Book 1, Number 49.

Form 4—10,000-7-26-'99.

Extract from Regulations to Secure a Full and Correct Record of Vital Statistics in the District of Columbia.

SECTION THIRD.—That any physician, accoucheur, midwife or other person in charge, who shall attend, assist, or advise, at the birth of any child within the District of Columbia, shall report to the Registrar aforesaid within six days thereafter, stating distinctly the date of birth, sex and color of the child or children born, its or their physical condition, whether still-born or not, full name, nativity, and residence of the parents, and the maiden name of the mother of such child or children.

RETURN OF A BIRTH.

To the HEALTH OFFICER, WASHINGTON, D. C.

ALWAYS WRITE WITH INK.

SPECIAL NOTICE TO MIDWIVES: { This Birth Return is to be used ONLY in case the child Breathes or shows other evidence of LIFE after birth. In other cases, viz:—of STILL-BIRTH—the Midwife must report IMMEDIATELY to the Physician to the Poor in the District in which the Birth occurred. }

1. Date of Birth _Jan. 26th 1901_
2. Full Name of Father _Gustav Richard_
3. Full Name of Mother _Mennie A Richard_
4. Father's Birthplace _Paris, France_
5. Mother's Birthplace (State or Country) _Illinois_
6. Was it a Male or Female? _Male_
7. Was it White or Colored? _White_
8. If Twins or Triplets, state their Sex and Color
9. Number of Children Mother has given birth to, including present birth _1_
10. Place of Birth (Street and Number) _# 1 Tyler St. Accordia_
11. Mother's Maiden Name _Eagles_   12. Father's Occupation _Watchmaker_
    Signature of Medical Attendant _J.B. Nichol_
    Address
    Signature of Midwife _Susie Fields_

Name of child, FRANK MONNIER RICHARD, added from supp. report filed March 14, 1967

Figure 17 - Birth Certificate for Frank Monnier Richard, 1901, Loose Returns of a Birth, Number 108245.

Supplemental Report of Birth

NAME OF CHILD

I Hereby Certify that the full name of the Male child born on January 26, 1901 to Justin E. and Minnie A. Engles Richard whose birth is officially registered in the Vital Statistics Section, Department of Public Health of the District of Columbia on Certificate No. 108245 is FRANK MONNIER RICHARD.

I further certify that this form cannot be executed by a parent because they are: (check one)

Deceased ☒ Physically incapacitated ☐
Unknown ☐ Mentally incapacitated ☐

Signature *Frank Monnier Richard*
Relationship to registrant
Signature of witness
Date Signed 10 March 1967

The name of the registrant has been proved by documentary evidence submitted to this office as follows: Affidavit of Personal Knowledge signed by Jessamin R. Lowe, age 80, related to the registrant as sister, in which it is certified that she has personal knowledge that the registrant was born in Washington, D. C. on January 26, 1901 to Justin E. and Minnie A. Engles Richard and that he was named FRANK MONNIER RICHARD

Chief, Vital Statistics Section

PHVS-4D   3-M   4/63

Figure 18 - Addendum to Birth Certificate for Frank Monnier Richard, 1901. Note the Form Provides No Space for Entry of Child's Name and a Supplement Report Was Necessary.

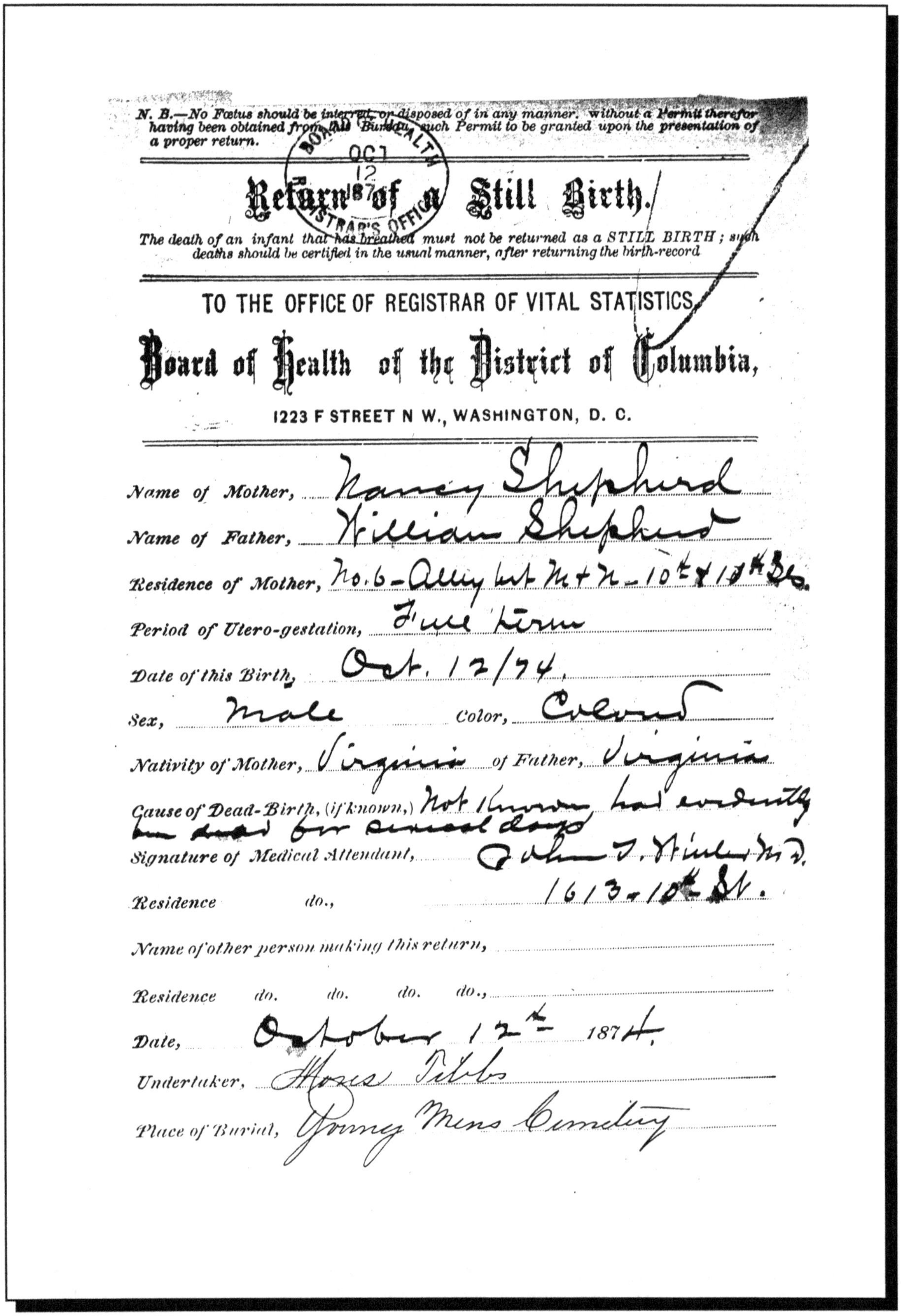

N. B.—No Fœtus should be interred, or disposed of in any manner, without a Permit therefor having been obtained from this Bureau, such Permit to be granted upon the presentation of a proper return.

OCT 12 1874 BOARD OF HEALTH REGISTRAR'S OFFICE

Return of a Still Birth.

The death of an infant that has breathed must not be returned as a STILL BIRTH; such deaths should be certified in the usual manner, after returning the birth-record

TO THE OFFICE OF REGISTRAR OF VITAL STATISTICS,

Board of Health of the District of Columbia,

1223 F STREET N W., WASHINGTON, D. C.

Name of Mother, Nancy Shepherd

Name of Father, William Shepherd

Residence of Mother, No. 6 - Alley bet M + N - 10th + 11th Sts.

Period of Utero-gestation, Full term

Date of this Birth, Oct. 12/74.

Sex, Male *Color,* Colored

Nativity of Mother, Virginia *of Father,* Virginia

Cause of Dead-Birth, (if known,) Not known had evidently been dead for several days

Signature of Medical Attendant, John T. Winter M.D.

Residence do., 1613 - 10th St.

Name of other person making this return,

Residence do. do. do. do.,

Date, October 12th 1874.

Undertaker, Moses Tibbs

Place of Burial, Young Mens Cemetery

Figure 19 - Return of a Still Birth, Infant Shepherd, 1874, Book 1.

Church Records

Church records, an excellent source of information on births, deaths, and marriages, are especially valuable for the years before 1850 when census records contained only the name of the head of the household. For this reason, our focus will be primarily on churches established in what is now the District of Columbia by 1850, although some churches discussed began a few years later and others are mentioned because of mergers. Your ancestor would probably have attended a nearby church, so the locations of the various churches have been researched, as well as whether and where there are extant records.

In making inquiries concerning church records, you will need to have the name or names and approximate date. Any information you have as to the name of the pastor or the exact church name that you have found may be helpful, especially when the church has moved or changed its name several times. Most of the church records are chronological and are not indexed. If persons at the church do research for you, there will sometimes be a request for a donation, since it may take a considerable amount of their time.

The District of Columbia Daughters of the American Revolution Genealogical Records Committee (D.C. G.R.C.) some years ago compiled and indexed a number of local church records. The Committee's reports are in bound volumes at the D.A.R. Library in Washington.

In his Centennial History of the City of Washington, published in 1892, author Harvey W. Crew discusses in Chapter XVI the churches in Georgetown and the city of Washington. In most cases are listed the church pastors over the years. This may be of interest if your ancestor was a clergyman. The information concerning pastors can also be useful in determining the religion of your ancestor, if you know from a newspaper or other source the name of a clergyman performing a marriage ceremony. A copy of this book is in several locations, including the small library off the Main Research Room at the National Archives, the D.A.R. Library, and the George Washington University's Gelman Library.

BAPTIST

◉ First Baptist Church. Organized 7 March 1802 by six members in a private home. They purchased a lot on the southwest corner of 19th and I streets and erected a church building which was occupied the following November. A new church was begun in July 1833 on the east side of 10th Street between E and F streets, N.W. In the 1850's the 10th Street property was sold and the First Baptist Church consolidated with the Fourth Baptist Church. The consolidated congregation moved in the 1890's to 16th and O streets, N.W. The Judge Lynn and Little John Boyden chapters of the D.A.R. compiled records for 1805-1885, in "Records of the First Baptist Church," in D.C. G.R.C., Vol. 82. This includes lists of members from 1802-1885; baptisms, 1845-1885; and teachers and pupils in Sunday School, 1859-1863. See LDS Microfilm #0845801. Contact: First Baptist Church of the City of Washington, 1328 16th Street, N.W., Washington, D.C. 20036; telephone (202) 387-2206.

◉ First Baptist Church. Soon after the original First Baptist Church built a new church in 1833, a large portion of the "colored" members of the congregation were formed into a separate organization and given the use of the old church building at 19th and I streets. They continued to use the name "First Baptist Church" for some time, but because the church was on 19th Street, the name was changed to "Nineteenth Street Baptist Church." The church reports no existing records. Contact: Nineteenth Street Baptist Church, 4606 16th Street, N.W., Washington, D.C. 20011; telephone (202) 829-2773.

A Guide to Records of the District of Columbia

◉ Second Baptist Church. Located on the corner of Fourth Street and Virginia Avenue, S.E., was organized June 1, 1810 with five members who were dismissed from the First Baptist Church. Close to the Navy Yard, it was sometimes called the Navy Yard Baptist Church. In 1957, the Second Baptist Church moved from the District of Columbia to suburban Maryland, having built a new church in College Park. Then in 1970, Second Baptist merged with University Baptist Church, and after the consolidation took the name University Baptist Church. Copies of the church records are on microfiche and available to researchers. Contact: University Baptist Church, 3515 Campus Drive, College Park, Maryland 20740; telephone (301) 422-1430.

◉ E Street Baptist Church. Located on E Street between Sixth and Seventh streets, N.W., was organized in 1842. A church was erected in 1843. A new church was dedicated at 10th and N streets, N.W., in 1902. The church, now the Temple Baptist Church, is presently located on Nebraska Avenue, off Ward Circle. Contact: Temple Baptist Church, 3850 Nebraska Avenue, N.W., Washington, D.C. 20016; telephone (202) 363-8371.

Historical Records Survey, District of Columbia. Bibliography of the Baptist Churches in the District of Columbia. (Washington, D.C., 1941). LC Call Number Z7845.B2 H53.

CATHOLIC

◉ St. Francis DeSales Catholic Church. Organized in 1821 by the Carrolls, Digges, Fenwicks and other Catholic families. A small chapel was then used. A church was erected in 1908 at Rhode Island Avenue and 20th Street, N.E. Contact: St. Francis DeSales Rectory, 2021 Rhode Island Avenue, N.E., Washington, D.C. 20018; telephone (202) 529-7451.

◉ St. Mary's Catholic Church. Began with about twenty families in 1844. A church was built on 5th Street near H Street, N.W., the lot being furnished by General Van Ness. A parsonage and school were added in 1866, and a new church erected in 1891. Write to the church, giving names and approximate dates and the research you request will be done by someone at the church. Contact: St. Mary's Catholic Church, 727 5th Street, N.W., Washington, D.C. 20001; telephone (202) 289-7770.

◉ St. Matthew's Catholic Church. Established c.1840, the church building at the corner of H and 15th streets, N.W., was consecrated May 15, 1842. In 1892 a new church was built on Rhode Island Avenue just off Connecticut Avenue. For information from the records, write to the church and the research will be done for you. Contact: St. Matthew's Cathedral, 1725 Rhode Island Avenue, N.W., Washington, D.C. 20036; telephone (202) 347-3215.

Philibert, Helene. Saint Matthew's of Washington, 1840-1940 (Baltimore, Md.: A. Hoen & Co., 1940). LC Call Number BX4603.W32.S33.

◉ St. Patrick's Catholic Church. Organized in 1794. In 1810, the congregation erected its first church building on F Street near 10th, N.W. A much larger church was completed during the Civil War on a lot on 10th Street, between F and G streets. History of the Records of St. Patrick's Church and School by Charles H. Wentz (1941), found at the D.A.R. Library, contains a list of the records of St. Patrick's church and school. These include baptisms from 1811, marriages from 1807, and confirmations and interments from 1860. See LDS Microfilm #0845824. Copy in Library of Congress, LC Call Number CD3169.S3 H5. Contact: St. Patrick's Rectory, 619 10th Street, N.W., Washington, D.C. 20001; telephone (202) 347-2713.

◉ St. Peter's Roman Catholic Church. Built in 1821 at the corner of 2nd and C streets, S.E. It

Church Records

was torn down in 1889 and replaced with a stone church on the same site. If you will write, giving names and approximate dates, someone at the church will research the records for the information you want. Contact: St. Peter's Rectory, 313 2nd Street, S.E., Washington, D.C. 20003; telephone (202) 547-1430.

◉ [Holy] Trinity Catholic Church, Georgetown. Located on the north side of N Street between 35th and 36th streets, was begun after the lot was purchased by Bishop Carroll in 1787. It was half completed by 1792 but probably not ready for worship until 1795, as the first record is that of a marriage on 6 April 1795. In the churchyard are two slabs covering marked tombs and it is believed that there are unmarked graves. A boys' school was opened in 1805 and a girls' school in 1808. The church in later years came to be known as Holy Trinity Church. Records of the D.C. G.R.C., Volume 47, give baptisms and marriages, 1795-1805, which were copied from Volume 175 of the Georgetown University Archives.

The records of Holy Trinity Church are at the Georgetown University's Lauinger Library, Special Collections Division, 37th and Prospect streets, Washington, D.C. 20057; telephone (202) 687-7444. At the library, a Guide to Genealogical Sources, lists Holy Trinity baptismal registers, 1795-1928; marriage registers, 1795-1908; confirmation registers, 1806-1834, 1853-1898; First Communicants and Confirmations, 1818-1836; marriage registers, 1795-1908; parish census, 1893; pew rent accounts, 1830-1958. There are also records of members of Georgetown Visitation Convent, 1799-1826, which gives both religious and family name, date of birth, entrance, profession and death, and records of burials at Holy Rood Cemetery 1819-1917. "Register of the Holy Trinity Church Archives" at the library mentions pew register records, 1851-1908, pew rents (colored), 1851-1871, and Holy Trinity school accounts, 1871-1879.

Kelly, Laurence J. History of Holy Trinity Parish, Washington, D.C., 1795-1945 (Baltimore, Md.: John D. Lucas Printing Company, 1945). LC Call Number BX4603.W32.H63.

EPISCOPAL

◉ Church of the Ascension. Organized in May of 1844. Marcia Burnes Van Ness, daughter of one of the original landowners in Washington, donated a site on H Street between 9th and 10th streets, N. W. A church was built in 1845. A new church at the corner of Massachusetts Avenue and 12th Street was completed in 1875. Early in the 1900's, Church of the Ascension merged with St. Agnes Church. Contact: Ascension and St. Agnes Church, 1217 Massachusetts Avenue, N.W., Washington, D.C. 20005; telephone (202) 347-8161.

Elliott, John Habersham (1832-1906). A Sermon Preached in Ascension Church, Washington, D.C. on the Fourth Sunday After Easter (Washington, D.C.: Gibson Brothers, Printers, 1874). LC Call Number BX5937.E54.S4.

Tyler, Frederick Stansbury (1882-   ). A Brief History of the Ascension Parish (Harrisburg, Pa.: The Evangelical Press, 1933). LC Call Number BX5980.W3.A7.

◉ Church of the Epiphany. Located on G Street between 13th and 14th streets, N.W., was built in 1844 on a site donated by Miss Louisa Harrison. The D.C. G.R.C. compiled and indexed the records of the Church of the Epiphany in two volumes, which have a slight overlap in dates. Volume 85 gives baptisms, confirmations, marriages and burials from 1842 to 1870. See LDS Microfilm #0845801. Volume 189 has baptisms, confirmations, marriages, funerals and communicants from 1869 to 1885. See LDS Microfilm #0848240. Contact: Church of the Epiphany, 1317 G Street, N.W., Washington, D.C. 20005; telephone (202) 347-2635.

A Guide to Records of the District of Columbia

Hall, Charles Henry (1820-1895). Reminiscences of Epiphany (Cambridge, Mass.: Riverside Press, 1873). LC Call Number BX5980.W3.E57.

◙ Christ Protestant Episcopal Church, Washington Parish. When organized in 1794 it was known as Christ's Church. The first meetings were in a modest building on New Jersey Avenue that had been a tobacco barn. In 1795 land was given and in 1807 a new church was opened for services on G Street between 6th and 7th streets, S.E., near the Navy Yard. Reports of the D.C. G.R.C., Vol. 69, has indexed births and deaths, 1795-1838; baptisms, 1836-1920; marriages, 1795-1921; confirmations 1809-1921; communicants, 1825-1921; burials 1865-1911; and families 1865-1873; the last giving not only names but ages and place of residence. See LDS Microfilm #0845778. Contact: Christ Church Capitol Hill, 620 G Street, S.E., Washington, D.C. 20003; telephone (202) 547-9300.

Ennis, Robert Brooks. "Christ Church, Washington Parish," Records of the Columbia Historical Society of Washington, D.C., 1969-1970 (Washington, D.C., By the Society, 1971), pp. 126-177.

◙ Christ Episcopal Church, Georgetown. Organized in 1817 by former members of St. John's Church of Georgetown. A church was erected in 1818 at the corner of O and 31st streets in Georgetown, and in 1885 a new one was built at the same location. Part II of Volume 27 of D.C. G.R.C. gives baptisms, marriages and funerals, 1820-1866; and confirmations, 1840-1864. There is an index to Part II. The G.R.C. records for Christ Episcopal are not the complete church records. If you inquire the church staff will do the research for you. Contact: Christ Church, Georgetown, 3116 O Street, N.W., Washington, D.C. 20007; telephone (202) 333-6677.

◙ Grace Episcopal Church. Established in 1851. A church was erected at the corner of D and 9th streets, S.W. The church was closed in 1957 and its extant records were transferred to the Washington Cathedral. You may call or write and make and appointment to come to the Cathedral to research the Grace Church records or write and research will be done for you. See D.C. G.R.C., Vol. 56; LDS Microfilm #0845776. Contact: Washington Cathedral, Mount St. Alban, Washington, D.C. 20016; telephone (202) 537-6200. There is a fee charged for research by personnel at the Cathedral.

Mitchell, Rose Trexler, comp. Parish Register of Grace Protestant Episcopal Church, Georgetown, D.C., 1863-1900 (1963). LC Call Number BX5980.W3.G7.

◙ St. Alban's Protestant Episcopal Church. Built in 1854 on the turnpike leading from Georgetown to Rockville, at what is now the intersection of Wisconsin and Massachusetts avenues, on the grounds of the Washington Cathedral. You may either call or write and they will check the records for you or make an appointment for you to come in. Contact: St. Alban's Church, Mount St. Alban, 3001 Wisconsin Avenue, N.W., Washington, D.C. 20016; telephone (202) 363-8286.

◙ St. John's Protestant Episcopal Church, Georgetown Parish. Organized as early as 1796. A lot was donated by Col. William Deakins and there a church begun. The building funds were quickly depleted and the church remained unfinished for 6 or 7 years. In 1803, building resumed and in 1804 a rector was chosen for the church, located at what is now 3240 O Street, N.W. D.C. G.R.C., Part I of Volume 27, has subscribers 1796 and 1843, pewholders, 1804 and 1821; vestry 1806-1838; communicants from 1841; baptisms of children 1821-1847 and adults 1842-1869; marriages and burials, 1821-1867. Part I of this volume is indexed separately. Transcriptions of marriages in St. John's Parish as performed by reverends William Hawley, Smith Pyne and John Lewis,

Church Records

were compiled and typed by the D.A.R. See LDS Library call number 975.3 V25d or LDS Microfilm #0924445. Contact: St. John's Church, 3240 O Street, N.W., Washington, D.C. 20007; telephone (202) 338-1796.

Ten Eyck, Dorothy Lauder. One Hundred and Fifty Years in the Life of St. John's Church, Georgetown (Washington, D.C., 1946). LC Call Number BX5980.W3.J56.

◉ St. John's Protestant Episcopal Church, Washington. Designed by Benjamin Latrobe, architect of the Capitol, and completed in 1816. On Lafayette Square, it is just opposite the White House and often called "The Church of Presidents." At the D.A.R. Library, two reports of the D.C. G.R.C. concern St. John's Church, St. John's Parish, Washington City. Volume 139 is a list of marriages from 1817 to 1870, which gives names, date and where the marriage took place. Volume 140 lists baptisms from 1817 to 1870, with date of birth, date of baptism, and names of child, parents and sponsors. Both volumes are indexed. See LDS Microfilm #0845809. Contact: St. John's Episcopal Church, Lafayette Square, 1525 H Street, N.W., Washington, D.C. 20005; telephone (202) 347-8766.

Green, Constance McLaughlin (1897-). The Church on Lafayette Square; A History of St. John's Church, Washington, D.C., 1815-1970 (Washington, D.C.: Potomac Books, 1970). LC Call Number BX5980.W3.J62.

Hagner, Alexander Burton (1826-1915). History and Reminiscences of St. John's Church, Washington, D.C., 1816-1905 (Washington, D.C.: 1906). LC Call Number BX5980.W3.J7.

◉ St. Paul's Episcopal Church, Rock Creek Parish. Located on Rock Creek Church Road, N.W., was the first Episcopal church in what is now the District of Columbia. The first church services were held in the spring of 1712. Originally part of Piscataway Parish, Prince George's Parish was created in 1726, and included the land between the Potomac and the Patuxent Rivers and extending indefinitely west. Rock Creek Church remained in Prince George's Parish until 1856, when Rock Creek Parish was formally created and the church itself resumed its original name, St. Paul's. The church was occasionally referred to in later records as both "St. Paul's Church, Rock Creek Parish" and "Rock Creek Church, St. Paul's Parish."

D.C. G.R.C., Volume 16, entitled "Rock Creek Church Records," lists for Piscataway Parish from 1693-1725, vestrymen, marriages, births and deaths; for Prince George's Parish; births, 1726-1792; baptisms, 1792-1828; communicants, 1820-1824; marriages, 1731-1745 and 1806-1813; funerals, 1796-1828; vestrymen, 1726-1826; for St. Paul's Church, Rock Creek Parish, baptisms, communicants, confirmations, marriages and funerals from 1849-1883. Unusual among church records are lists of bachelors over the age of 25 who were taxed in 1758, 1759 and 1761 by the Maryland Assembly to finance the French and Indian War. See LDS Microfilm #0845769. Contact: St. Paul's Church, Rock Creek Church Road and Webster Street, N.W., Washington, D.C. 20011; telephone (202) 726-2080.

◉ Trinity Protestant Episcopal Church. First established in 1828 on 5th Street between D and E streets, N.W. Partly through the philanthropy of William W. Corcoran, a new church was built in 1850 at 3rd and C streets, N.W. The church was closed in March of 1934 and the records were transferred to the Washington Cathedral. "Inventory of Washington Cathedral Archives" prepared by the District of Columbia Historical Records Survey of the Works Projects Administration in 1940 lists the Trinity Church records at the Cathedral as being: register, 1848-1933; baptisms, 1859-1896; marriages, 1871-1890; burials, 1878-1890; treasurer's accounts, 1871-1878; and an undated book of confirmations. Research may be done at the Cathedral. There is a fee charged for research by personnel at the Cathedral. Contact:

A Guide to Records of the District of Columbia

Washington Cathedral, Mount St. Alban, 3001 Wisconsin Ave., N.W., Washington, D.C. 20016; telephone (202) 537-6200.

LUTHERAN

◙ German Evangelical Lutheran Church. Later known as the Concordia Lutheran Church, was organized in 1833 by a small band of Germans meeting for a time at the City Hall. Then a church was erected on the corner of 20th and G streets, N.W. A copy of the original records of the Concordia Lutheran Evangelical Church in the United Church, Washington, D.C., is available on LDS Microfilm #1303264. The text is in English and German and includes baptisms, marriages and deaths, 1833-1943; minutes, 1876-1884; and membership lists. In 1975 the Concordia Lutheran Church merged with the Union United Methodist Church forming the United Church of Christ. It is requested that you use the microfilm copies of the records for research. Contact: The United Church, 1920 G Street, N.W., Washington, D.C. 20006; telephone (202) 331-1495.

◙ St. Paul's English Lutheran Church. Established in 1842. In 1844 the cornerstone of a church building was laid at the intersection of H and 11th streets, N.W. D.C. G.R.C., Volume 106, has baptisms, 1842-1900; marriages, 1842-1890; and deaths, 1850-1874. See LDS Microfilm #0845805. In 1927, St. Paul's merged with Epiphany Lutheran Church and the combined congregations moved to Connecticut Avenue and Everett Street, N.W. Contact: St. Paul's Lutheran Church, 4900 Connecticut Avenue, N.W., Washington, D.C. 20008; telephone (202) 966-5489.

◙ Trinity German Evangelical Lutheran Church. Organized in 1851; erected a church at the corner of 4th and E streets, N.W. The church at this location is known today as First Trinity Lutheran Church. Church records are in German script, described as "almost unreadable" and in poor condition. Contact: First Trinity Lutheran Church, 309 E Street, N.W., Washington, D.C. 20001; telephone (202) 737-4859.

METHODIST EPISCOPAL

◙ Anacostia Methodist Episcopal Church. The church was organized in 1845 in a building known as Danforth Chapel, on the river road near old Bridge Street, which is apparently the road now known as Martin Luther King, Jr. Avenue. The congregation moved in 1859 to Ryan Chapel in Uniontown and in 1922 dedicated a new church at 14th and U streets, S.E. The Anacostia Methodist Episcopal Church was closed about 1977 and its records deposited with the Lovely Lane Museum in Baltimore. To look at the records, call or write the museum and arrange to come in. Contact: Lovely Lane Museum, 2200 St. Paul Street, Baltimore, Maryland 21218; telephone (410) 889-4458.

◙ Asbury Methodist Episcopal Church. Erected in 1849 at the corner of 11th and K streets as a "colored church." The Foundry Methodist Episcopal Church was repaired that year and in order to use the basement for Sunday School, the church floor was raised and the galleries, until then occupied by the colored members, were taken down. A separate church, Asbury Methodist Episcopal, was built for the colored. The church reports that there are no extant records. Contact: Asbury United Methodist Church, 11th and K streets, N.W., Washington, D.C. 20001; telephone (202) 628-0009.

Sluby, Paul Edward, Sr. Asbury: Our Legacy, Our Faith, 1836-1993 (Washington, D.C.: Asbury United Methodist Church, 1993). LC Call Number BX8481.W3 S58 1993.

◙ Dumbarton Avenue Methodist Episcopal Church, Georgetown. Founded in 1792, was the first church of this denomination established in the District of Columbia. Although doctrines of this church were preached in Georgetown as

Church Records

early as 1772, the first meetings were probably held in a cooper shop near the intersection of Gay and Congress streets. It was 1793 or 1794 before a small brick church was erected on Montgomery Street. The 1830 Georgetown directory states that in 1806 the congregation had so increased it became necessary to take down the old church and erect another at the same location. The site for a new church on Dumbarton (referred to as "Dumbarton" in some records) Avenue was acquired in 1849. Part I of D.C. G.R.C., Volume 14, entitled "Records of Dumbarton Avenue Methodist Episcopal Church of Georgetown" lists ministers, 1772-1890; members, 1821-1860; marriages, 1823-1838; 1862-1866; and deaths, 1849-1892. Part I has a separate index. See D.C. G.R.C., Volume 14; LDS Microfilm Roll #0845769. Contact: Dumbarton United Methodist Church, 3133 Dumbarton Street, N.W., Washington, D.C. 20007; telephone (202) 333-7212.

Donovan, Jane. Records of Dumbarton United Methodist Church, Volume I - Baptisms and Marriages, 1813-1991 (Bowie, Md.: Heritage Books, Inc., 1993). LC Call Number F193.D66 1993.

◉ Emory Methodist Church. Located at 6100 Georgia Avenue, N.W., was formerly Emory Methodist Church South, Brightwood, D.C., and earlier, Emory Chapel. It was organized in 1832. Abner C. Pierce, owner of Pierce's Mill on Rock Creek, gave land for a school and church. A log chapel was built and called Emory Chapel in honor of Methodist Bishop John Emory. In 1843, a larger log-frame church was built wherein the white congregation used the first floor and the "colored" the gallery. Nearby houses and the red brick church built in 1856 were torn down during the Civil War to build Fort Stevens. The congregation was reimbursed for the brick church and in 1870 built a stone chapel on the Seventh Street Pike, later Brightwood Avenue, now Georgia Avenue. D.C. G.R.C., Volume 263, gives the membership, 1832-1955; baptisms, 1891-1917; and marriages, 1891-1912. It is not indexed. See LDS Microfilm #0848240. Contact: Emory United Methodist Church, 6100 Georgia Avenue, N.W., Washington, D.C. 20011; telephone (202) 723-3130.

Ray, Laura Collison, Margaret Fisher, H.T. Waesche and Gerald E. Keene. A History of Emory Methodist Church, 1832-1962; One Hundred and Thirtieth Anniversary (Washington, D.C., 1962). LC Call Number BX8481.W3.E47.

◉ Foundry Methodist Episcopal Church. Established in 1814 when Rev. Henry Foxall purchased a lot at the corner of 14th and G streets where he erected a church and presented it to the trustees. It is said that Mr. Foxall erected the church in thanks to God that the British had not destroyed his cannon foundry in Georgetown during the War of 1812. D.C. G.R.C., Volume 15, Part I, lists baptisms, 1818-1837; and marriages, 1818-1862. This section is indexed, then early members are listed and indexed. See LDS Microfilm #0845769. If you need further information from the church records, it is preferred that you write and research will be done for you. Contact: Foundry United Methodist Church, 1500 16th Street, N.W., Washington, D.C. 20036; telephone (202) 332-4010.

◉ Fourth Street Methodist Episcopal Church. Located on 4th Street between South Carolina Avenue and G Street, S.E., later known as the Trinity Methodist Church, was the pioneer organization of this denomination in Washington City. By 1802, the Methodists were meeting at Greenleaf's Point, in a building at South Capitol and N streets. From 1807 to 1811, the congregation met at Dudley Carroll's barn on New Jersey Avenue, south of E Street. A lot was purchased in 1810 on 4th Street, S.E., near South Carolina Avenue. The following year the church, called at the time "Ebenezer," was dedicated. The city directory in 1860 refers to the church as "East Washington Station," in 1880 as the "Fourth Street Church," and then, beginning in 1895, as "Trinity Church." About 1961, Trinity merged with three other Methodist

A Guide to Records of the District of Columbia

churches: Waugh, 3rd and A streets, N.E.; North Carolina Avenue, Eighth Street and North Carolina Avenue, S.E.; and Wilson Memorial, 11th Street, S.E. The church formed was the Capitol Hill United Methodist Church at 5th Street and Pennsylvania Avenue, S.E.

D.C. G.R.C., Volume 188, "Trinity Methodist Church," has in Part I the trustees' minutes, 1810-1826; marriages at Ebenezer Station, 1827-1834; marriage register, 1837-1891; and baptisms, 1870-1875. Part II has baptisms, 1848-1867 and 1875-1890. Each of the two parts is indexed separately. See LDS Microfilm #0845817. If you need further information from the church records, call or write and make an appointment to come in. Contact: Capitol Hill United Methodist Church, 421 Seward Square, S.E., Washington, D.C. 20003; telephone (202) 546-1000.

◙ Israel Bethel African Methodist Episcopal Church. Organized in 1820, was the first African church in the city of Washington. For a time, the members met at Simm's Rope-Walk at 3rd Street and Pennsylvania Avenue, S.E. (A ropewalk is a long covered walk or building where ropes are manufactured.) In 1822, they purchased a lot at 1st and B streets, S.W., and built a church which was replaced by another at the same location in 1874. In 1930, a new church was built at New Jersey Avenue and Morgan Street, N.W. Today the Israel Metropolitan Christian Methodist Episcopal Church is on Randolph Street, N.W. Contact: Israel Metropolitan Christian Methodist Episcopal Church, 557 Randolph Street, N.W., Washington, D.C. 20011; telephone (202) 723-5795.

◙ John Wesley Church. Organized in 1849 and a church built in 1851 at Connecticut Avenue and L Street, N.W. In 1902 the congregation sold this building and purchased another on 18th Street, N.W., between L and M. The present site located at 14th and Corcoran streets was acquired in 1913. Because of a fire in 1979, the church has no 19th century records. Contact: John Wesley African Methodist Episcopal (A.M.E.) Zion Church, 1615 14th Street, N.W., Washington, D.C. 20009; telephone (202) 667-3824.

◙ Little Ebenezer Church. Founded in 1838 as a "colored church." From its beginnings, the Fourth Street Methodist Episcopal Church, known then as "Ebenezer," had been interracial. In April 1838, the black members established their own church. Assisted by the white members, they purchased a lot on the corner of 4th and D streets, S.E., and built a small frame church that they called "Little Ebenezer." By 1880, the city directory referred to the church as "Ebenezer." The church building has been twice replaced at the same site. Contact: Ebenezer United Methodist Church, 420 D Street, S.E., Washington, D.C. 20003; telephone (202) 544-9539.

◙ McKendree Chapel of the Methodist Episcopal Church. Organized in 1844, was on Massachusetts Avenue, between 9th and 10th streets, N.W. About 1939 the congregation moved to South Dakota Avenue at 24th Street, N.E. For information from the records, write to the church and research will be done for you. Contact: McKendree United Methodist Church Study, 2421 Lawrence Street, N.E., Washington, D.C. 20018; telephone (202) 529-3075.

◙ Mount Zion Church. Organized in 1816 by the black members of the Dumbarton Avenue Methodist Church in Georgetown. They purchased a lot on Mill Street near West Street (what is now 27th Street near P), and built their church. It was in the 1830 Georgetown directory as "The African Church ... a small brick building on Mill Street." The church was originally known by its members as "The Meeting House" and "The Little Ark." The name of the church was later changed to Mount Zion Methodist Episcopal Church and in 1875 a lot was purchased to build a new church. In 1880 the congregation held its first service in the new church on 29th Street between Dumbarton

Church Records

Avenue and O Street, N.W. Contact: Mount Zion United Methodist Church, 1334 29th Street, N.W., Washington, D.C. 20007; telephone (202) 234-0148.

◉ Ryland Chapel of the Methodist Episcopal Church. Located on D and 10th streets, S.W., was organized in 1843 and its house of worship completed a year or two later. About 1940, the congregation moved to a new church building at Branch Avenue and S Street, S.E. They have records beginning in 1852. Staff prefer that you call or write and make an appointment to come in to look at the records yourself. Contact: Ryland Epworth United Methodist Church, 3200 S Street, S.E., Washington, D.C. 20020; telephone (202) 582-4006.

◉ Second Colored Wesleyan Church. According to a history of black churches by author Nina H. Clarke, this church was built in 1848 at 23rd Street, N.W., between L and M. Ms. Clarke states this was the original name of the present Union Wesley African Methodist Episcopal Zion Church. The Churches and Pastors of Washington, District of Columbia," by Lorenzo Dow Johnson (1805-1867), published in 1857, lists "Second Colored Church" on Missouri Avenue between 6th and 7th streets. See LC Call Number F203.2.A1 J6. The 1858 and 1860 city directories list "Second Colored" on Missouri Avenue and also list a "Union Wesley Chapel" on 23rd Street, N.W., near L Street. At this time, the connection between the two churches is not clear. Union Wesley African Methodist Episcopal Zion Church remained on 23rd Street until 1963, when it relocated to Michigan and Eastern avenues, N.E. Write to the church and they will check their records for you. Contact: Union Wesley A.M.E. Church, 1860 Michigan Avenue, N.E., Washington, D.C.; telephone (202) 526-1242.

Clarke, Nina Honemond. History of the Nineteenth Century Black Churches in Maryland and Washington, D.C. (New York: Vantage Press, 1983). LC Call Number BR555.M3 C58 1983.

◉ Trinity Methodist Church. See "Fourth Street Methodist Episcopal Church."

◉ Union Bethel African Methodist Episcopal Church. Organized before 1846 when the city directory listed the church on M Street, N.W., between 15th and 16th streets. An 1855 map and a book published in 1857, The Churches and Pastors of Washington, District of Columbia", by Lorenzo Dow Johnson (1805-1867), also listed Union Bethel at the same location, as did subsequent directories. The name of the church appears to have changed by 1890 when the city directory gives the name of the church on M Street, N.W. near 15th Street as the "Metropolitan African Methodist Episcopal Church." In 1900 the city directory notes that the Metropolitan African Methodist Episcopal Church was organized in 1838. For information concerning their records, write to the church. Contact: Metropolitan African Methodist Episcopal Church, 1518 M Street, N.W., Washington, D.C. 20005; telephone (202) 331-1426.

Kohler, Sue A. Sixteenth Street Architecture, Volume 2 (Washington, D.C.: Commission on Fine Arts, 1988), pp. 219-237. LC Call Number NA735.W3 K644.

◉ Union Chapel Methodist Episcopal Church. Located at the corner of 20th Street and Pennsylvania Avenue, was founded in 1846. The Union United Methodist Church merged with the Concordia Lutheran Evangelical Church in 1975 to form the United Church of Christ. A microfilm copy is available of the original records. Text is in English and German, and includes baptisms, 1833-1943; marriages, 1833-1944; deaths, 1833-1944; minutes, 1876-1884; and membership lists. See LDS Microfilm #1303264. Because the church records are in poor condition, it is requested that you use the microfilm copies. Records of Union Methodist Episcopal Church, 1860-1883, can be found on LDS Microfilm #1303264. Contact: The United Church, 1920 G Street, N.W., Washington, D.C. 20006; telephone (202) 331-1495.

A Guide to Records of the District of Columbia

◉ Wesley Chapel of the Methodist Episcopal Church. Located at the southwest corner of 5th and F streets, N.W., was organized in 1823. A new church was erected on Connecticut Avenue between Jenifer and Jocelyn streets in the 1920's. D.C. G.R.C., Volume 86, concerning First Wesley Chapel, 5th and F streets, N.W., lists probationers, 1865-1883; baptisms, marriages, and membership, 1866-1882. See LDS Microfilm #0845802. Contact: Wesley United Methodist Church, 5312 Connecticut Avenue, N.W., Washington, D.C. 20015; telephone (202) 966-5144.

METHODIST PROTESTANT

◉ Congress Street Methodist Protestant Church. Located on 31st Street in Georgetown, was organized in 1828. (What is now 31st Street was originally named Congress Street.) The 1830 Georgetown city directory states that the church, on Congress Street between Bridge and Gay streets, was dedicated in 1829. About 1951 Congress Street Church, Mount Tabor Methodist Church and Aldersgate Methodist Church merged, forming St. Luke's United Methodist Church, which used the Mount Tabor Church building on Wisconsin Avenue for several years. In 1954, St. Luke's built a new church at Calvert and Wisconsin. Contact: St. Luke's United Methodist Church, 3655 Calvert Street, N.W., Washington, D.C. 20007; telephone (202) 333-4949.

◉ Central Methodist Protestant Church. Organized in April of 1829 when members of the Methodist Episcopal church left their church to form the "Associate Methodist Church," later to be known as the "Methodist Protestant Church." The first church, called "The Tabernacle," was at 12th and H streets. The Ninth Street Church, on 9th Street between E and F, N.W., was built in 1835, and a church on Rhode Island Avenue and 1st Street, N.W., was dedicated in 1902. When the Rhode Island Avenue Methodist Protestant Church was closed in 1958, the last pastor reported finding no records before c.1952.

◉ First Methodist Protestant Church. Located on the corner of 5th Street and Virginia Avenue, S.E., was organized in 1830 from the Fourth (Ebenezer) Methodist Episcopal Church. They bought a school at 6th and G streets, S.E., to use as a church. In 1844, was built a church at 5th Street and Virginia Avenue, S.E., known as the East Washington Station. The congregation moved in 1897 to 4th Street between E and G streets, S.E., and in 1945 merged with Bradbury Heights to form the First United Methodist Church of Bradbury Heights, now on Bowen Road, S.E. The pastor reports that they have membership records 1845-1920 and some baptism and marriage records. Contact: First United Methodist Church of Bradbury Heights, 4323 Bowen Road, S.E., Washington, D.C. 20019; telephone (202) 583-1244.

PRESBYTERIAN

◉ Central Presbyterian Church. Records for 1868-1918 are found on LDS Microfilm #1550288 and #1516274. Original records are at the library of the Union Theological Seminary in Richmond, Virginia.

Taylor, James Henry (1871-   ). Woodrow Wilson in Church, His Membership in the Congregation of the Central Presbyterian Church, Washington, D.C., 1913-1924 (Charleston, S.C., 1952). LC Call Number E767.T3.

◉ Eastern Presbyterian Church. Records from 1875 to 1955 have been microfilmed by the LDS Church, including baptisms, marriages, deaths, and lists of ministers and church officials. See LDS Microfilm #1862755, four rolls designated items 6-9.

Church Records

◉ Eckington Presbyterian Church. Formerly North Capitol Presbyterian Church. Records, 1896-1900, are on LDS Microfilm #0525735 and #0913458.

◉ F Street Presbyterian Church. Organized in 1803 by persons who had been connected with the Associate Reformed Presbyterian Church in Philadelphia before the federal government was moved to Washington. Dissatisfied with the First Presbyterian Church, they left to start the F Street Church. In 1859 the F Street Church was consolidated with the Second Presbyterian Church.

◉ Fifteenth Street Presbyterian Church. Organized 14 May 1842 as the "First Colored Presbyterian Church of Washington." Forty members of this organization worshiped in Cook's schoolhouse at 14th and H streets until they were able, with the assistance of the First, Second and Fourth churches, to erect a small frame building on 15th Street between I and K streets in 1853. Contact: Fifteenth Street Presbyterian Church, 1701 15th Street, N.W., Washington, D.C. 20009; telephone (202) 234-0300.

Sluby, Paul Edward, Sr. Sessional Minutes, Volumes I-III of the Fifteenth Street Presbyterian Church (First Colored Presbyterian Church), Washington, D.C. (Washington, D.C.: Columbian Harmony Society, 1981). LC Call Number BX9211.W3.F4527 1981. Minutes, 1841-1890; elders, 1841-1888; baptisms, 1842-1859, 1874-1881; marriages, 1843-1854, 1874-1878; funerals, 1874-1882; and church register, 1841-1887.

◉ First Presbyterian Church. Originated as early as 1795. The first services were held in a carpenter shop erected for the use of workmen engaged in building the President's House, then in a frame chapel erected on F Street near St. Patrick's Church. In 1812 a church was dedicated on South Capitol Street, with President Madison among its contributors. In 1827 a church was built on 4-1/2 Street West near C Street. First Presbyterian merged with Church of the Covenant in 1930, the combined congregations taking the name Covenant-First Presbyterian Church and using Covenant's church at the intersection of 18th Street, N Street and Connecticut Avenue. The name was changed in 1947 to National Presbyterian Church and by 1968 National Presbyterian moved to its present location on Nebraska Avenue.

At the D.A.R. Library, "First Presbyterian Church of Washington, D.C." records have been compiled by the Monticello Chapter of the D.A.R., including births, 1841-1855; marriages 1841-1880; deaths, 1841-1866; and members 1856-1865 have been listed and indexed. See LDS Microfilm #0845824. The church records have been put on microfilm and you may call or write the church and make an appointment to look at the microfilm copies. Contact: National Presbyterian Church, 4101 Nebraska Avenue, N.W., Washington, D.C. 20016; telephone (202) 537-0800.

◉ Fourth Presbyterian Church. Established in 1828. The first church building was dedicated in 1829, a one-story structure on 9th Street, N.W., without seats or chimneys. When a new building was erected in 1840 on 9th between G and H streets, N.W., it was the largest church then in the city. In 1929, construction of a new church began at 13th and Fairmont streets, N.W. Fourth Presbyterian moved to suburban Maryland in 1956, locating on River Road in Bethesda. The records are available for research if you will call or write and make an appointment. Contact: Fourth Presbyterian Church, 5500 River Road, Bethesda, Maryland 20816; telephone (301) 320-3600.

Kurtz, Grace W. The Story of the Fourth Presbyterian Church of Washington, D.C., Bethesda, Maryland: A Past to Remember, A Future to Mold (South Hackensack, N.J.: Custombook, 1978). LC Call Number BX9211.B39 F684.

A Guide to Records of the District of Columbia

◉ Georgetown Presbyterian Church. Established as a result of a movement begun in 1780, when Rev. Stephen B. Balch preached to a few persons in Georgetown. The congregation built a small church, the Bridge Street Presbyterian Church, at the corner of Bridge and Washington streets (now M and 30th streets), which was replaced by a much larger one in 1821. In 1871 the West Street Presbyterian Church was built on West Street (now P Street), near 31st, the present location of the Georgetown Presbyterian Church. Reports of the D.C. G.R.C. contain three volumes concerning the Georgetown Presbyterian Church. In Volume 75, the Journal of Trustees, 1806-1850, is transcribed and indexed; Volume 79, covers 1850-1873; and Volume 80, covers 1873-1908. There is an 1850 list of pewholders; a few tombstone inscriptions in the Presbyterian Burying Ground in 1892 when the bodies were removed; and the ledger of the collector for the graveyard, 1806-1822. All three volumes are indexed. See LDS Microfilm #0845800. Contact: Georgetown Presbyterian Church, 3115 P Street, N.W., Washington, D.C. 20007; telephone (202) 338-1644.

Schaffter, Dorothy. The Presbyterian Congregation in Georgetown, 1780-1970 (Washington, D.C.: The Session, 1971). LC Call Number BX9211.W3 G463 1971. Also see LDS Microfilm #1845437.

◉ Metropolitan Presbyterian Church. D.C. G.R.C. Volume 96; LDS Microfilm #0845804. Original church records, 1864-1954, were microfilmed by the LDS Church and are found on roll #186244, designated items 1-6. Records include baptisms and deaths from 1864, marriages from 1865, and session minutes from 1878.

◉ New York Avenue Presbyterian Church. After the above consolidation, dedicated a new church on New York Avenue between 13th and 14th streets in 1860. It claimed, rightly, that its history dated back to 1803. In D.C. G.R.C., Volume 92, Part I, "New York Avenue Presbyterian Church," lists baptisms, 1815-1869, and members from the time of the F Street Church to 1869. The list of communicants, 1821-1845, has a column "to what church dismissed," which indicates to what city or to what church in Washington the person moved, a useful genealogical clue. This Part I of Volume 92 is separately indexed. See LDS Microfilm #0845803. Contact: New York Avenue Presbyterian Church, 1313 New York Avenue, N.W., Washington, D.C. 20005; telephone (202) 393-3700.

Edgington, Frank E. A History of the New York Avenue Presbyterian Church: One Hundred Fifty-Seven Years, 1803 to 1961 (Washington, D.C.: Cooper-Trent Lithograph Corporation, 1962). LC Call Number BX9211.W3 N55 1962. Compilation lists elders of the F Street Church, 1803-1853; elders of the Second Church, 1821-1856; and elders of the New York Avenue Church, 1859-1960; trustees, 1822-1960; deacons, 1853-1960; clerks, 1821-1948; and school superintendents, 1851-1958.

◉ Second Presbyterian Church. Organized on May 9, 1820, at a meeting first held in a corridor of the Navy Department building on 17th Street. After consolidation in 1859 with the F Street Church, the two congregations formed the New York Avenue Church. Another church, organized in 1903 as the Second Presbyterian Church, changed its name in 1919 to the Church of the Pilgrims. Records from that church, 1902-1987, are on LDS Microfilm #1550289, #1516275, and #1550289. Originals are at the library of the Union Theological Seminary in Richmond, Virginia. Contact: Church of the Pilgrims, 2201 P Street, N.W., Washington, D.C. 20037; telephone (202) 387-6612.

◉ Seventh Street Presbyterian Church of Washington. Organized in 1853, the site for a church on 7th Street between D and E, S.W. was donated by Charles Stott. In 1873 the congregation changed the name of their church to the "Westminster Presbyterian Church" and, in 1900, to "Westminster Church Memorial."

Church Records

Later, it became "Westminster United Presbyterian Church" and, in 1983, "Westminster Presbyterian Church." In 1965, the church moved to I (Eye) Street, S.W. D.C. G.R.C., Volume 95, concerns Westminster Church Memorial and gives records of elders, 1853-1935; deacons, 1853-1902; members, 1853-1942; infant baptisms, 1853-1928; marriages, 1868-1921; and deaths, 1855-1921. After 1872 the listing of deaths has information regarding age, place of death and where buried. See LDS Microfilm #0845804. Contact: Westminster Presbyterian Church, 400 I (Eye) Street, S.W., Washington, D.C. 20024; telephone (202) 474-7700.

◉ Sixth Street Presbyterian Church. Located at the corner of 6th Street and Maryland Avenue, held its first public services in 1852 in "Island Hall." Sixth Street Presbyterian, now known as Sixth Presbyterian Church, moved in 1916 to 16th and Kennedy streets, N.W. Contact: Sixth Presbyterian Church, 16th and Kennedy streets, N.W., Washington, D.C. 20011; telephone (202) 723-5377.

SOCIETY OF FRIENDS (QUAKER)

◉ Friends Meeting House. A brick structure was built in 1811 on I Street between 18th and 19th streets, N.W. There was also a school and, on 19th above Columbia Road, a burying ground. The 1860 city directory lists two Friends' Meeting Houses: Hicksite on I Street near 20th Street, N.W. and Orthodox at 468 9th Street West. Quaker Records in Maryland, by Phebe R. Jacobsen states that as early as 1783 the Friends were meeting in Alexandria, and in 1802 a monthly meeting was established there. In 1807, a meeting was settled in the city of Washington and placed under the care of the Alexandria Monthly Meeting. A few extant records of the Washington and Alexandria meetings, beginning in 1803, are on microfilm at the Hall of Records, Annapolis, Maryland (M 569). The Friends Religious Society of the National Capital Area Association reports a list of members 1821-1900. For information, write to Willna Uebrick-Pacheli, 3304 Dona Avenue, Alexandria, Virginia 22303.

UNITARIAN

◉ First Unitarian Church. Established in 1820; a church building dedicated in 1822. Soon after 1870, it was decided that the church at the corner of 6th and D streets was poorly located, with the center of population moving rapidly northwest. A new church building was erected in 1877 at 14th and L streets, N.W. and the name of the congregation was changed to All Souls' Church. About 1922, All Souls' moved to its present location on 16th Street, N.W. Contact: All Souls' Church, 16th and Harvard streets, N.W., Washington, D.C. 20009; telephone (202) 332-5266.

Conway, Moncure Daniel (1832-1907). The Old and New: A Sermon Containing the History of the First Unitarian Church in Washington City (Washington, D.C.: Buel and Blanchard, Printers, 1855). LC Call Number BX9861.W3.C6 1855.

Other Church Finding Aids and Sources:

Dixon, Benjamin Franklin (1892-   ). General Garfield's Church: Centoddities, 1843-1943 (Washington, D.C.: Alpha C.E. Press of National City Christian Church, 1946).

Gatti, Lawrence P. (1914-   ). Historic St. Stephens': An Account of Its Eighty-Five Years, 1867-1952 (Washington, D.C., 1952). LC Call Number BX4603.W32.S36.

Haslup, Alice Emma, comp. History of Rosedale Methodist Church From 1896 to 1924 (Washington, D.C.: Press of C.H. Potter & Co., Inc., 1924). LC Call Number BX8481.W8.R6.

A Guide to Records of the District of Columbia

Leonard, William Andrew (1848-1930). <u>Historical Address Delivered at the Formal Opening of St. Mary's Chapel for Colored People in St. John's Parish, Washington, D.C.</u> (Washington, D.C.: Gibson Brothers, Printers, 1887). LC Call Number Microfilm 30404 BX.

Historical Records Survey. <u>A Directory of Churches and Religious Organizations in the District of Columbia, 1939</u> (Washington, D.C.: District of Columbia Historical Records Survey, 1939). See also LDS Microfilm #1036761. LC Call Number BR560.W35 H35 1939.

Miller, William Alexander. <u>Historical Sketch of Mount Vernon Place Church, Washington, D.C., With a Full List of Pastors Since the Foundation of the Church in 1850 and Anecdotes of Some Early Families, 1850-1939</u> (Washington, D.C., 1939). LC Call Number BX8481.W3.M6.

Sluby, Paul Edward, Sr. and Wanda Harris. <u>Minutes of the Berean Baptist Church, Washington, D.C.</u> (Washington, D.C.: Columbian Harmony Society, 1982). LC Call Number BX6480.W3.B473 1982. Minutes for the period February 23, 1877 to January 5, 1905.

Washington, D.C. Grace Reformed Church. <u>100th Anniversary of Grace Reformed Church, 1877-1977</u> (Washington, D.C.: Grace Reformed Church, 1977). LC Call Number BX9581.W33.W37 1977.

Wilbur, William Allen. <u>Chronicles of Calvary Baptist in the City of Washington</u> (Washington, D.C.: Jud & Detweiler, Inc., 1914). LC Call Number BX6480.W3.C3.

Figure 20 - David C. Catlett, Disinterment Permit Within Payne's Burial Ground, 1914.

Cemetery Records

In 1866, author Christian Hines, in his <u>Early Recollections of Washington City</u>, stated that during his youth there were graveyards scattered throughout Washington City, including small, private ones. As the city grew, graveyards were abandoned and while sometimes the remains were moved, often they were not.

Of importance to researchers of District of Columbia cemeteries is an ordinance adopted by the City Council in June 1852. The ordinance prohibited the location of new burial grounds within the limits of Washington City, and resulted in many new cemeteries being established north of Boundary Avenue during the ensuing years. Many small church cemeteries could not be expanded, and in several cases, a decision was made to close the cemetery and re-inter the remains elsewhere.

In making inquiries concerning burials at cemeteries, give the full name of the deceased (or as much as you have) and approximate date of death. Sometimes tombstones have information, such as place of birth, that is not on the office records at the cemetery, or the reverse is also true. Other family members may be buried in nearby plots, and a visit to the cemetery could be rewarding as well as interesting. If you request the cemetery to do research from their records, there is sometimes a fee charged or a request for a donation in keeping with the time spent.

A detailed "Necropolis" list of all places of burial in the District of Columbia in 1882 can be found in William H. Boyd's <u>Boyd's Directory of the District of Columbia</u> (Washington, D.C.: J. Bradley Adams, et al., 1882), pp. 779-780. Each of the entries therein has been included in the list below. A more thorough listing can be found in Pippenger's "District of Columbia Interments (Index to Deaths)," detailed under Death Records in this guide.

CEMETERIES AND BURIAL GROUNDS

❏ <u>Adas Israel Cemetery</u>. Burials from 1870 to 1919 are found on microfiche in the Library of Congress. LC Call Number Microfiche 96/79 F. Contact: Adas Israel Cemetery, 1400 Alabama Avenue, S.E., Washington, D.C. 20032; telephone (202) 562-5831.

❏ <u>Baptist Cemetery</u>. Located in 1882 near Drovers' Rest in Georgetown.

❏ <u>Battleground National Cemetery</u>. The 1880 city directory shows Battle Ground Cemetery at 7th Street Road near Brightwood. Battleground National Cemetery is discussed in <u>Civil War Cemeteries of the District of Columbia</u>, by Paul E. Sluby, Sr. The cemetery at 6625 Georgia Avenue, N.W. was established as a burial ground for Union soldiers who lost their lives in the Battle of Fort Stevens when the Confederate troops attacked on July 11 and 12, 1864. Fort Stevens, one of the forts built to defend the city, is at 13th and Quackenbos streets, N.W. From various sources Sluby has compiled and indexed a list of interments at Battleground. "Preliminary Inventory of the Records of the National Park Service," (PI #166) compiled in 1966 by Edward E. Hill, lists as Item 119 "Register of Burials at Battleground National Cemetery." This is a single volume with entries for individual burials; giving name, rank, company, regiment, date of death, grave mark and sometimes other information. Dates of death from 1864 to 1936. This record is available through the Civil Reference Branch, Room 13E of the National Archives on Pennsylvania Avenue.

❏ <u>Beckett's Burial Ground</u>. Square 1089. Described in the 1880 city directory as being on C Street between 16th and 17th streets, S.E. Proprietor was William Beckett.

A Guide to Records of the District of Columbia

❑ Belts [Family] Burial Ground. North of Tennallytown (1882).

❑ Brightwood Cemetery. No specific location given in the 1882 city directory.

❑ Cephas [Family] Burial Ground. On Conduit Road near Drovers' Rest; John Cephas, proprietor (1882).

❑ Chapel's [Private] Burial Ground. Northeast of Tennallytown; J.E. Chapel, owner (1882).

❑ [Georgetown] College Burial Ground. On the present campus of Georgetown University.

❑ Columbian Harmony Cemetery. Sometimes called Harmonial or Harmoneon. The burial ground was founded in 1825 by a society primarily composed of freedmen. The original cemetery was in Square 475, at the intersection of Boundary (Florida Avenue) and 5th Street, N.W., as noted on an 1854 map and described as the "African" cemetery. The cemetery was moved in 1856 to a site between Rhode Island Avenue and Brentwood Road, N.E. Most of the persons buried there were colored, but there were some whites and persons of other races. In 1960, remains of 37,000 dead were moved from the Brentwood location to the Harmony Memorial Park as were the remains from Payne's Cemetery, which had been located on Benning Road, S.E., across from Woodlawn Cemetery. A few extant records of Payne's Cemetery are at Harmony. Contact: Harmony Memorial Park, 7101 Sheriff Road, Landover, Maryland 20785; telephone (301) 772-0900.

Military burials at Harmony Cemetery during the Civil War years of 1863-1864 are listed in Civil War Cemeteries of the District of Columbia, detailed below.

Sluby, Paul Edward, Sr. and Stanton Lawrence Wormley, Jr. Records of the Columbian Harmony Cemetery, Washington, D.C., 1831-1899 (Washington, D.C.: By the Compilers, 1993), 7 vols. LC Call Number F193.S5837 1993.

Sluby, Paul Edward, Sr. and Stanton Lawrence Wormley, Jr. Civil War Cemeteries of the District of Columbia Metropolitan Area (Washington, D.C.: Columbian Harmony Society, 1982).

❑ Congressional Cemetery. Established in 1807 by a few individuals of different Christian denominations in the eastern part of the city. They purchased Square 1115 between E, G, 18th, and 19th streets, S.E. It was agreed that as soon as the purchasers were reimbursed for the cost of the land and the improvements, the entire property would be placed under the direction of the Protestant Episcopal Church, which was undivided in 1812. The cemetery may be found called "Congress Ground" or "Washington Parish Burial Ground," and "Washington Cemetery," and later, "Congressional Cemetery." It has no direct connection with Congress, but Congress has erected in the cemetery over 200 cenotaphs (empty tombs or monuments in honor of persons who are buried elsewhere) for senators or representatives who died between 1807 and 1850. Some members of Congress are, however, buried under a cenotaph there. The cemetery comprises over 32 acres.

At the D.A.R. Library, Congressional Cemetery records are transcribed and indexed to 1862. There are four volumes entitled "Washington Parish Burial Ground (Congressional Cemetery)," in the reports of the D.C. G.R.C. Volume 23 consists of tombstone inscriptions, 1790-1818, and interments and removals from cemetery Book No. 1, April 25, 1820 to April 8, 1839. Volume 24 has interments and removals from cemetery Book No. 2, July 23, 1839 to July 16, 1849; Volume 25, is for cemetery Book No. 3, July 16, 1849 to September 28, 1856; Volume 26, for cemetery Book No. 4, January 1, 1857 to May 31, 1862. See LDS Microfilm #0845770 and #0845771.

Cemetery Records

Original records from the office at the cemetery, for the period 1820-1988, were microfilmed by the Genealogical Society of Utah in 1978. See LDS Microfilm #1530459, #1530519-1530522, #1530542 for indexes; #1030816-1030822 for records of interments, journal, range and vault books.

Genealogical inquiries must be presented in writing, accompanied by a $25.00 research fee. Contact: Congressional Cemetery, 1801 E Street, S.E., Washington, D.C. 20003; telephone (202) 543-0539.

❑ Convent Burial Ground. There is a burial ground at the Convent of the Georgetown Visitation, at 35th and P streets, N.W. Extant records are with the Georgetown University Library, Special Collections.

❑ Dangerfield [Family] Burial Ground. No location given in the 1884 city directory; Henry Dangerfield, superintendent.

❑ Dean's [Private] Burial Ground. On Sheriff Road, listed in the 1882 city directory.

❑ [Eastern] Methodist Cemetery. In 1824 the trustees of the Methodist Society at Ebenezer Station, commonly called the Fourth Street Methodist Church, purchased Square 1102, bounded by 17th, 18th, E and D streets, S.E., directly north of Congressional Cemetery. On that site, they established the Eastern Methodist Cemetery, also known as Ebenezer Cemetery or Old Ebenezer. In 1892 relocation activity began, the vast majority of the remains were reinterred in Congressional Cemetery.

Sluby, Paul Edward, Sr. The Transcribed Ledger of the Eastern Methodist Cemetery (Also Called Old Ebenezer), 1823-1893, Washington, D.C. (Washington, D.C.: Columbian Harmony Society, 1981). LC Call Number F193.S584.

❑ Ebenezer Cemetery. Also known as the Methodist Burial Ground, was used primarily by the black community (see Eastern Methodist Cemetery above).

❑ Francis DeSales Cemetery. Sometimes referred to as Queens Chapel Cemetery, on Evarts Street, N.E., just off Queens Chapel Road, is mentioned in "Tombstone Inscriptions Virginia, Maryland, North and South Carolina, Washington, D.C.," in D.C. G.R.C., Volume 59. A few tombstone inscriptions dating 1805-1842 were copied before the remains were reinterred in 1936 at Mount Olivet Cemetery.

❑ Garden's [Private] Burial Ground. Near Anacostia Road; Alex. Garden, proprietor in 1882.

❑ Glenwood Cemetery. Located on Lincoln Road, N.E., about two miles north of the Capitol. Incorporated July 27, 1854, it has always been non-sectarian. Removals have been made here from a number of other cemeteries. Glenwood was described in the 1882 city directory as being a beautiful "City of the Dead" on a 90-acre tract. The D.A.R. Library has record abstracts in D.C. G.R.C. Volumes 30, 48 and 163. Parts I and II of Volume 48 cover Plat Book A with entries from c.1840 to 1939. Volume 163 also covers parts of Plat Book A. Volume 30 covers Plat Book B; the earliest death date being 1788, and 1934 the latest. (The earliest appears to have been removed there from another cemetery.) See LDS Microfilm #0845772, #0845775 and #0845816. A sketch and dedication of the cemetery done in 1854 is at LC Call Number YA14402 (Rare Book Collection).

Interment cards, 1854-1888, can be found amongst eight rolls of microfilm by the LDS Church. Cards give varying amounts of information, many give lot owners and other burials in a particular lot. These are listed below:

A Guide to Records of the District of Columbia

Roll	Description
#1530875	Jno. Rowan Abbey to Nany J. Camp, and contains historical and subscriber information about the cemetery
#1530876	Virginia B. Camp to Lawrence M. Farley
#1530877	Martha E. Farley to Helen Hoskins
#1530884	Henry M. Hoskins to Nicholas Mandanyohl
#1530885	Peter Mandas to James Nevitt
#1530936	James C. Nevitt to Vallora L. Shives
#1530937	David A. Shovar, Sr. to Welda A. Welsh
#1530938	Sallie K. Welsh to Katie Zuschnitt, and contains corrections and other additional cards

Contact: Glenwood Cemetery, 2219 Lincoln Road, N.E., Washington, D.C. 20002; telephone (202) 667-1016.

❑ Good Hope Burial Ground. On Hamilton Road; Wm. Batson, proprietor in 1882.

❑ Graceland Cemetery. Established in 1872 and is listed in the city directories as being at 15th and H streets, N.E. Graceland's location is also described as the northeast corner of Benning and Bladensburg roads, which is essentially the same. City directories do not list the cemetery after 1905. Most of the remains were moved to Woodlawn Cemetery before Graceland was closed. Destroyed.

❑ Hebbon's [Family] Burial Ground. Listed in the 1882 city directory at Broad Branch Road; proprietor Eliza Hebbon.

❑ Hillsdale Burial Ground. In Hillsdale, an eastern suburb of Washington; proprietor Sol. G. Brown in 1882.

❑ Holmead's Burial Ground. Holmead's, also called Western Burial Ground, was one of the first burying grounds in Washington. It occupied Square 109, between 19th and 20th streets, and S and Boundary (now Florida Avenue) streets. It was commonly called "Holmead's Cemetery" after Anthony Holmead who owned the property before the city was divided into squares. Square 109 was set aside as a cemetery and, until 1816, was the most popular burying ground in Washington. The last interment was made c.1860. In his study of the cemetery, historian Paul E. Sluby, Sr. states Holmead's was begun in 1794, but that by 1884 it was in a state of disrepair. It is not listed in the 1882 city directory. The land became valuable as the city grew and was sold. Remains were reintered at Rock Creek and Graceland cemeteries. In 1895, those at Graceland were moved again to Woodlawn Cemetery. Destroyed.

Sluby, Paul Edward, Sr. and Stanton Lawrence Wormley, Jr. Holmead's Cemetery (Western Burial Ground), Washington, D.C. (Washington, D.C.: Columbian Harmony Society, 1985). LC Call Number F193.S582 1985.

❑ Holy Rood Cemetery. On Wisconsin Avenue near 35th Street, N.W. was established by Trinity Catholic Church (later Holy Trinity) in Georgetown. The 1880 directory of Washington describes the location then at High and Fayette streets. "Rood" is an Anglo-Saxon word, the ecclesiastical meaning of which is cross or crucifix, so that the name could be said to mean "holy cross." The records of Holy Rood Cemetery are at Georgetown University Library, Special Collections Division. At the library, "Records of Holy Rood Cemetery" describes three boxes of records, plus oversize items, that include registers, map, lot books, records of interments, 1817-1917. "Register of Holy Trinity Church Archives" notes that Box 5, folder 13, contains a record of Holy Rood Cemetery lot owners 1864-1931.

Cemetery Records

❏ Methodist Burial Ground. Described in the 1880 city directory as being immediately opposite the Congressional burial ground.

❏ Howard's [Private] Burial Ground. Listed in the 1882 city directory for Anacostia Road; Robt. Howard, superintendent.

❏ Insane Asylum. (see St. Elizabeth's Hospital)

❏ Jenkins' [Private] Burial Ground. On the Jenkins family farm; Thomas Jenkins, proprietor in 1882.

❏ Jones' Chapel Burial Ground. The 1882 city directory gives location as Bennings Station; Wm. Henson, superintendent.

❏ McPhearson's [Private] Burial Ground. In Hillsdale; Wm. Pinney, sexton in 1882.

❏ Macedonia Burial Ground. Near Sheridan Avenue in Hillsdale; Henry Waddy, sexton in 1882.

❏ Methodist Cemetery. Located on Murdock Mill Road, N.W., immediately behind Eldbrooke Methodist Church at River Road. It is discussed in D.C. G.R.C., Volume 59. Tombstone inscriptions in the Methodist Cemetery have been copied and there is a list of unmarked graves. The G.R.C. list gives name of the deceased, age and date of death.

❏ Moore's [Family] Burial Ground. Later known as Rosemont Cemetery. Predominantly a black burial area, once located in Hillsdale at 3134 Stanton Road, S.E.. The cemetery was established c.1850 by Hillsdale area resident Jacob Moore as his family's private burial ground. Public use began c.1880, and burials continued to c.1927 when it became known as Rosemont Cemetery. Moore's burial ground occupied the greater portion of Square 5879. Destroyed.

Sluby, Paul Edward, Sr. and Stanton Lawrence Wormley, Jr. Rosemont Cemetery (Formerly Moore's), Washington, D.C. (Washington, D.C.: Columbian Harmony Society, 1993). LC Call Number F193.S58395 1993.

❏ Mount Olivet Cemetery. Located on Bladensburg Road, N.E., was established in 1858 by the four Catholic parishes of St. Patrick's, St. Peter's, St. Matthew's and St. Dominic's. For written inquiries, contact: Mount Olivet Cemetery, 1300 Bladensburg Road, N.E., Washington, D.C. 20002; telephone (202) 399-3000.

Mount Olivet Cemetery. Regulations of Mount Olivet Cemetery, Near Washington City, D.C. (Washington, D.C.: H. Polkinhorn, Printer, 1858). LC Call Number RA629.W3.M6.

❏ Mount Pleasant Plain Cemetery. Also known [concurrently] as the Young Mens Burial (Colored) Ground. Located in 1882 about 1 mile northwest of Columbian College. It is in the vicinity of Adams Mill Road above the National Zoo where a grove of trees now stands on a hill.

❏ Mount Zion Cemetery. According to historian Paul E. Sluby, Sr., the cemetery was composed of two separate but adjacent burying areas in Georgetown, the Old Methodist Burying Ground and the Female Union Band Society Burying Ground. In 1808 the Montgomery Street Church, known after 1850 as the Dumbarton Avenue United Methodist Church, purchased property near 25th and Q streets, N.W. and established the "Old Methodist Burying Ground." In 1842, the Female Union Band Society, a group of free Negro women, purchased the adjacent 1 ½ acres for a cemetery. The Mount Zion United Methodist Church in 1879 leased

A Guide to Records of the District of Columbia

from the Dumbarton Avenue Church a major portion of their cemetery for 99 years. The two burial grounds are in Squares 1288 and 1289, behind the 2500 and 2600 blocks of Q Street, N.W. From grave markers and other documented records, Sluby lists in his book interments from about 1810 to 1945.

Sluby, Paul Edward, Sr. Mt. Zion Cemetery: Washington, D.C., Brief History and Interments (Washington, D.C.: Columbian Harmony Society, 1984). LC Call Number F193.S5827 1984.

Sluby, Paul Edward, Sr. The Old Methodist Burying Ground, Georgetown, Washington, D.C. (Washington, D.C., 1975). LC Call Number F193.S583. A section of the Mt. Zion Cemetery as distinguished from the adjacent Female Union Bank Society Burial Ground section.

❑ Oak Hill Cemetery. Located at 30th and R streets, N.W., is located on the heights of Georgetown bordering on Rock Creek. It was a densely wooded tract known as Parrott's Woods when it was purchased by William W. Corcoran in 1849. He spent $70,000 on improvements and conveyed the land to the Oak Hill Cemetery Company, which obtained a charter from Congress in 1849. A large group of reinterments at Oak Hill includes remains from the Old Presbyterian Church Cemetery at 34th and Q. "Oak Hill Cemetery Records," in D.C. G.R.C., Volume 17, contains an indexed listing of burials from 1849 to 1869, with date, name, age, lot number and notes about removals and owners of lots. See LDS Microfilm #0845769. Some compiled tombstone inscriptions are on LDS Microfilm #0874221.

Original records were microfilmed by the LDS Church. Rolls #1543685 to #1543689 contain entries from the interment index. Rolls #1543689 and #1543690 are of the lot owner index. Microfilm records are found as follows:

Roll	Description
1543685	Ada Rebecca Alexander Abbaticchio to Richard D. Cutts
1543686	Hildreth Dahlgren to Malvina R. Hurley
1543687	Malvina R. Hurley to George Lewis Peckham
1543688	George Lewis Peckham to Helen H. Waters
1543689	Helen R. Waters to Mary E. Zollinger

For information concerning burials at Oak Hill, you may call (202) 337-2835, or write to Oak Hill Cemetery, 3001 R Street, N.W., Washington, D.C. 20007.

❑ Payne's Burial Ground. Located in 1882 at Bennings Station with John Payne, superintendent. Extant records for the period April 18, 1907 to October 29, 1947 were published by Paul Edward Sluby, Sr. and Stanton Lawrence Wormley. See LDS Microfilm #1697777.

Sluby, Paul Edward, Sr. and Stanton Lawrence Wormley, Jr. Records of Payne's Cemetery, Washington, D.C. (Washington, D.C.: Columbian Harmony Society, 1991), 4 vols. LC Call Number F193.S5835 1991.

❑ Potters Field. At several locations, for the burial of indigents. (see Washington Asylum)

❑ Presbyterian Cemetery. Formerly located in Hawkins & Beatty's Addition to Georgetown on Market Street between 4th and 5th streets, now 33rd and Q. Additional information about this cemetery is found under the above discussion of the church. In records of Georgetown undertaker Joseph F. Birch, found at the D.A.R. Library, entitled Records of Birch's Funeral Home, is found included two books in which Birch listed "Burials in the Presbyterian Grave Yard." The first book covers the period 1856 to 1862 and the second from 1863 to 1896. (The

Cemetery Records

last entries concern disinterments.) The undertaker provided the date, the name of deceased and the site of burial in the cemetery. Other of Birch's records are described below. See LDS Microfilm #0887587. Records for the earliest years of the cemetery are not known to have survived. Destroyed.

Sluby, Paul Edward, Sr. and Stanton Lawrence Wormley, Jr. <u>Presbyterian Cemetery Records (Georgetown), Washington, D.C., 1856-1897</u> (Washington, D.C.: Columbian Harmony Society, 1990).

Wesley Methodist Church. <u>Records of Wesley Methodist Church, Washington, D.C.</u>, unpublished manuscript, 1942. Copy in LDS Library, call number 975.3 V2d. Contains some inscriptions from the Presbyterian Burying Ground.

❏ <u>Prospect Hill Cemetery</u>. Begun in 1858 as a German Lutheran cemetery, has been non-sectarian for many years. The entrance to the cemetery is at 2201 North Capitol Street. Cemetery records were microfilmed by the LDS Church, and are found as described below.

Roll	Description
1530939	History of Prospect Hill Cemetery Society of Washington, D.C., 1858-1950, by P.G. Gleis; Interment Index for Chr. Abel to Mary K. Gott
1531004	Interment Index for Mary K. Gott to Louis Philip
1531005	Interment Index for Louis Philip to Mrs. Zyprecht
1531006	Lot Owners Daniel A. Abbott to Edward Metzler
1531007	Lot Owners Edward Metzler to Mrs. Zyprecht

Contact: Prospect Hill Cemetery, 2219 Lincoln Road, N.E., Washington, D.C. 20002; telephone number (202) 667-0676.

❏ <u>Quaker Burial Ground</u>. Some history and details of the Friends Burying Ground in Georgetown, and a list of its sponsors, as well as some of the surnames of prominent families buried there (Shoemaker, Seaver, Scholfield, McPherson, Janney), can be found in Edward Shoemaker's, <u>Some Account of the Life and Family of George Shoemaker, For Half a Century Flour Inspector of Georgetown, D.C.</u> (West Washington, D.C.: L.E. Mankin, 1882). An account details that Jonathan Shoemaker and wife Hannah Lukens moved from Cheltenham near Philadelphia, Pennsylvania to Northumberland County, Pennsylvania. In the early 1800's, they moved to Georgetown, D.C., and later to land near Alexandria, Virginia. The burial ground is not listed in the 1882 Washington city directory. See LDS Microfilm #1429794.

❏ <u>Rock Creek Cemetery</u>. Located immediately north of the Soldiers' Home on Rock Creek Church Road. It contains 100 acres upon which is St. Paul's Episcopal Church, Rock Creek Parish. St. Paul's manages the cemetery. A portion of the ground has long been used for burials, and the records go back to 1719.

At the D.A.R. Library, D.C. G.R.C., Volume 72, entitled "Interments in Rock Creek Cemetery" is an indexed listing of interments copied from Books A and B, which appear to be from 1801 to 1931. This is on LDS Microfilm #0845779. There are notations occasionally that the body was removed from the Old Presbyterian Cemetery, Mount Olivet or some other cemetery. Also at the D.A.R. Library is the book "Inscriptions from Tombstones in Rock Creek Cemetery, Sections A to I Inclusive," which was compiled in 1928 by the District of Columbia Society of the Daughters of American Colonists. The earliest date appears to be 1775 and the latest 1925.

Original records were microfilmed by the LDS Church, as described below. The first sequence is for interment index cards, followed by section books and interment ledgers.

A Guide to Records of the District of Columbia

Roll	Description
1530545	Albert Abajian to Alice I. Briscoe; introductory material
1530546	Alice I. Briscoe to Fannie Lander Demaree
1530547	Jas. Delzell to Medora E. Grim
1530582	Medora E. Grim to Chas. H. Johnson
1530583	Chas. H. Johnson to Susan H. Leidy
1530669	Alexandra L. Leigh to Nicholas Myshencoff
1530772	Catherine Nadin to Norman E. Ryon
1530773	Abigail Cooper Sabin to Norman W. Tapp
1530774	Wm. A. Tapp to Laura T. Zytkoskee; churches, homes, vestries
1579719	Sections A-K
1579720	Sections L-W; includes Section V for St. John the Baptist Russian Orthodox Church
1579721	Sections 4-10, 11-R, 14-15, 15-A, 16-17, 30, PV-B
1579722	Interment Ledgers, 1775 to March 7, 1920
1579723	Interment Ledgers, February 8, 1920 to 1930

Inquiries concerning burials at Rock Creek should be made in writing, addressed to Rock Creek Cemetery, Rock Creek Church Road and Webster Street, N.W., Washington, D.C. 20037; telephone number (202) 829-0585.

Sluby, Paul Edward, Sr. and Stanton Lawrence Wormley, Jr. Rock Creek Cemetery, Washington, D.C.: Old Interment Records, 1822-1906 (Washington, D.C.: Columbian Harmony Society, 1992), 4 vols. LC Call Number F193.S5839 1992.

❏ Rosemont Cemetery. See "Moore's Cemetery." Destroyed.

❏ St. Elizabeth's Hospital Cemetery. This burial ground is discussed in Civil War Cemeteries of the District of Columbia by Paul Edward Sluby, Sr. The hospital was established in 1855 and called the Government Hospital for the Insane. Through the 1880's, references on District of Columbia death certificates document burial at the "Hospital." During the Civil War, the hospital was used to receive and care for the men wounded in battle. The men were reluctant to write home that they were in a hospital for the insane, so they referred to it as "St. Elizabeth's," since they were in an area which was part of a parcel by that name which was granted in 1663 to George Thompson. Later the hospital's name was officially changed to "St. Elizabeth's." One burial area here was used during the Civil War and another was established afterward. A list of interments as compiled by Paul E. Sluby, Sr., gives name of deceased, company and battalion of service, rank, date admitted to hospital, gravestone number, and date of death. The list covers the period c.1863 to 1879.

Sluby, Paul Edward, Sr. Civil War Cemeteries of the District of Columbia Metropolitan Area (Washington, D.C.: Columbian Harmony Society, 1982). LC Call Number E494.S62 1982.

❏ St. Mary's [German] Catholic Cemetery. Established on Lincoln Road, N.E. in the 1850's. Listed in the 1880 city directory as "St. Mary's German Catholic Cemetery," it was originally on O Street between North Capitol and First Street, N.E. For information, you may write to St. Mary's Catholic Cemetery, 2121 Lincoln Road, N.E., Washington, D.C. 20002; telephone (202) 635-7444. There is no office at St. Mary's since it is under the same supervision as Mount Olivet Cemetery where records are kept.

❏ St. Matthew's Catholic Cemetery. Once located in Square 236 on U Street, between 13th and 14th streets, N.W. Destroyed.

Cemetery Records

❑ St. Patrick's Catholic Cemetery. Located on Boundary (Florida Avenue) between North Capitol and 3rd Street, N.W. was the burial ground for St. Patrick's Church, which was organized in 1797. In the late 1850's, the remains at St. Patrick's were exhumed and re-interred at Mount Olivet Cemetery, as were those from St. Peter's and St. Matthew's.

❑ St. Peter's Catholic Cemetery. Formerly located in Square 808 between 4th and 5th, H and I streets, N.E., according to an 1855 map of the city of Washington. Remains were reinterred at Mount Olivet Cemetery. Destroyed.

❑ Scaggs' [Family] Burial Ground. Located on Anacostia Road; Sarah Scaggs, superintendent in 1882.

❑ Shoemaker's Farm [Family] Burial Ground. Near Pierce's Mill; owned by Pierce Shoemaker in 1882.

❑ Smith's [Family] Burial Ground. On Hamilton Road; Richard Smith, sexton in 1882.

❑ Soldiers' Home Cemetery. Location in the 1880 city directory is described as Harewood Road. Established in 1861 when, within days after the Battle of Bull Run, commissioners at the Soldiers' Home offered to the Secretary of War six acres of land within the grounds as a burial place for officers and men. The cemetery was enlarged to over 15 acres in 1883. Union soldiers and sailors who died during and after the Civil War were buried there and, by 1874, "117 citizens, employees, etc.," Most of the burials are soldiers who were living at the Soldiers' Home at the time of their death. Contact: Soldiers' Home Cemetery, 21 Harewood Road, N.W., Washington, D.C. 20011; telephone (202) 829-1829.

Vilas, Martin Samuel. The Veterans of the National Soldiers' Home (Burlington, Ver.: Free Press Association, 1915). LC Call Number UB384.D5.V6.

❑ Washington Asylum Burial Ground. (or Potters Field). Later D.C. General Hospital.

❑ Washington Hebrew Congregation Cemetery. Located is at 1380 Alabama Avenue, S.E. An 1880 city directory describes the Jew's Burial Ground at about 1½ miles from the government insane asylum. Washington Hebrew Congregation, Washington, D.C., Interment List, 1856-1911, a microfilm copy of original records at the American Jewish Archives, Cincinnati, Ohio, and is available on LDS Microfilm #1013426. A record of the burials in the old section of Washington Hebrew Cemetery was compiled by the Jewish Genealogical Society of Greater Washington and the Jewish Historical Society of Greater Washington, and can be found on an uncirculating copy of microfiche by LDS (#6334374), and LC Call Number Microfiche 96/80 F. Contact: Washington Hebrew Congregation, 1380 Alabama Avenue, S.E., Washington, D.C. 20032; telephone (202) 562-1807.

❑ Western Burial Ground. (see Holmead's Burial Ground).

❑ Woodlawn Cemetery. Woodlawn was established in 1895 at 4611 Benning Road, S.E.. Remains from more than 6,000 burials were reinterred here from the now destroyed Graceland Cemetery. Woodlawn is a predominantly black cemetery, but in the period 1895 to 1918, from 8 to 31 whites were buried there yearly. Historian Paul E. Sluby, Sr. has compiled a listing of 550 Woodlawn Cemetery inscriptions from markers that could be located in 1972 and 1973. Copies of Woodlawn records for the years 1895 to 1972 are on microfilm at Howard University, Moorland-Springarn Research Center, in Washington, D.C.

A Guide to Records of the District of Columbia

Sluby, Paul Edward, Sr. and Stanton Lawrence Wormley, Jr. <u>Woodlawn Cemetery, Washington, D.C.: Brief History and Inscriptions</u> (Washington, D.C.: Columbian Harmony Society, 1984). LC Call Number F193.S585 1984.

Other Finding Aids and Sources:

Exton, Peter and Dorsey Kleintz. <u>Milestones Into Headstones: Mini Biographies of Fifty Fascinating Americans Buried in Washington, D.C.</u> (McLean, Va.: E.P.M. Publications, Inc., 1985). LC Call Number CT215.E98 1985.

Pippenger, Wesley E. <u>District of Columbia Interments (Index to Deaths), January 1, 1885 to July 31, 1874</u> (Westminster, Md.: Willow Bend Books, 1999).

Ridgely, Helen West. <u>Historic Graves of Maryland and the District of Columbia: With the Inscriptions Appearing on the Tombstone in Most of the Counties of the State and in Washington and Georgetown</u> (Baltimore, Md.: Genealogical Publishing Co., 1967). LC Call Number F180.R55 1967.

Sluby, Paul Edward, Sr. and Stanton Lawrence Wormley, Jr. <u>Civil War Cemeteries of the District of Columbia Metropolitan Area</u> (Washington, D.C.: Columbian Harmony Society, 1982). LC Call Number E494.S62 1982.

Sluby, Paul Edward, Sr. and Stanton Lawrence Wormley, Jr. <u>Selected Small Cemeteries of Washington, D.C.</u> (Washington, D.C.: Columbian Harmony Society, 1987). Includes discussions of Eldbrooke Methodist Cemetery, Franciscan Monastery Cemetery, Georgetown Visitation Convent, Institutional Burying Ground, Jesuit Community Cemetery, Queen Farm Burying Ground, Sheriff Farm Burying Ground, Sibley Farm Burying Ground, Union Baptist Cemetery, and Veitch Farm Burying Ground.

United States Military Academy, Quartermaster. Post Cemeterial Records, 1816-1908. 5 vols. For the burial ground at West Point, N.Y. Registers of interment, 1816-1907, 1889-1908. Plotbook, 1908. National Archives, Record Group 404, Item 278.

DISINTERMENT PERMITS

By law enacted March 3, 1901, one of the records kept by the District of Columbia Health Department was for disinterment of remains. An authorization for disinterment and reinterment of a dead body was issued by the Registrar after an application was signed by the next of kin or legal representative of the deceased, and approved by the Commissioner of Public Health. Disinterment permits for the period 1912 to 1957 (number 7,480 to 20,899), are at the D.C. Archives. The permit provides for: name of deceased, date of death, color, sex, age, place of death, name of person authorizing removal, from what cemetery, to what cemetery, date of reinterment. Permits on green paper are filed chronologically and are bound in groups of 150. See Figure 20.

Court Records - Record Group 21

The records of the several United States courts for the District of Columbia comprise Record Group 21 in the National Archives. Much of the descriptive material given below was taken from a preliminary inventory of the record group which was prepared in 1962 by Janet Weinert.

One of the minimum requirements of using this mass of records is that all references to a particular item be complete and precise. You must request specific items and, obviously, you will not be brought 1,770 feet of law case files to rummage through. Personnel at the National Archives indicate that some of the descriptions may be misleading and some records do not contain genealogical information.

The staff in Room 13E will be glad to make suggestions concerning your research if you will let them know what you are looking for and the names and time period involved.

The chancery cases in the Circuit Court and, later, equity cases in the Supreme Court are excellent sources for genealogical information. Both are indexed by names of the parties to the suit. Chancery and equity cases often involve partition, sale or title to inherited land, and frequently name heirs and their family relationships. The criminal dockets for the Supreme Court show the history of the case, including name, case number, crime, verdict, sentence, and sometimes a list of witnesses.

UNITED STATES CIRCUIT COURT
For the District of Columbia

Congress in 1801 created a circuit court of the District of Columbia, which continued until 1863. Court sessions were held alternately in each of the two counties, Alexandria and Washington, until Alexandria was retroceded to Virginia in 1846. Since Alexandria's records have been retained by Virginia, the list below concerns only records of Washington County. The Circuit Court continued in operation until March 3, 1863, when it was abolished and all jurisdiction was vested in the Supreme Court of the District of Columbia. Each entry is followed in the right margin with a number which corresponds to the item in the record group's locator catalog that is maintained at the National Archives.

◘ Law, Appellate and Criminal Records. From 1801 until 1838, when the Criminal Court for the District of Columbia was created, civil suits at law, appeals, and criminal cases were docketed together. After that date, criminal cases no longer came before the Circuit Court except on appeal. From 1801 until 1809, equity cases also appeared in these dockets as well as in the chancery dockets; however, all papers appear to have been filed with the chancery records.

Description	Entry
Docket Books, June Term 1801 to January Term 1863. 134 vols.	1
Minute Books, June Term 1801 to January Term 1863. 21 vols.	2

See LDS Microfilm #0940130 to 0940135; National Archives Microfilm M1021. This court held sessions in the counties of both Washington and Alexandria until July 1846 when Alexandria County was retroceded to the State of Virginia. The records for Alexandria were returned to Virginia, hence the microfilm covers only those for Washington County. The minutes relate to cases involving slavery and the slave trade,

A Guide to Records of the District of Columbia

usury, trespass, bankruptcy, and procedures, and the ejection of tenants. There are a few cases involving the evasion of customs duties and maritime law. In almost all cases, the minutes simply list the case and give a brief account of the action taken.

Description	Entry
Copies of Minute Books, October 1848 to June 1858. 2 volumes.	3
Judgment Record, 1809-1810, 1813, 1849-1850, 1856-1860. 6 volumes.	4
U.S. Cases on Civil Docket, 1839. 1 volume.	5
Case Papers Containing Appearances, Trials, Imparlances, Judicials, etc., 1802-1863. 480 feet, 385 boxes.	6
References for Cases Referred to Arbitrators, 1802-1820. 2 boxes.	7
Criminal Appearances, 1809-1833. 2 boxes.	8
Civil Appearances, 1818-1863. 15 boxes.	9
Supersedeas Bonds Holding Collection of Judgment Pending Appeal, 1832-1863. 2 boxes.	10
Prison Bounds Bonds to Secure Release of Debtors, 1834-1844. 1 foot.	11
Rough Bundles of Accounts, Discharges, Grand Jury Lists, and Other Papers Not Related to Specific Cases, 1809-1863. 4 boxes.	12
Unidentified Papers. 1 box.	13

◘ Chancery Records. The basis of equity jurisdiction in the Federal courts was laid in the original Judiciary Act of 1789, to be exercised where an adequate remedy at law may not be obtained. In the District of Columbia chancery jurisdiction was exercised by the Circuit Court from the time it was founded in 1801 until it was dissolved in 1863. From 1801 until 1809, chancery cases were docketed both in the general dockets under the heading "equity" and in the regular chancery docket series. All of the papers seem to have been filed with the main chancery series.

Description	Entry
Index, A-Z, 1801-1863. 2 volumes, 5 inches.	14
Dockets of Chancery Docket Cases and Petitions for Partitions Docket, 1801-1830. 3 volumes, 6 inches.	15
Docket of Chancery Rules Cases and Old Divorce Docket, 1803-1863. 6 volumes, 10 inches.	16
The equity dockets for the period March 24, 1863 to June 15, 1938, essentially continue the series kept by the old Circuit Court that was dissolved in 1863. This record group, format X, contains 136 volumes arranged chronologically by date of court proceedings, and thereunder alphabetically by surname of parties.	
Petition Docket, 1810-1824. 1 volume, 2 inches.	17
Proceedings, 1801-1819, 1835-1836. 4 volumes, 1 foot.	18
Records, 1848-1858, 1861. 4 volumes, 1 foot.	19
Dockets and Rules Case Files, 1804-1863. 110 boxes.	20
Petitions for Partition, 1803-1863. 3 boxes.	21
Equity Papers, Mainly Injunctions and Subpoenas, 1809-1814. 1 box.	22
Old Divorces, 1860-1863. 1 item.	23

◘ Bankruptcy Records. These records pertain to proceedings under the Insolvency Law of 1803 for the District of Columbia except for the period February 1842 to March 1843 when the Bankruptcy Act of 1842 was in effect.

Court Records - Record Group 21

Description	Entry
Insolvency Minutes, 1836-1850. 1 volume, 3 inches.	24
Bankruptcy Docket, 1842-1843. 1 volume, 3 inches.	25
Insolvents Case Papers, 1814 to January 1842, and April 1843 to 1850. 28 boxes.	26
Bankruptcy Case Papers, February 1842 to March 1843. 2 boxes.	27

◘ <u>Habeas Corpus Records</u>. The writ of habeas corpus is generally regarded as the most famous writ in law, having been employed for many centuries to remove illegal restraint on personal liberty. Accordingly, the First Congress in the original Judiciary Act (1 Stat. 81) gave to all the U.S. courts the power to issue writs of habeas corpus. Most of the cases in this court involved persons alleged to be fugitive slaves.

Description	Entry
Segregated Habeas Corpus Papers, 1820-1863. 2 boxes. See LDS Microfilm #1601546 and 1601546	28

◘ <u>Slavery Records</u>. Manumission and emancipation papers, 1821 to 1861, are discussed in further detail on Page 72 of this Guide. The entries below are for items found in Record Group 21.

Description	Entry
Index to Record, Vol. 1, 1821-1828. 1 volume.	29
Manumission and Emancipation Record, 1821-1862. 5 volumes and index. (Commonly called "Free Negro Registers")	30
Fugitive Slave Cases, 1821-1861. 1 box.	31
Manumission Papers, 1857-1863, 1 box. See LDS Microfilm #1299308; National Archives Microfilm M433	32
Emancipation Papers, 1862-1863. 2 boxes. See LDS Microfilm #1299307; National Archives Microfilm M433	33

Provine, Dorothy S. <u>District of Columbia Free Negro Registers, 1821-1861</u> (Bowie, Md.: Heritage Books, Inc., 1996), 2 volumes. Abstracts of the record books in Entry 30. The record book for 1846 to a portion of 1855 has been lost. LC Call Number F205.N4 P76 1996.

◘ <u>Lien Law Records</u>. These papers are notices of liens required to be filed with the clerk of the court by the Lien Law of 1833, as a condition precedent to their validity as against third persons without notice. When the Circuit Court was abolished in 1863, this function was taken over by the Supreme Court of the District of Columbia. The dockets of both courts forming a single series, they are filed with the latter court's records.

Description	Entry
Lien Law Papers, 1833-1862. 2 boxes.	34

A Guide to Records of the District of Columbia

◘ <u>Marriage Records</u>. Marriage records are discussed elsewhere in this Guide. The bulk of the early original loose marriage licenses for the District of Columbia are not known to have survived with exception of those listed below.

Description	Entry
Marriage Licenses, 1837-1862. 1 box.	35

UNITED STATES DISTRICT COURT
For the District of Potomac and the District of Columbia

By an act of February 13, 1801 (2 Stat. 96), a new district was formed consisting of the territory of Columbia and called the District of Potomac. Court was held in the courthouse in Alexandria twice yearly, in April and October. This act was superseded April 29, 1802 (2 Stat. 156) by an act which stated that the chief judge of the Circuit Court of the District of Columbia was required twice yearly to hold a District Court of the U.S. in and for the said District. Court continued to be held in Alexandria until 1844 when it moved to the courthouse in Washington. In 1863, the functions of the District Court were taken over by the Supreme Court of the District of Columbia.

◘ <u>General Records</u>. The following records are those that cannot be identified with a specific case. They include a group of papers dealing with the administration of the court, such as appointment papers, bonds, and oaths of office. The minute book also reflects the administrative work of the court as well as giving a record of cases handled. Beginning in 1808, the minute book contains naturalization entries which in most cases give the age and place of birth of the person naturalized. Related records can be found in the Supreme Court of the District of Columbia.

Description	Entry
Minutes. 1801-1863. 1 volume. 3 inches.	36
Papers Showing Administration of the Court, 1855-1862. 1/4 inch.	37
Item missing as of April 16, 1976	

◘ <u>Admiralty Records</u>. Most of the District Court records concern admiralty cases: civil, criminal, and prize. The reason for this seems to be that in all other cases of violation of Federal law this court had concurrent jurisdiction with the Circuit Court for the District of Columbia; and the natural result was that such cases were disposed of in the Circuit Court.

Description	Entry
Admiralty Docket, 1857-1863. 1 volume. 1 inch.	38
Case Files, 1839-1863. 4 boxes.	39

Court Records - Record Group 21

◘ Copyright Records. These records are title pages to works for which copyright was sought in the District of Columbia, which, by terms of the original copyright law of May 31, 1790, were required to be filed with the clerk of the United States District Court where the author resided. In a few cases, the entire work instead of the title page is filed.

Description	Entry
Title Pages of Works For Copyright, 1854-1863. 1 box. 4 inches.	40

UNITED STATES CRIMINAL COURT
For the District of Columbia

Before 1838, all criminal cases were handled by the United States Circuit Court for the District of Columbia. An act of July 7, 1838, created a one-judge criminal court for the District of Columbia which was to hold alternate sessions in each of the counties of the District, i.e. Washington and Alexandria. It also required that the district attorney, marshal, and clerks of the Circuit Court perform the same functions in relation to the new criminal court. A review of judgments of the criminal court was provided in the form of a writ of error to the Circuit Court. This court continued in operation until 1863 when its functions were taken over by the Supreme Court of the District of Columbia.

◘ General Records

Description	Entry
List of Convictions Obtained by the Court, 1831-1853. 1 volume. 1 inch.	41
Criminal Court Dockets, 1838-1863. 80 volumes. 8 feet.	42
Criminal Court Minutes, 1838-1863. 24 volumes. 4 feet.	43
Record of Criminal Proceedings, 1844-1859. 7 volumes. 1 foot.	44
Case Papers, Appearances, Trials, Judicials, etc., 1838-1863. 50 boxes.	45
Criminal Appearances, 1838-1861. 4 boxes. 2 feet.	46
Recognizances, 1839-1861. 1 box.	47
Unidentified Papers. 1 box.	48

UNITED STATES SUPREME COURT
For the District of Columbia

The Supreme Court of the District of Columbia was established in 1863. It took over all functions previously vested in the Circuit, District and Criminal Courts. On July 22, 1863, the Supreme Court set up the following organizations: the General Term, which handled admissions of attorneys, removal of officials, and other general matters and also acted as a court of appeal; the Circuit Court, which heard law cases; the District Court; the Criminal Court; and Special Terms, which heard equity cases and acted as an orphans court. This organization continued until 1936 when the court was recognized into its present form.

A Guide to Records of the District of Columbia

◘ General Records

Description	Entry
General Term Minutes, 1863-1903. 8 volumes. 2 feet. Volume 5 missing on September 25, 1991	49
Records Location Register, c.1890. 1 vol. 3 inches.	50

◘ Law Records. These records include both law cases tried when the Supreme Court was sitting as a Circuit Court and the Municipal Court cases were docketed in the Supreme Court. The docketed volume <u>Appearance Docket Circuit Court and Judicials Supreme Court</u> appears to be a transition volume for some of the cases started in the old Circuit Court and completed in the Supreme Court. With the abolition of the old Circuit Court, its method of filing papers by stages of the case such as appearances, trials, etc., was also abolished. In the Supreme Court all papers in each case are filed together by the same docket number.

Description	Entry
Law Dockets, 1863-1934. 110 volumes. 26 feet.	51
Appearance Docket Circuit Court and Judicials Supreme Court, 1863. 1 volume. 2 inches. See note above.	52
Law Minutes, 1863-1934. 88 volumes. 20 feet.	53
Rule Book, Chronological Listing of Rules Made by the Court Relating to Individual Cases, 1864-1922. 1 volume. 3 inches.	54
Index to Judgments in Cases at Law, 1863-1895. 4 volumes. 9 inches.	55
Index to Ejectment Suits at Law, March 24, 1863-1935. 2 volumes. 3 inches.	56
Index to Attachments, 1876-1920. 1 volume. 2 inches.	57
Stet Calendar Showing Date Case Inactivated and Final Disposition of Case, 1894-1922. 1 volume. 2 inches.	58
Judgments of Municipal Court Docketed in the Supreme Court of the District of Columbia, 1928-1933. 2 volumes. 7 inches.	59
Law Case Files, 1863-1934. 1,771 boxes.	60
Bonds for Appeals to Court of Appeals of the District of Columbia, 1901-1917. 1 item.	61
Certified Copies of Municipal Court Judgments and Proceedings Filed in the Supreme Court to Become Liens Upon Land, 1928-1933. 17 items.	62

◘ Equity Records. These records consist of those cases in equity tried by the Supreme Court in Special Term. Up until 1907, adoption records were filed and docketed along with the rest of the equity papers. After that, however, the adoption dockets and papers were maintained as a separate series. These records are largely a continuation of the chancery records kept by the old Circuit Court; the equity dockets begin with number 7, thus continuing the Chancery Rules series which ended with number 6.

Description	Entry
Equity Index, 1863-1902. 7 volumes. 2 feet.	63
Equity Dockets, 1863-1899. 41 volumes. 10 feet.	64
Equity Minutes, 1863-1900. 57 volumes. 13 feet.	65
Memorandum Book (Order Book) Containing Requests by Lawyers for Action by the Clerk,	

Court Records - Record Group 21

	Entry
March 1869 to March 1870. 1 volume. 2 inches.	66
Order Books of Clerks' Orders Regarding Procedure, 1863-1903. 19 volumes. 4 feet.	67
Adoption Dockets, 1907-1937. 3 volumes. 4 feet.	68
Equity Case Files, 1863-1899. 1,652 boxes. 640 feet.	69
Trustees, Appeal, Receivers, and Other Bonds in Equity Cases, 1864-1909. 9 boxes.	70
Bonds Filed by Complainants in Equity Injunction Undertakings, 1878-1903. 1 box.	71
Equity Cases Auditors Reports, 1878-1945. 11 feet.	72
Adoption Case Files, 1907-1937. 12 boxes. 30 feet.	73

◘ Criminal Records. Papers include both criminal cases tried by the Supreme Court and the records of actions by the Grand Jury. For the period 1873-1889, habeas corpus cases are included in the criminal dockets.

Description	Entry
Criminal Dockets (Including Habeas Corpus Cases, 1873-1879), 1863-1934. 54 volumes. Volume 42 missing as of September 25, 1991	74
Criminal Minutes, 1863-1934. 94 volumes. 22 feet.	75
Grand Jury Dockets, 1868-1870 and 1924-1946. 30 volumes. 6 feet.	76
Criminal Case Files, 1863-1934. 494 boxes.	77
Grand Jury Case Papers, 1924-1946. 21 boxes.	78

◘ Habeas Corpus and Extradition Records. Papers in this section include requests for writs of habeas corpus and requests by the states upon the District of Columbia for extradition of persons wanted in their states and believed to be in the District. A few criminal cases are found in the habeas corpus dockets for 1863. For the period 1873-1889, the habeas corpus cases are docketed in the criminal dockets.

Description	Entry
Habeas Corpus Dockets, 1863-1873 and 1889-1933. 4 volumes. 1 foot.	79
Habeas Corpus Minutes, 1891-1931. 3 volumes. 7 inches.	80
Habeas Corpus Case Files, 1863-1933. 51 boxes.	81
Requisitions for Extradition, 1868-1877. 1 box.	82

◘ District Court Cases. Papers mostly relate to admiralty cases arising out of the Civil War in the period 1863-1868, and to cases involving land in the District of Columbia in the period 1869-1929.

Description	Entry
Typed Index to Dockets, 1863-1921. 1 item. 6 inches.	83
General Orders of the Court Relating to Admiralty Cases and Miscellaneous Papers, 1863-1873. 6 inches. Missing as of April 16, 1976	84
District Court Case Files, 1863-1929. 185 boxes.	85

A Guide to Records of the District of Columbia

◘ Lien Law Records. (See description above.)

Description	Entry
Index to Mechanics Liens. 9 volumes. No dates. 2 inches.	86
Lien Record, Beginning in Circuit Court and Continuing in Supreme Court of the District of Columbia, 1833-1934. 21 volumes. 4 feet.	87
Mechanics Lien Case Files, 1863-1924. 35 boxes.	88

◘ Bankruptcy Records. Records created under the Bankruptcy Act passed March 2, 1867, which provided for both voluntary and involuntary bankruptcy. This act was repealed on June 7, 1878. A few of the entries in the minute book go beyond that date, including some from 1892 to 1897, which were made by the District Court for the District of Columbia instead of the Supreme Court General Term; but all are of cases instituted under the act of 1867.

Description	Entry
Bankruptcy Dockets, 1867-1878. 2 volumes. 6 inches.	89
Bankruptcy Minutes, 1867-1889 and 1892-1897. 1 volume. 3 inches.	90
Bankruptcy Case Files, Act of 1867, 1867-1878. 53 boxes.	91
Bankruptcy Bonds. No dates. 1 foot.	92
Item missing as of April 16, 1976	

◘ Appointments. Records of appointments of justices of the peace, constables, and notaries public made by the Department of Justice and approved by the Supreme Court of the District of Columbia in General Term.

Description	Entry
Bonds of Justices of Peace and Constables, 1887-1907. 1 box.	93
Bonds of Notaries Public, Lists of Notaries, Copies of Their Seals, Recommendations and Receipts for Publishing Court Notices, 1860-1893. 1 box.	94

◘ Licenses. These records are licenses of physicians and midwives, issued by the Board of Medical Supervisors of the District of Columbia under the authority of an act of June 3, 1896, to regulate the practice of medicine in the District of Columbia. Licenses were issued to physicians who graduated from a medical school, who were licensed in one of the states, or who passed an examination.

Description	Entry
Physicians' License Registers, 1896-1939. 5 volumes. 1 foot.	95
Midwife License Registers, 1897-1926. 3 volumes. 5 inches.	96

◘ Naturalization Records. The first naturalization act was passed March 26, 1790. This act has been modified many times especially by the passage of the alien and sedition acts in 1798 and their repeal in 1802. However, the basic structure has remained unchanged. The alien filed before any United States

Court Records - Record Group 21

Court a declaration of intention to become a citizen. After a certain length of time he went again to court and took the oath of allegiance to the U.S. This was modified in 1906 by centralizing control of immigration and naturalization under the Bureau of Immigration and Naturalization in the Department of Commerce and Labor. In 1911 this Bureau was split in two, and naturalization functions were undertaken by the Naturalization Service, which was placed under the Department of Labor in 1914. On June 10, 1933, these bureaus were reunited to form the Immigration and Naturalization Service, which was transferred to the Department of Justice in 1940. However, the naturalization papers are still issued by the course. Up until 1863, District of Columbia naturalizations were issued chiefly by the Circuit Court and after that date by the Supreme Court. Since all of the records from the earliest date have been kept as a single series, these records are all filed under the Supreme Court of the District of Columbia.

Naturalization records are actually court records, but because many researchers do not think of them as such, we have given them a separate heading. To use the records, you need to ask for specific items, with names and approximate dates. The naturalization index is the best starting place. Following the name of the person in the index, there are abbreviated references to sources of information. These abbreviations are explained in the front of the index. Before persons could become naturalized, they usually had to apply several years in advance. The applications for naturalization in the Declarations of Intention and Supporting Papers records are not only applications filed in the District of Columbia, but in other jurisdictions, which may show where your ancestor was prior to his arrival in the District of Columbia. The Declarations of Intention to Become Citizens give the person's name, age, and his native country, with a renunciation of allegiance to the ruler. In some cases the town or county of origin is given. The first naturalization record is of August 4, 1802.

Abbreviations Used:

C.C.M. Nos. 1 to 12	Naturalization Circuit Court Minutes, 1847-1863. (Also see Entry 2 and Microfilm M1021 at the National Archives)
Crim. M.	Criminal Minutes, Supreme Court of the District of Columbia
Dec. of Int.	Declarations of Intention, 1818-1865 (Also see Entry 99)
D.C.M.	Naturalization District Court Minutes, 1801-1863 (Also see Entry 36)
G.T.M.	General Term Minutes, Supreme Court of the District of Columbia (Also see Entry 49)
J.A.S. Nos. 1 & 2	Naturalization Circuit Court Minutes by John A. Smith, 1848-1858 (Also see Entry 2 and Microfilm M1021 at the National Archives)
L.M.	Law Minutes, Supreme Court of the District of Columbia (Also see Entry 53)
N.P.	Naturalization Papers (Also see Entry 105)
N.R. Nos. 1 to 5	Naturalization Records, Supreme Court of the District of Columbia (Also see Entry 101)
O.M. Nos. 1 to 17	Naturalization Minutes of the Circuit Court, 1801-1837
O.N.R. No. 1 & 2 Old	Naturalization Records, 1824 to 1863 (Also see Entry 100)
R.B.	Naturalization Papers Found in Rough Bundles (Also see Entry 105)

Description	Entry
Naturalization Index, 1802-1909. 1 volume. 3 inches.	97
Naturalization Index Stubs, Containing Certificate Number, 1906-1926. Arranged alphabetically. 2 feet.	98
Declaration of Intention, with Supporting Papers. 1802-1903. 8 feet.	

Newspapers

There were many newspapers published in the 18th and 19th centuries in Georgetown and Washington. Extant issues are at various locations; some are originals, others are on microfilm. There are many gaps for which there are no known issues. Use of abstracts and indexes that have been prepared for some newspapers may save countless research hours.

A ledger of subscriptions to the *States and Union* newspaper, 1858-1861, is found in Record Group 351 of the National Archives (Entry 78). The record gives name and address of the subscriber, date paid, terms of the subscription, and amount paid.

At the Washingtoniana Division of the Martin Luther King Memorial Library are microfilm copies of a number of local newspapers as given below.

◙ Georgetown and Washington Papers

Daily Globe, 1857-1858, 1864
Daily Morning Chronicle, 1862-1866
Evening Star, Washington Star, 1852-1981
National Era, Jan. 1847-Mar. 1860
New National Era, Sept. 1870-Sept. 1874
Washington Bee, 1882-1922
Washington Federalist, 1801-1803
Washington Times, Washington Times Herald, 1895-1953

The *Washington [Evening] Star*, Dec. 1852-1981, is also at the Maryland Room of the Montgomery County Regional Library in Rockville, Maryland. The Peabody Room at the Georgetown Regional Library has bound copies of two 19th century Georgetown newspapers:

Federal Republican and Commercial Gazette, 1812-1813
Georgetown Courier, 1865-1876

The Newspapers and Current Periodicals Room at the Library of Congress has by far the most complete collection of Georgetown and Washington newspapers. Some newspapers had both a regular city edition and a "country edition," which might be of special interest to those who lived in Washington County. A chronological list at the Library indicates whether the paper was daily (d), weekly (w) or semi-weekly (sw). Early local newspapers that are found at the Library of Congress are listed below with microfilm roll numbers.

◙ Georgetown Papers

The Centinel of Liberty or George-town and Washington Advertiser, Museum and Washington and George-town Advertiser, 1796-1801. Microfilm #3306.
The Columbian Chronicle, Dec. 1793-May 1796.
Columbian Gazette (Union), 1829-1833. Microfilm #3048.
Courier, 1812
Federal Republican, Daily Federal Republican, 1812-1816. Microfilm #1004, 3052.
Georgetown Advocate, 1841-1856. Microfilm #1005.
Georgetown Daily Advertiser, 1839-1841. Microfilm #3026.
The George-town Weekly Ledger, 1790-1792.
Georgetown Columbian & District Advertiser, 1826-1828
[Georgetown] Independent American, 1809-1811. Microfilm #1004, 2891.
The Messenger, National Messenger, 1816-1821. Microfilm #2799.
The Metropolitan, 1820-1826. Microfilm.
The Olio, 1802-1803. Microfilm #2944.
The Senator, 1814
The Times and Patowmack Packet, 1789-1791.
Washington Federalist, Oct. 1800-1809. Microfilm #3216.

◙ Washington Papers

Atlantic World, 1807
American Auditor, 1826
The Cabinet, 1801
The Columbian Observer, 1821
Columbian Register, 1828-1829
Columbian Centinel, 1826-1827. Microfilm #2799.

A Guide to Records of the District of Columbia

Description	Entry
Declaration of Intention to Become Citizens, 1818-1926, filed chronologically and numerical. 21 volumes. Note: After 1906, the declarations are numbered	99
Naturalization Record, Old Circuit Court. O.N.R. Vol. 1, 1824-1840; Vol. 2 (an index), 1836-1868. 2 volumes. 6 inches.	100
Naturalization Record, Supreme Court, N.R., 1866-1906. 7 volumes. Note: Indicates age and place of birth of alien up to 1903; after that date more information is given.	101
Petition and Record, Forms Supplied by the Bureau of Immigration and Naturalization and Successor Agencies, 1906-1926; Some Military Naturalizations in Vol. 23, Beginning May 16, 1918. 55 volumes. 9 feet. Volumes 24 to 28 missing on November 20, 1991	102
Military Naturalization Index Stubs, 1918-1924, alphabetical. 3 items.	103
Military Petitions Issued Under Act of May 9, 1918, 1918-1920, chronological and numerical. 28 volumes. 4 feet.	104
Declarations of Intention With Supporting Papers, N.P., 1802-1903, chronological with four boxes of alphabetical index at beginning. 18 boxes.	105
Applications for Naturalization, 1903-1910. 1 foot.	106
Depositions Taken in Support of Petition for Naturalization Under Act of June 29, 1906, 1906-1925. 5 feet.	107

◘ Justice of the Peace Records

Description	Entry
Miscellaneous Volumes. 60 volumes. 5 feet.	108

◘ Probate Records. Discussion of entries 109 through 128 have been moved to the "Probate, Administrations and Guardianships" section at page 6 of this guide.

◘ Appellate Jurisdiction. The General Term of the Supreme Court of the District of Columbia acted as a court of appeal which heard appeals from other court sessions and inferior courts and commissions. The records described below consist of appeals from decisions of Police Court, justices and Municipal Court, the Rent Commission, and the Commissioner of Patents. All the appeals are taken to the General Term of the Supreme Court except those from Police Court, which are appealed first to the Criminal Court.

Description	Entry
District of Columbia Docket of Appeals from the Police Court to the Criminal Court of the District of Columbia, 1890-1895. 1 volume. 3 inches.	129
Appeals Case Files, 1870-1893. 12 boxes.	132
Appeals Case Files, 1890-1895. 1 item.	130
Case Files of Appeals From Justices Court, 1907-1909, and Municipal Court, 1909-1919. 1 item.	133
Case Files of Appeals From the Rent Commission, 1922-1924. 6 boxes.	134
Docket of Appeals From Decisions of the Commissioner of Patents, 1870-1893. 1 volume. 3 inches.	131

A Guide to Records of the District of Columbia

The Columbian Star, 1822-1826
Mrs. Colvin's Weekly Messenger, 1822-1828
[Daily] National Intelligencer, var., 1800-1829. See LDS Microfilm #0176493-0186564 for issues through March 1, 1852; single issues on LDS Microfilm #0226231 and #0233821.
Daily National Journal, 1824-1829
Impartial Observer and Washington Advertiser, 1795
The Monitor, 1808-1809
National Journal, 1823-1829
National Observer, 1822
National Palladium, 1823
Spirit of "Seventy-Six," 1809-1814. Microfilm #3216.
United States Telegraph, 1826-1829
Universal Gazette, Nov. 1800-1809
Washington City Chronicle, 1828-1829
Washington City Weekly Gazette, 1815-1820
Washington Gazette, 1796-1798, 1817-1826
Washington Republican & Congressional Examiner, 1822-1824
We the People, 1828

In the *Evening Star*, *Washington Star*, and the *Sunday Star*, between 1890 and 1952, were regular feature stories on aspects of local history. The articles are an interesting source of information on a specific area in Washington, i.e., roads, churches, cemeteries. The Martin Luther King Memorial Library has three indexes to these articles:

Coyle, John F. Index to Articles on Washington in the Evening Star, 1890-1893
Shannon, J. Harry. Index to The Rambler in the Sunday Star, 1912-1927
Proctor, John Claggett, Index to Articles on Early Washington From the Sunday Star, 22 January 1928 to 7 September 1952

Finding Aids and Sources:

Brigham, Clarence Saunders. History and Bibliography of American Newspapers, 1690-1820 (Worcester, Mass.: American Antiquarian Society, 1947).

Dixon, Joan Marie. National Intelligencer and Washington Advertiser Newspaper Abstracts, 1800- ___ (Bowie, Md.: Heritage Books, Inc., 1996-). Ongoing series.

Leach, Frank Willing (1855-1943). Extracts of Some of the Marriages and Deaths Printed in the National Intelligencer, Washington, D.C., Between the Years 1806-1958. Manuscript at the Historical Society of Pennsylvania, Philadelphia, Pa., and as LDS Microfilm #0441391.

Metcalf, Frank J. and George H. Martin. Marriages and Deaths, 1800-1820, From the National Intelligencer, Washington, D.C. (Washington, D.C.: National Genealogical Society, 1968). Extracted from the NGS Quarterly, published in book form to 1820. Metcalf's abstracts appeared in the Quarterly, June 1938 to Sept. 1942. Martin took over for Metcalf and continued in the Quarterly in Sept. 1948. A microfilm set of the notices, 1800-1850, with index, was sold by NGS, Arlington, Va. See LDS Microfilm #0929472-0929474.

Pippenger, Wesley E. The Georgetown Courier, Marriage and Death Notices, Georgetown, District of Columbia, November 18, 1865 to May 6, 1876 (Westminster, Md.: Willow Bend Books, 1998). LC Call Number F193.P58 1998.

Pippenger, Wesley E. Daily National Intelligencer, Washington, D.C., Marriage and Death Notices, January 1, 1851 to December 30, 1854 (Westminster, Md.: Willow Bend Books, 1999). LC Call Number F193.P555 1999.

Sluby, Paul Edward, Sr. Newspaper Obituary Clippings From the Baltimore Afro-American and the Washington Afro-American: For the Year 1992 (Baltimore, Md.: Afro-American Company of Baltimore City, 1994).

Wright, F. Edward, comp. Abstracts of the Newspapers of Georgetown and the Federal City, 1789-1799 (Westminster, Md.: WillowBend Books, 1986; reprinted 2000). LC Call Number F193.W75 1986.

Miscellaneous Records

GENERAL GOVERNMENT

In 1976, Dorothy S. Provine compiled <u>Preliminary Inventory of the Records of the Government of the District of Columbia</u>, which details items found in Record Group 351 of the National Archives. The introduction therein lists material in other record groups in the Archives that relates to the District of Columbia. There are 196 entries in the inventory. There are numerous entries in the guide which detail financial records, lists of correspondence, minutes and journals. Items most used for genealogical research are on microfilm in the microfilm research room on the fourth floor at the National Archives. Some of particular interest are discussed below. Original records from Record Group 351 are available for review by submitting a request through the Civil Reference Branch in Room 13E at the National Archives.

◘ <u>Appointments</u>. Registers of Appointments in the District of Columbia Government 1871-1880. 1 vol. (Entry 23). Appointments include commissioners, trustees of public schools, physicians to the poor, engineers, Metropolitan Police, justices of the peace and to the offices of the collector, treasurer, assessor. Usually gives name of appointee, position, salary, amount of bond, date of removal or resignation and remarks. Indexed by name.

◘ <u>Architectural Drawings</u>. As part of building permits, drawings for the period 1958 to 1982 are at the D.C. Archives. Most of these are stored in tubes.

◘ <u>Articles of Incorporation</u>. Records for the period 1870-1954, generated by the Recorder of Deeds, are at the D.C. Archives. Index volumes for the period 1870-1957. Includes reservation of name, articles of incorporation, amendments, annual reports, statement of changes, service of process, revocations.

◘ <u>Bawdy Houses</u>. A list of bawdy houses in the city of Washington, 1864-1865, including those identified as "coloured," is found in Record Group 393 at the National Archives, Provost Marshal's Department, 22nd Army Corps, Vol. 298, begin page 106.

◘ <u>Board of Architects</u>. Created in 1924 as the Board of Examiners and Registrars of Architects. At the D.C. Archives is found Board minutes and correspondence, 1925-1969, and 1975-1989. There are separate registration files of architects for the period 1925 to 1967.

◘ <u>Board of Health</u>. Minutes from the Board of Health cover the period 1822 to October 4, 1841, and 1876 to 1878. Subjects mentioned include outbreaks of diseases in the area, quarantines, changes in health laws, etc. Also discussed are special problems of German and Irish laborers in the city as well as those of free Negroes and slaves. The bound volumes are at the D.C. Archives.

◘ <u>Children</u>. Records of the Board of Children's Guardians. Include: History of Committed Feebleminded Children, 1884-1907, 2 vols. (Entry 151); Record of Children Received, July 4, 1893 to January 5, 1912, 1 vol. (Entry 152); Children's History, 1893, 1897-1906 and 1909-1913, 7 vols. (Entry 153); Directory of Placed-Out Children, July 7, 1893 to July 31, 1908, 1 vol. (Entry 154); Record of Children in Temporary Custody, November 9, 1897 to July 19, 1909, 3 vols. (Entry 155); Histories of Children Committed to the Industrial Home School for White Children, 1896-1917, 2 vols. (Entry 157). Records give varying information, but usually the name of child, age, race; sometimes physical condition, birthplace,

A Guide to Records of the District of Columbia

religion, name, address and birthplace of parents.

◘ Docket Book. A docket book for the Justice's Court, July 8, 1878 to May 5, 1882. Unnumbered series, alphabetical index. At the D.C. Archives.

◘ Employment. Applications for Employment in the Bureau of Streets, Avenues and Alleys, 1871-1874. 1 vol. (Entry 81). File number, name of applicant, residence, date of application, position desired, by whom recommended and action taken on application.

Roster of Employees, 1876-1878. 1 vol. (Entry 24). List of employees in local offices. Usually gives name of employee, position, salary, and remarks concerning date of appointment, salary changes and information on dismissals or resignations.

A register of employees of the Office of Public Buildings and Grounds covers the period 1871-1918. Entry 108 of Record Group 42 at the National Archives is arranged by division of the Office. Schedules show employee name, state from which appointed, position, salary. Other information often included is age, birthplace, citizenship, marital status, dependents, names of relatives in the Government service, and remarks about military service.

◘ Engineer Department. The Office of the Chief Clerk, Engineer's Department, was created by an Act of June 20, 1874 (18 Stat. 3) out of part of the old Board of Public Works. Records for the period 1897 to 1950 include among other items, plats, maps and charts, licenses and inspection cases, wharf property data, zoning, work orders in cemeteries, and traffic fatalities. At the D.C. Archives. A separate index is available.

◘ Habeas Corpus. Habeas Corpus case records, 1820-1863, are on two rolls of Microfilm M434 at the National Archives. These concern orders to produce a prisoner and show cause for capture. Records in chronological order include writs, orders of court and other papers. Most of the cases relate to persons alleged to be fugitive slaves. Originals are at the National Archives. See LDS Microfilm #1601546.

◘ Jail and Prison Records. Records of the District of Columbia jail, for the period May 1, 1863 to October 31, 1906, are at the prison in Lorton, Virginia. These include: Record of Deaths, July 1, 1895 to February 25, 1904; Record of Commitment, 1878-1882 and 1858-1902; Weekly Reports Ledger for Washington Asylum, January 7, 1894 to July 6, 1902; the Runaway Slaves Ledger; and the Old Capitol Prison journal. Records about Central Guard House (1863-1865), Carroll Prison (1863-1865), Old Capitol Prison (1863-1865), Fort Stanton (1861-1865), Russell Barracks (1866-1867), and Sedgwick Barracks (1868-1869) can be found in the National Archives' Record Group 393, "Records of U.S. Army Continental Commands."

◘ Licenses. Registers of Licenses, 1818-1876. 24 vols. (Entry 72). An act of May 3, 1802 (2 Stat. 195), which incorporated the city of Washington, empowered the corporation to license and regulate certain activities, including: auctions; retailing of liquor; hackney carriages, wagons, carts, and drays; pawnbrokers; theatrical productions; and other amusements. Entries vary between volumes, but lists usually show date, licensee, type of license, address of business. Arranged chronologically or by name of licensees.

◘ Manufactured Goods. An account book concerning duties on manufactured goods, 1815-1817. (Entry 71). Duties were imposed on sales of iron, nails, brads, and sprigs; candles; hats; umbrellas; paper; playing cards; saddles and bridles; boots; beer, ale, and porter; tobacco, cigars, and snuff; leather; and gold, silver and plated ware and paste work. The volume is a record book of bonds, licenses, and

Miscellaneous Records

duties kept by James H. Blake, Collector of the District of Columbia.

◘ Police Records. Metropolitan Police Force Service Records, 1861-1930. (Entry 118). Entries for members appointed from 1861 to 1917, giving name of the appointee; date and position to which appointed; and a summary of service, including information on promotions, resignations, discharges, suspensions, fines, misconduct charges, and other official personnel actions.

Register of Appointments to the Metropolitan Police Force, 1861-1930. (Entry 117). Name and date and place of birth of appointee, where and when naturalized, age, former occupation, number in family, home address, date of appointment and resignation or dismissal. There are also notes concerning promotions, reason for dismissal, and death. Alphabetical by first letter of surname.

Registers of Oaths of Office, 1862-1865 and 1868-1875. (Entry 120). Entries include name and signature of appointee and date. Arranged chronologically.

Arrest Books, 1869-1906. (Entry 127). Lists of arrests for the 3rd and an unidentified precinct. Entries usually give the date, name, age, race, nationality, occupation, marital status, complaint, name of complainant, and disposition of case.

General files of the Metropolitan Police Department, 1936-1965, are at the D.C. Archives.

Sylvester, Richard. District of Columbia Police (Washington, D.C.: Gibson Brothers, 1894). The author held various positions in the Police Department, including major and superintendent of police, 1898-1915. LC Call Number NV8148.W3 S8.

◘ Register of Licensed Physicians and Midwives. For the period 1896-1928 (before 1918, physicians only), 2 volumes. A Register of Practicing Physicians, prior to an Act of 1896, is sequenced alphabetically. Annual registration cards dubbed "Healing Art," for the period 1943-1954, include medical and surgical persons. Each of these items is at the D.C. Archives.

◘ Tax Assessments. General Assessment Books for the City of Washington 1814-1940. (Entry 46). Arranged by square and lot number, except the volumes covering 1874-1879, which are by surname. Information varies, but usually gives square and lot number, square footage of lot, value and owner's name. Some volumes give assessed value of improvements or personal property. Assessors' lists of property valuations were compiled every 5 years through 1871, and annually thereafter.

Tax Books for the City of Washington 1824-1879. (Entry 47). Annual record of the payment of taxes on real and personal property. Arranged by ward before 1837, by name of property owner after 1837. Two wards bound in one volume.

General Assessment Books for the County of Washington, 1855-1864 and 1868-1879. (Entry 193). List of assessments of real property, usually giving name of owner, location of property, acreage, lot number, value of land and value of improvements.

Tax Books for Washington County, 1871-1879. (Entry 194). Record of payment of assessments, giving name of person, location of property, acreage, lot number, and value of land and improvements.

MILITARY

Residents of the District of Columbia who served in the military in the earliest years of the District's existence would be included in an index to compiled service records of volunteer soldiers who served from 1784 to 1811. This is available on nine rolls of Microfilm M694 at the National Archives.

A Guide to Records of the District of Columbia

Names of those who served during the War of 1812 will be found on 234 rolls of Microfilm M602 at the National Archives, called "Index to Compiled Service Records of Volunteer Soldiers Who Served during the War of 1812." The index gives the man's name, rank and unit. After you have located your ancestor in the index, note the information given and from that you will be able to put in a request to look at the original papers, which can be photocopied.

The records of volunteer Union soldiers serving during the Civil War has no complete index. President Lincoln in 1861 called for 75,000 militiamen from the states and territories loyal to the Union and most soldiers served in units formed in the state of residence. However, a re-enlisting soldier was not necessarily assigned to the same unit in which he had served and there were special units composed of persons from different areas. You may find it necessary to check more than one index to locate your ancestor.

At the National Archives on three rolls of Microfilm M538 is the index to compiled military service records of volunteer Union soldiers who served in organizations for the District of Columbia. A similar index is on microfilm for organizations from Maryland. The index for the U.S. Colored Troops is on 98 rolls of Microfilm M589, and that for the Veteran Reserve Corps is found on 44 rolls of Microfilm M636. The Reserve Corps was composed of men unfit for active duty because of wounds or disease. As with the War of 1812 records, you can request to see the original papers. Records of the enlisted men sometimes give age, occupation and description.

When you know the unit in which your ancestor served, you may want to check "Compiled Records Showing Service of Military Units in Volunteer Union Organizations" on 225 rolls of Microfilm M594 at the National Archives. These will tell something of the unit's activities, stations, movements and organization, but do not contain information about individual soldiers. For a District of Columbia unit, see Roll 10.

If you find no record of an ancestor in a volunteer unit and yet have been told or have evidence to show that he was in the Union Army during the Civil War, there is another set of military records at the National Archives covering this period. Many of the men joined the regular Army instead of a volunteer unit. These will be found in "Registers of Enlistments in the United States Army, 1798-1914" (M 233). The names are indexed in each of eight chronological periods and for the Civil War years give name, organization, description, date and place of birth, and enlistment information.

At the National Archives, on microfilm, are numerous other military records, including those of Confederate soldiers, the U. S. Military academy, Indian Wars, Patriot War, Mexican War and Spanish-American War. "Returns from U.S. Military Posts 1800-1916," includes some posts in the District of Columbia. Navy enlistments before, during and after the Civil War are covered in "Index to Rendezvous Reports."

◘ Pension and Bounty Land. Pension and bounty land records contain far more personal information than do military service records and if you are fortunate enough to locate an ancestor in the files, your search will probably be well rewarded. Bounty land warrants were certificates giving eligible veterans rights to free land in the public domain, based on service in wartime between 1775 and 1855. Pension applications and records of pension payments for veterans, their widows and other heirs were based on service in the Armed Forces of the United States between 1775 and 1916. The applications show veteran's name, rank, unit, service, residence, age and birthplace, while the widow or heir's applications also contain information concerning marriage and the date of the veteran's death. There are various types of proof of service and often affidavits of witnesses.

Miscellaneous Records

REVOLUTIONARY WAR

◘ <u>Pension Application Files and Bounty Land Warrants</u>. Revolutionary War pension and bounty land warrant application files, 1800-1900, are on 2,670 rolls of Microfilm M804 at the National Archives. These contain both pension and bounty land warrant applications, arranged in alphabetical order. The original records typically are not accessible to patrons.

WAR OF 1812

The War of 1812 created a rich source of genealogical material for the District of Columbia. There are not only military service records, but pension and bounty land applications made many years after the war. Records of the District of Columbia militia units during the War of 1812 show great activity in August of 1814. British troops landed at Benedict in Charles County and District of Columbia militia were mobilized to defend the city. After defeating the Americans at Bladensburg, the British captured the city of Washington and set fire to nearly all the government buildings. In the process, they destroyed a considerable amount of public records, including records of service during the Revolutionary War.

◘ <u>1812 War Militia</u>. The names of Richard S. Briscoe's company of militia in the city of Washington in 1811, 1813 and 1814, are listed in <u>Early Recollections of Washington City</u> by Christian Hines.

◘ <u>1812 Bounty Land Warrants</u>. Bounty land warrants were issued under Congressional Acts of 1850, 1852 and 1855, which applied to veterans of several wars, including the War of 1812. Unless combined with a pension file, these bounty land applications are not indexed, but if you fill out a request form in the Microfilm Research Room at the National Archives stating the veteran's name and company as given in the military record, bounty land records will be searched. If an application exists it will be made available to you in the Main Reading Room on the second floor.

Pension and bounty land records refer to the military unit in which a soldier served. If the District of Columbia ancestor lived in Maryland during the War of 1812, check Maryland militia records. War of 1812 military bounty land warrants, 1815-1858, are found on 14 rolls of Microfilm M848 at the National Archives. It is partially indexed, includes warrants issued under the Acts of 1812, 1814 and 1842 for service during the War of 1812.

◘ <u>1812 Pension Application Files</u>. The index to the War of 1812 pension application files is on 102 rolls of Microfilm M313 at the National Archives, and covers pensions for those who served from 1812 to 1815.

CIVIL WAR

◘ <u>Civil War Pension Application Files</u>. The general index to pension files, 1861-1934, which includes Union soldiers in the Civil War, is on 544 rolls of Microfilm T288 at the National Archives.

Virginia provided for Confederate veterans and their widows and dependents with three pension acts: 1888, 1900 and 1902. These acts varied in the persons they covered, what qualified an applicant for pension, and the amount paid. The Act of 1888 provided pensions for soldiers, sailors and marines who were maimed or disabled during the war and for widows of men who were killed during the war. This act applied to natives of Virginia who enlisted from Virginia or any other state in the Confederate service and who were residing in Virginia at the time of application. The Act of 1900 extended that of 1888. The 1902 act made for additional restrictions on who could apply for pension. It was amended by later acts to lengthen the deadline for filing and to make minor changes.

A Guide to Records of the District of Columbia

This act contained a section for servant pensions which appears to have been for blacks. Many pension files provide age, place of birth, how many years the veteran resided in a particular place, and length of service rendered. Applications are arranged alphabetically by locality and thereafter alphabetically by surname of the applicant. The card index, though incomplete, is arranged alphabetically by name of veteran, widow or servant. Disallowed pensions are not indexed.

Original records and index from The Library of Virginia, Richmond, Virginia, were filmed on 219 microfilm rolls. For microfilm copies of the indexes, 1888-1934, see LDS Microfilm #1439763-1439775. For pension applications under the Act of 1888 (by county then city), see LDS Microfilm #1617178-1617194. Applications filed under the Act of 1900 (by county then city) are on LDS Microfilm #1763903- 1763939, #1763869-1763902, #1985938-1985939, #1822821-1822923. Disallowed applications are found on rolls #1822924, #1838463 and #1838464.

◘ Other Civil War Topics. A publication entitled War History of the 'National Rifles' Company A, Third Battalion District of Columbia Volunteers 1861 (Wilmington, Delaware, Ferris Bros. 1887) is at the George Washington University's Gelman Library. The company was organized in November of 1859 and reported for active duty April 15, 1861. The book's muster roll gives the name, rank and date mustered in, with an additional column, "remarks," which may be a notation concerning death in battle or service in other companies.

◘ Soldiers' Home. Provisions to establish national homes for disabled volunteer soldiers were passed by Congress in 1866. This was to provide residences for honorably discharged veterans who were without adequate means of support. The United States Soldiers' Home in Washington, D.C., now called the U.S. Soldiers' and Airmen's Home, is at Rock Creek Road and Upshur streets, N.W.

Record Group 231 at the National Archives consists of records of the U.S. Soldiers' Home in Washington. The general and monthly registers of members, 1852-1941, are arranged chronologically and then alphabetically by surname. An entry usually shows the name of member (resident), date of admission, military history, physical description, date and place of birth, occupation at time of admission, marital status, size of family and remarks. Hospital records for the U.S. Soldiers' Home consist of registers of persons admitted to the hospital, 1872-1943. They show member's name, age, date and place of birth, military unit, diagnosis, date of admission and discharge or death, and remarks. Death records, 1852-1942, give date, name, age, nativity and cause of death. Case files for deceased members, 1880-1942, arranged alphabetically, include member's military and home history; date, place and cause of death; date and place of burial. Original records for the U.S. Soldiers' Home are at the National Archives, through the Military Service Branch, Room 8E.

◘ Washington Light Infantry Battalion of Volunteers. A muster roll exists at the National Archives of the men in the Washington Light Infantry Battalion of Volunteers, who left home April 12, 1861, to serve for 3 months as a battalion, after which most of the men re-enlisted in other battalions. The Infantry was reorganized in 1870. There are minute books, a list of 1880 members, and a scrapbook.

◘ Veterans' Census Schedules. In 1890 a special census was taken of Union veterans of the Civil War and widows of veterans. The schedules show the name of the veteran, or his name and that of his widow if he had died; his rank, company, regiment or vessel; dates of enlistment and discharge; length of service; post office address; disability incurred by veteran; and remarks.

These records are with other census records at the National Archives on 118 rolls of Microfilm M123. The booklet entitled "Federal Population

Miscellaneous Records

Censuses 1790-1880," in listing the states for which there are extant records of the 1890 Veterans' Census, has those for the District of Columbia under "Washington, D.C., and Miscellaneous."

WORLD WAR I

Draft cards of the District of Columbia Selective Service System during World War I, 1917-1918, are found on 19 rolls of Microfilm M1509 at the National Archives. The original records are maintained at the National Archives in East Point, Georgia. Draft cards are arranged alphabetically by state, then alphabetically by county or city, then alphabetically by surname of the registrants. See LDS Microfilm #1570933-1570936, #1556832-1556838, and #1556843-1556848. Cards for Indians, prisoners, insane, those in hospitals, and late registrants are found on LDS Microfilm #2022331 item 6 and #2022332 item 1.

OTHER MILITARY

◘ District of Columbia Militia. Listed in the Preliminary Inventory of the Records of the Adjutant General's Office, Record Group 94 (PL #17), as Entry 332, is a one-volume "Register of Officers of the Militia of the District of Columbia 1813-1830." This gives the name of the officer, rank, regiment, brigade, date of appointment and remarks. In the back of the book is a section concerning the First and Second Legions of the Militia of the District of Columbia for the years 1802 to 1811. This section contains the names of men to whom commissions were offered, for what rank, the date and, in some cases, a notation that they declined the commission.

Also part of Record Group 94, but apparently not in the Preliminary Inventory, are three volumes entitled "Register of Commissions of the District of Columbia Militia, Adjutant General's Office, April 19, 1887 to February 15, 1899." The first two volumes, which are indexed, cover the year 1887 to 1909. In them are copies of the actual commissions, which had been signed by Grover Cleveland, William McKinley or Theodore Roosevelt, as the case may be, and give the officer's name, rank, company, battalion and date of the commission. The third volume, unindexed, is a record of the officers by regiment, and dates from 1887 to 1939.

"Militia of the District of Columbia 1828-1832," on LDS Microfilm #0020449, contains records from the Historical Society of Pennsylvania, Philadelphia, Pa., which were with the roll record of the 7th Company, 84th Regiment of Philadelphia militia. The District of Columbia records are the roll of Captain Francis Asbury Dickins' Company of infantry, including: the 2nd regiment, 1st brigade, 1828-1829; 6th company, 3rd regiment, 3rd brigade, 1830; and 6th company, 1831-1832. The names of the men are given and their rank. During one of the years covered, the records give a square number after each man's name. The square numbers, along F Street between 10th and 15th, N.W., may indicate where the men lived.

◘ Register of Militia of the District of Columbia, Together with the Militia Laws of the United States, by Brooke Williams of the Adjutant General's Office, was published in June 1831, and is a listing of the officers of the First, Second and Third Regiments, giving their rank and date of commission. The book is in the George Washington University's Gelman Library.

"Washington Light Infantry Corps," in the manuscript collection of the Historical Society of Washington, D.C., has minute and letter books beginning in 1840 and a list of members, 1840-1853.

◘ Registers of Cadet Admissions, 1800-1953. 7 volumes. Arranged by year of admission and thereunder alphabetically by name of cadet, except for the period 1800-1818 when names were entered by date of admission. Record shows U.S. Military Academy cadet's name, date of admission, age when admitted, source of

A Guide to Records of the District of Columbia

appointment, place of birth (from 1839), date of birth (from 1890). Also included are date and circumstances a cadet left the Academy (graduation, dismissal, discharge, death). National Archives, Record Group 404, Item 192.

Military Finding Aids and Sources:

Merrill, Samuel Hill. The Campaigns of the First Maine and First District of Columbia Cavalry (Portland, Me.: Bailey & Noyes, 1866). LC Call Number E511.6 1st M. See LDS Microfilm #1454570.

Pierce, Alycon Trubey. Selected Final Pension Payment Vouchers, 1818-1864: District of Columbia (Westminster, Md.: Willow Bend Books, 1998). LC Call Number F193.P54 1998.

Pompey, Sherman Lee. Genealogical Notes on the District of Columbia During the American Civil War (Albany, Ore.: By the Author, 1984). See LDS Microfilm #1750789. LC Call Number E501.3.P65 1984.

Wells, Charles J. Maryland and District of Columbia Volunteers in the Mexican War (Westminster, Md.: Willow Bend Books, 1991). LC Call Number E409.7.W45 1991.

Wills, Mary Alice. The Confederate Blockage of Washington, D.C., 1861-1862 (Parsons, W.Va.: McClain Printing Company, 1975). LC Call Number E600.W55.

Wright, F. Edward. Maryland Militia, War of 1812, Volume 7 - Montgomery County (Silver Spring, Md.: Family Line Publications, 1986)

Wright, F. Edward. Maryland Militia, War of 1812, Prince George's County (Silver Spring, Md.: Family Line Publications, 1986). LC Call Number E359.5.M2 W8.

EMANCIPATION AND MANUMISSION

In April 1862, legislation was passed which abolished slavery in the District of Columbia and required slave owners to free their slaves with compensation. Commissioners were appointed to investigate the claims for compensation and make payments. A supplementary Act in July provided that slaves whose owners did not file could themselves petition for freedom and also enlarged the original Act to include slaves employed in the District whose owners lived elsewhere.

Emancipation papers resulting from the Act of April 16, 1862, are on three rolls of Microfilm M433 at the National Archives. See reference under Record Group 21 on Page 55 of this Guide. Included in this series is owners schedules which were filed to request compensation. These not only have the name, age and sex of the slave, but description. Sometimes a notation such as "she has learned to read" or "waiter, very intelligent." Occasionally, there is information concerning the owner that is of genealogical importance, when, for instance, the owner is listed as guardian for another or gives the name of the person from whom he inherited the slave. Many of the schedules filed by the freed slaves contain little information, but some are fascinating. One told of having left the city for fear of being colonized in Africa and going to her father who was the slave of a certain man in Montgomery County. A few affidavits were filed which state that the Negro was born free.

◘ Board of Commissioners for the Emancipation of Slaves in the District of Columbia. The records of the Board of Commissioners for the Emancipation of Slaves in the District of Columbia, 1862-1863, are on six rolls of Microfilm M520 at the National Archives. See LDS Microfilm #1299303-1299306. This series includes three bound volumes and a number of unbound records of the Board. The records were transmitted to the First Auditor of the Treasury Department in 1866 by F.E. Spinner,

Miscellaneous Records

Treasurer of the U.S., who, on the recommendation of the First Comptroller of the Treasury Department, had been designated as the agent for payment of monies awarded by the Board of Commissioners.

An act of April 16, 1862 (12 Stat. 376), abolished slavery in the District of Columbia. Under section 3 of the act the President was authorized to appoint a board of three commissioners, who were residents of the District, to examine petitions for compensation from former owners of freed slaves in the District. Pursuant to this act, Daniel R. Goodloe, Horatio King, and Samuel F. Vinton were appointed. In June 1862, John M. Broadhead was appointed to replace Mr. Vinton. A clerk of the circuit court served as clerk of the Board.

An act of July 12, 1862 (12 Stat. 538), provided that petitions could be received from slaves whose owners had not presented petitions for compensation. The petitions received under this act were filed separately from those received under the act of April 16, and are reproduced on Roll 6 of the M520 microfilm series.

The records of the Board include the following:

1. A bound volume of the minutes of the meeting of the Board of Commissioners, April 28, 1862 to January 14, 1863, contains the official summary of activities of the Board, arranged chronologically by date of session. A name and subject index is at the front of the volume.

2. A bound volume of a record of petitions filed under the act of April 16, 1862, for the period April 29 to July 15, 1862, showing the date the petition was filed, number of the petition, name of petitioner, names of slaves, value of slaves as claimed in the petition. Arranged chronologically and thereunder by petition number. An index by name of petitioner is at the front of the volume.

3. A bound docket book kept by the Board, dated April to December 1862, relating to the petitions filed under the act of April 16, 1862, showing the number of the petition, name of claimant, and a summary of action taken. Arranged by petition number. An index is at the front of the volume.

4. An unbound summary list of amounts awarded to claimants who filed petitions under the act of April 16, 1862, showing the number of the petition, name of claimant, number of servants, amount awarded by the Board, and the signature of the claimant. Arranged by petition number.

5. An unbound final report by the Board of Commissioners of the Secretary to the Treasury, dated January 14, 1863. Accompanying this narrative report are three tables that present data in chronological order about petitions filed under both acts, with alphabetical index.

6. Unbound petitions filed with the Board of Commissioner pursuant to acts of April 16 and July 12, 1862. The petitions filed under the first act were numbered consecutively as they were received by the Board and are arranged numerically. Those filed under the second act were not numbered and are arranged chronologically.

For petitions filed under the Act of April 16, 1862, numbers 1 to 966, and those filed under the act of July 12, 1862, there is a printed index found in the House of Representatives Report, Executive Document No. 42, 38th Congress, 1st Session.

All records of the Board that are listed above, except the petitions, are reproduced on Roll 1 of the M520 microfilm series. The petitions are reproduced on Rolls 2 through 6. Original records reproduced on microfilm are part of Record Group 217 in the National Archives.

A Guide to Records of the District of Columbia

◘ Freedmen's Records. The Freedmen's Bureau, created by Congress after the Civil War, helped former slaves make the transition to citizenship and aided destitute freedmen and refugees. "Records of the Assistant Commissioner for the District of Columbia Bureau of Refugees, Freedmen, and Abandoned Lands 1865-1869" are on 21 rolls of Microfilm M1055 and contain indexed letters, orders and notations. The Bureau maintained freedmen's schools, cooperated with benevolent societies issuing supplies to destitute, supervised labor contracts, helped black soldiers and sailors collect bounty claims, pensions and back pay, procured transportation for freedmen who wished to travel north to seek employment, supervised freedmen's farms in Maryland and Virginia, and made decisions about orphan children.

A special record group concerning schools is titled "Records of the Superintendent of Education for the District of Columbia, Bureau of Refugees, Freedmen, and Abandoned Lands, 1865-1872" and found on 24 rolls of Microfilm M1056 at the National Archives. The record group is described in a pamphlet bearing this number that is available from the National Archives. The Bureau was established in the War Department by an act of March 3, 1865. Congress assigned to the Bureau responsibilities that previously had been shared by military commanders and by agents of the Treasury Department. The duties included supervision of all affairs relating to refugees, freedmen, and the custody of abandoned lands and property. This microfilm series is also available from the LDS Church, on 23 rolls. The collections includes: letters received; endorsements; reports of operations; records of rations issued; records relating to the relief of destitute (some at the Freedmen's Hospital); abandoned or confiscated lands; freedmen's applications for transportation, 1866-1868 (roll #1605553; and personnel records for officers and laborers employed by the Bureau.

EDUCATION

Three universities were established and began classes in the District of Columbia before 1900. Their records are of interest if your ancestor attended one of them. Occasionally, the records can provide a valuable genealogical clue. A change in the name of the next of kin or name of the person paying tuition may indicate a death has occurred.

◘ George Town Academy. Later Georgetown College, and now Georgetown University, was founded in 1789 and students were admitted in 1791. Although established by the Roman Catholic Church, it was for "students of every religious profession." There are records of tuition payments dating back to the 1790's, and some information on alumni. Extant records are in the Georgetown University's Lauinger Library, Special Collections Division.

◘ Columbian College. Now George Washington University, began in 1819 when a lot was purchased consisting of 47 acres about half a mile beyond Boundary Avenue between 14th and 15th streets, N.W., for the formation of a college under the direction of the Baptist General Convention. The college was chartered by Congress in 1821 and trustees were to be of every denomination, as were professors and pupils. The college opened in 1822 and the first commencement was in 1824. It became George Washington University in 1904 and moved to its present quarters on G Street between 20th and 21st, N.W., in 1912. At George Washington University, records concerning when the person attended, field of study and name and address of next of kin are at the Registrar's Office, and commencement programs, alumni catalogues and alumni achievement awards are in the Gelman Library, Special Collections Division.

A copy of the "George Washington University General Alumni Catalogue," published in 1917, is at the Mormon Library. It names the alumni beginning with the three graduates in 1814, and gives degree, year graduated, place of death,

Miscellaneous Records

and sometimes occupation and position held. The catalogue is indexed and lists graduates only, not all students.

◘ Howard University. Established in 1867, when General Oliver Otis Howard, head of the Freedmen's Bureau and an upstanding Congregationalist, received from Congress a charter to incorporate Howard University. The university included white trustees, faculty and students from the first but the education of black leadership has always been its primary intention. The Registrar's Office of the University has records concerning dates of attendance, whether the student graduated and grades and the Archivist has graduate directories.

Contact: Howard University, 2400 Sixth Street, N.W., Washington, D.C. 20059; telephone (202) 636-6100.

BUSINESSES

A vital source for research into business history is of course the city directories. In 1834, we see for the first time in a city directory a list of hotels, boarding houses, and messes; and locations of public offices and the names of the clerks therein employed. It is not until 1858 that William H. Boyd's directory of Washington and Georgetown contains a separate business directory. These appear consistently from 1862 forward. The extant directories are listed on Pages 4-5 of this Guide.

On occasion a business directory was published entirely separate from the city directory. An undated one, c.1885, by Bard & Company of New York, is entitled "Classified Business and Professional Directory of Washington, D.C. [and Alexandria]." It lists businessmen and their establishments by category; very similar to the yellow pages we are familiar with today. There is even a run of more than 12 pages full of lawyers!

◘ Freedman's Savings and Trust Company. The company was incorporated by an act of Congress approved March 3, 1865, as a banking institution established in the city of Washington, for the benefit of freed slaves. The company failed in 1874. The main office was in Washington but there were branches in a number of other cities.

"Registers of Signatures of Depositors in Branches of the Freedman's Savings and Trust Company 1865-1874" (M 816) is at the National Archives. The registers called for account number, name of depositor, date, birthplace, place brought up, residence, complexion, employer or occupation, age, wife or husband, children, father, mother, brothers, sisters, remarks and signature. Unfortunately, in many instances very little information is given. On the other hand, some of the depositors were noted as "free born" and in one case, under "Remarks," it was stated that the depositor was born in South Carolina and named his former master, that the depositor had gone with his master to Richmond during the War and went over to the Union Army.

"Indexes to Deposit Ledgers in Branches of the Freedman's Savings and Trust Company 1865-1874" (M 817) serves as an index to the registers.

The early books sometimes also contain the name of the former master or mistress and the name of the plantation.

See also LDS Microfilm as: accounts 1865-1871, roll #0928574; and accounts 1872-1874, roll #0928575.

Finding Aids and Sources:

Hynson, Jerry M. District of Columbia Runaway and Fugitive Cases, 1848-1863 (Westminster, Md.: Willow Bend Books, 1999).

Neimeyer, David E. Freedman's Savings and Trust Company: Depositor Signature Card Entries for Washington, D.C., 1865-1868 (Westminster, Md.: Willow Bend Books, 2000).

Collections

MANUSCRIPT COLLECTIONS

There are manuscript collections at most of the libraries and historical societies listed elsewhere in this guide. The very extent of the collections frequently discourages the genealogist but if mention of an ancestor can be found, it will add interest to your family history. Taking into consideration the time period and social and economic position of your ancestor, the staff at the library or historical society may be able to suggest a particular manuscript collection.

◘ Library of Congress. In the Manuscript Division at the Library of Congress, the Diaries of George Washington are well-indexed and there are references to residents of George Town and surrounding areas. The Thomas Jefferson Papers are extensively indexed and contain some letters written to him by local citizens during the years he was in Washington. William W. Corcoran (1798-1888), who established the Corcoran Gallery of Art, was born in Georgetown (his father was twice elected mayor) and sympathized with the South during the Civil War. His papers are indexed in the card file at the Library of Congress.

Samuel Davidson (d. 1810) was a Georgetown merchant whose ledger and day book at the Library of Congress were a record of transactions from 1789 to 1810. There are several accounts per page, debits (Dr=debtor) on the left and credits on the right. For most of the accounts, Davidson gave the person's name, sometimes stating whose son he was, his occupation, place of residence and occasionally nationality or to what city he had moved. Account holders were not only from Georgetown and Washington, but Virginia, Montgomery County, and towns in Maryland as far away as Cumberland. Despite the fact the collection is not indexed, the handwriting is easy to read and Davidson's occasional comments (such as the one about a man who robbed his house, "as damned a villain as ever was hanged") make interesting browsing. A plat book, 1791-1809, of land called Port Royal which lay within the city of Washington and belonged to Samuel Davidson can be found in the Library of Congress, at LC Call Number G1277.P6G46.M3 1809.

Also at the Library of Congress is the Thomas Beall of George collection. His account books, 1794 to 1811, are difficult to decipher and not helpful, but Beall's ledger, 1802 to 1811 has notations concerning the account holder's occupation, residence, and occasionally "son of," "brother of," or "widow of." A few of the account holders are Negroes, and there is a notation as to owner's name. Several times Beall wrote in the date that someone he knew "departed this life." In the collection also are "Notes taken from the ledger of Colonel Thomas Beall of Georgetown, giving names, dates and occupation of early residents of the District of Columbia and Montgomery County," which is alphabetized.

◘ Maryland Historical Society. At the Maryland Historical Society, the ledger of Brooke Beall, a merchant in George Town, covers the period 1790 to 1795. (MS 111) It is not indexed, but is only a single volume and can be quickly scanned. For each account, on the left page are listed the items purchased, services rendered or cash advanced. On the right page, marked "Contra," are payments made on account, almost always made by someone else, in the form of crop tobacco, merchandise or services, that were owed to the account holder. As a result of this method of payment, there are many persons named who lived in George Town or traded there.

◘ D.A.R. Library. In the Office of the Historian General at the D.A.R., there is a card index to genealogical references in their manuscript collection for material received before 1970.

Collections

◘ **Historical Society of Washington, D.C.** The Historical Society publishes "Guide to Research Collections," which briefly describes its holdings, including its manuscript collection.

GENEALOGIES

Most researchers into family history are well aware of the potential value of work done by other genealogists. There are bound books, notebooks, family charts and files of loose letters and notes in many repositories in the District of Columbia and surrounding suburbs to be read and evaluated. Genealogies may include those that are impressive, bound books with five serious errors per page, charts based on Great-Aunt Matilda's memory (which was far from accurate), or excellent, well-documented family histories and letters written 40 or 50 years ago that provide marvelous clues to family researchers.

There are genealogies and family charts available in the Local History and Genealogy Room of the Library of Congress, the D.A.R. Library, the Maryland Historical Society, Maryland State Archives, National Genealogical Society, Montgomery County Historical Society, the Maryland Room of the Montgomery County Regional Library in Rockville, Prince George's County Genealogical Society, the Peabody Room of the Georgetown Library and a few at the Historical Society of Washington and Prince George's County Memorial Library in Hyattsville. Of these repositories, local libraries and local historical societies provide greatest emphasis on families in the Washington area.

MAPS AND PLAT BOOKS

A number of maps, plans and atlases, for the period 1792 to 1915 are found in Record Group 351 at the National Archives (Entry 98). A guide on the cartography holdings at the National Archives is available from that institution. Another comprehensive map collection is that at the Geography and Map Division of the Library of Congress. This collection may be considered the most accessible in the area. Some of the maps for the District of Columbia are large scale, with considerable detail, and actually show the houses, other buildings and their location.

Between c.1802 to 1804, Nicholas King (1771-1812) prepared a number of manuscript plats of the city of Washington. These showed numbered squares or blocks, other numbered areas known as appropriations or reservations, names of streets, and lines of the holdings of the original proprietors. A copy of 1934 was made by William P. Elliot. See Entry 40 of the Record Group 42 inventory at the National Archives.

At the Library of Congress the 1857 map by A. Boschke is the earliest detailed map of the area, but covers Washington City only. The 1861 map by A. Boschke, entitled "Topographical Map of the District of Columbia," covers the District and is fascinating. For the outlying areas, there are names of property owners, the houses, mills, rivers and streams, woods, orchards and cleared areas, roads, lanes and driveways. You can see the lane from farmhouse to cleared area.

An 1865 map at the Library of Congress, "Defenses of Washington: Extract of Military Map of N. E. Virginia," shows the location of Tennallytown, Uniontown, the forts, roads and, in some cases, property owners. See Figure 23.

The 1878 "Atlas of 15 Miles Around Washington Including the County of Prince George, Maryland," by G.M. Hopkins, containing land ownership maps of Prince George's County, also covers a few areas of the District of Columbia, such as Tennallytown and Pleasant Grove.

Beginning in 1887, there are plat books by G.M. Hopkins, which give the names of some of the homeowners in the city, particularly those who own a block of houses, and the property owners in the more rural areas. The plat books for 1903 and later were done by G. William Baist. If you

A Guide to Records of the District of Columbia

are lucky to find a copy of the Baist plans, you will normally encounter them in very poor condition.

The fire insurance maps of Washington, D.C. begin with an 1888 map by Sanborn Map Publishing Company. These maps were made for fire insurance companies as an aid to setting insurance rates. The 1888 maps cover only the built-up portions of the city, but the 1903 maps extend to outlying areas and by 1916 include parts of Montgomery and Prince George's Counties. For each building, the fire insurance maps give the street number, outline the building, and show the number of stories, placement of windows and whether brick or frame. By noting the churches, schools, shops, livery stables, bake houses, wagon shops, wood and coal yards, tin shop, boat yard and all the places of business, the character of each neighborhood is set out.

There is a card index to maps at the Library of Congress and maps which you request will be brought to you. Some maps may be photocopied and others, such as those bound in large books, may be traced, with Mylar sheets used to protect the map.

At the Martin Luther King Memorial Library, the map collection is in drawer files, so that you may browse through them. At the Historical Society of Washington, D.C., there is also a good map collection and personnel who will help. Both these research centers have the plat books. There are maps at the George Washington University's Gelman Library.

Finding Aids and Sources:

Cosentino, Andrew J. and Richard W. Stephenson. City of Magnificent Distances, The Nation's Capital: A Checklist (Washington, D.C.: Library of Congress, 1991). List and commentary on maps in the Library's collection which deal with the District of Columbia. LC Call Number F191.5.C67 1991.

Historical Society of Washington, D.C. Master's Theses and Doctoral Dissertations on the History of the District of Columbia: Occasional Paper Number 1 (Washington, D.C.: By the Society, no date).

King, Nicholas. The King Plats of the City of Washington in the District of Columbia, 1803 (Washington, D.C.: N. Peter, Photo-Lithographer, 1888). LC Call Number G1275.K5 1888.

Martin, Joseph. A New and Comprehensive Gazetteer of Virginia, and the District of Columbia (Charlottesville, Va.: J. Martin, 1835; reprinted 2000 by Willow Bend Books). Contains a copious collection of geographical, statistical, political, commercial, religious, moral and miscellaneous information, collected and compiled from the most respectable and chiefly from original sources. LC Call Number F224.M38. See LDS Microfilm #0897469.

Noel, Francis Regis and Margaret Brent Downing. The Court-House of the District of Columbia (Washington, D.C.: Judd & Detweiler, Inc., 1919). LC Call Number F204.C86 N7.

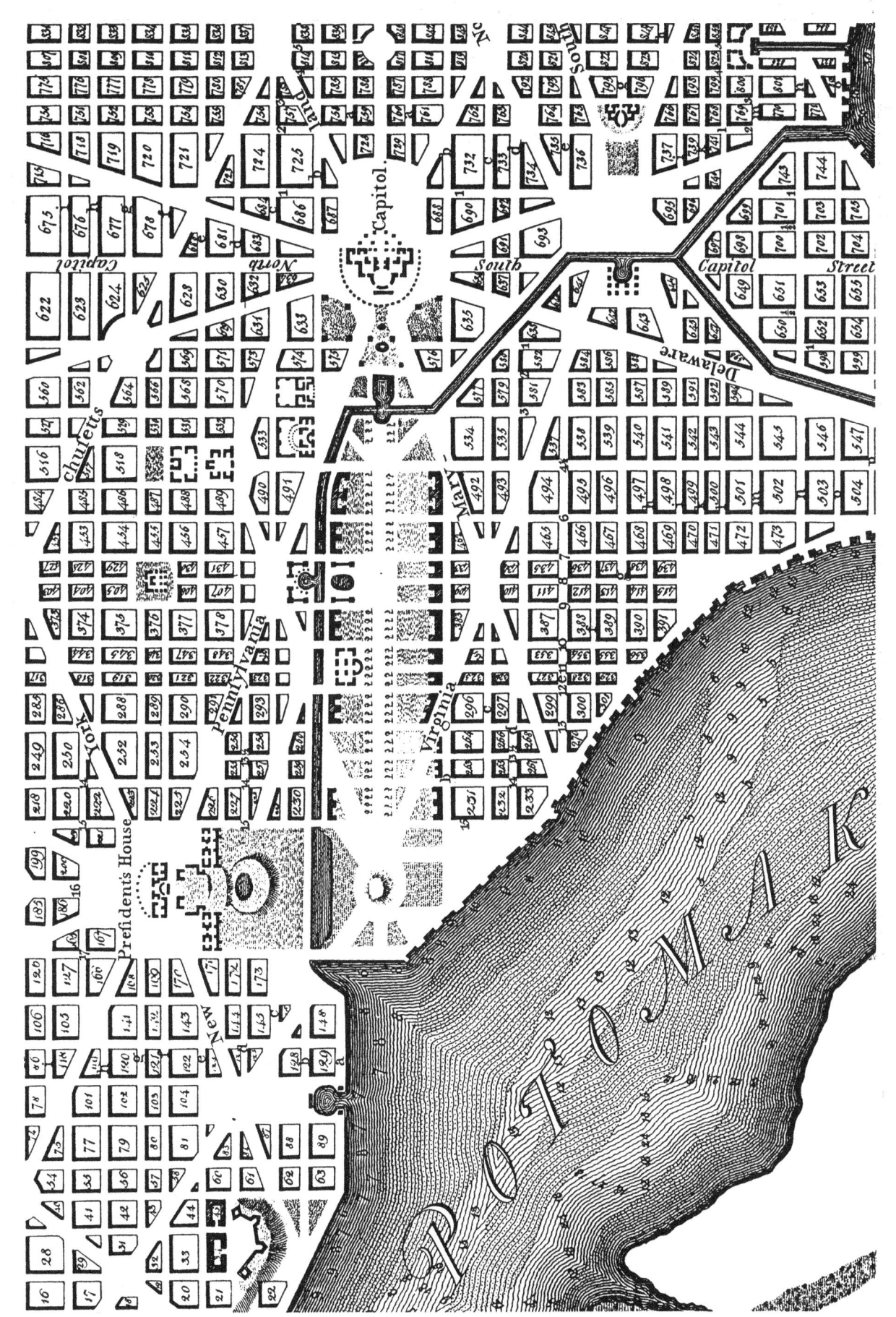

Figure 21 - Central Portion of the Ellicott Plan of Washington, 1792.

Figure 22 - "View of the City of Washington in 1792." Inscribed that it is reproduced in the style of that time from historical data and sketches, by Arthur B. Cutter, U.S. Army Corps of Engineers, Office of the District Engineer, Washington, D.C. Original in the Library of Congress, Geography and Map Division.

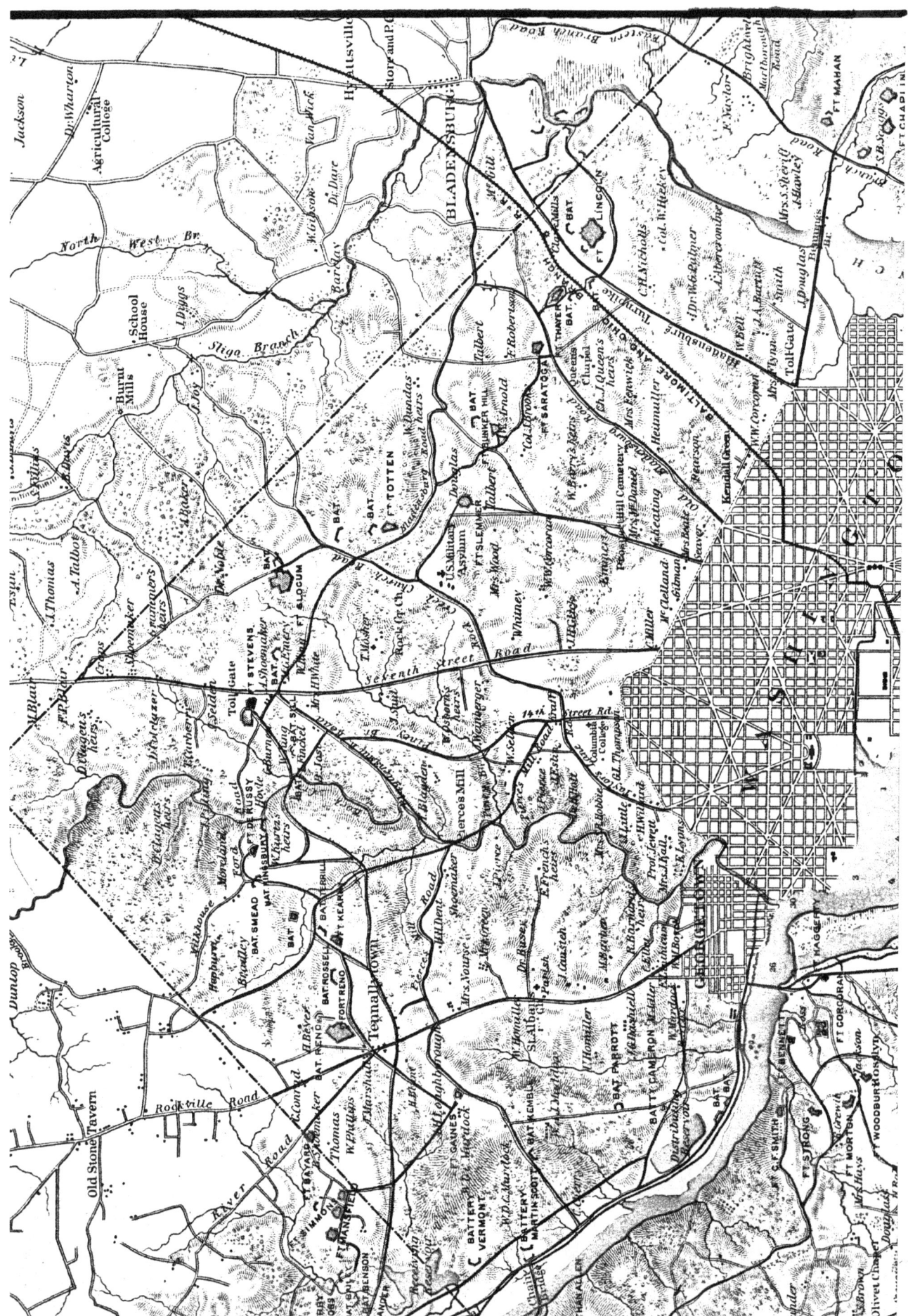

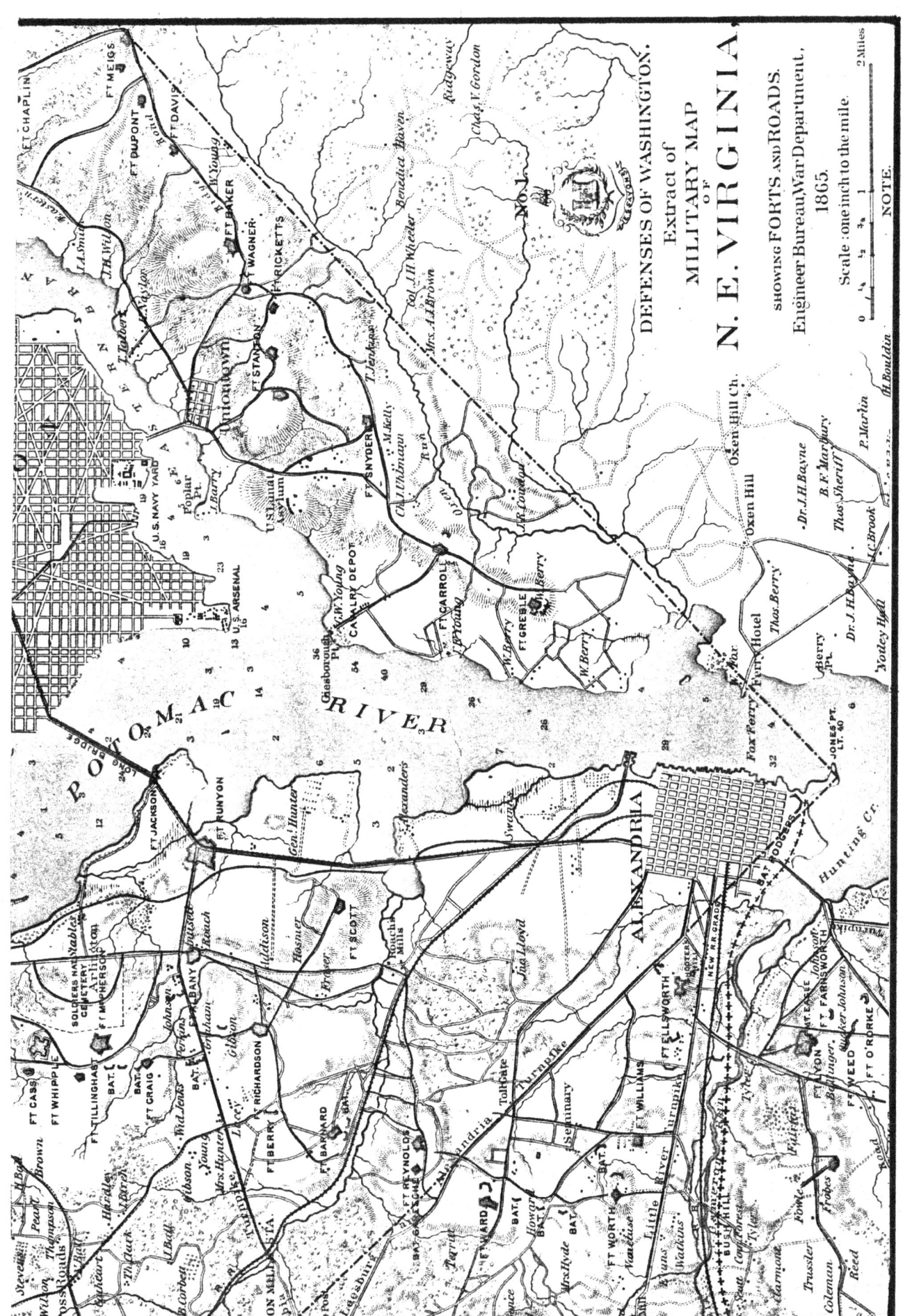

Figure 23 - "Defenses of Washington: Extract of Military Map of N.E. Virginia," 1865, by War Department, Engineer Bureau.

Research Locations

The Washington metropolitan area is rich in research facilities and records repositories relative to District of Columbia research. Note that some public and university libraries may curtail hours during summer months or vacation periods. Verify operating hours with a phone call. Some entries have an encircled number that corresponds to a location on the map in Figure 23.

Daughters of the American Revolution (D.A.R.) Library
1776 D Street, N.W. ❶
Washington, D.C. 20006-5303
(202) 879-3229
http://dar.library.net/

Monday-Friday, 8:45 a.m. to 4:00 p.m.
Sunday, 1:00 to 5:00 p.m., except Sundays followed by a Monday holiday and the Sunday after Christmas.
Closed to non-members 2 weeks each April during D.A.R. Continental Congress
Current user fees can be found D.A.R.'s Internet home page.

District of Columbia
Office of Public Records (D.C. Archives)
1300 Naylor Court, N.W. ❷
Washington, D.C. 20001
(202) 727-2052
Located off O Street between 9th and 10th Streets, N.W. Call to make an appointment.
Open Monday-Friday, 9:00 a.m. to 4:00 p.m.

District of Columbia Marriage Bureau
Room 4485
500 Indiana Avenue, N.W. ❸
Washington, D.C. 20001
(202) 879-4840
Open Monday-Friday, 9:00 a.m. to 4:00 p.m.

District of Columbia Recorder of Deeds
Room 300 ❹
515 D Street, N.W.
Washington, D.C. 20001
(202) 727-5374
Open Monday-Friday, 8:15 a.m. to 4:30 p.m.

District of Columbia Register of Wills
Probate Division
Room 5008 ❸
500 Indiana Avenue, N.W.
Washington, D.C. 20001
(202) 879-1499 or 879-4800
(202) 879-1010, for copies of wills, access to administrative case files after 1960
Open Monday-Friday, 9:00 a.m. to 4:00 p.m.

District of Columbia Department of Human Services
Vital Records Division ❺
825 North Capitol Street, N.W., Room 1312
Washington, D.C. 20002
(202) 442-9009
Open Monday-Friday, 8:00 a.m. to 3:30 p.m.

Church of the Latter Day Saints
Genealogical Library
10000 Stoneybrook Drive
Kensington, Maryland 20895
(301) 587-0042
Open Monday-Saturday, 9:00 a.m.- 5:00 p.m.;
Tuesday-Thursday, 7:00 p.m.-10:00 p.m.

George Washington University
Gelman Library, Special Collections
Room 207 ❻
2130 H Street, N.W.
Washington, D.C. 20052
(202) 994-7549
Open Monday to Friday, Noon to 5:00 p.m.

Research Locations

Georgetown Regional Library
Peabody Room ❼
Wisconsin Avenue & R Street, N.W.
Washington, D.C. 20007
(202) 727-1353
As hours are restricted, it is suggested you call before visiting.

Georgetown University, Lauinger Library
Special Collections Division
37th and O Streets, N.W., 5th Floor ❽
Washington, D.C. 20057
(202) 687-7444
Open Monday-Friday, 9:00 a.m. to 5:30 p.m.

Historical Society of Washington, D.C.
1307 New Hampshire Avenue, N.W. ❾
Washington, D.C. 20036
(202) 785-2068
http://www.hswdc.org/welcome.htm
Library Open Wednesday to Saturday, 10:00 a.m. to 4:00 p.m.

Library of Congress ❿
First Street & Independence Avenue, S.E.
Washington, D.C. 20540
  General Research Information: (202) 707-6500
  Reading Room Hours: (202) 707-6400
  Copyright Information: (202) 707-3000
  Online catalog searchable on Internet at:
    http://catalog.loc.gov/.
  Geography and Maps - Madison Building, Room LMB01, (202) 707-6277
    Open Monday-Friday, 8:30 a.m. to 5:00 p.m., closed Saturday
  Local History and Genealogy - Jefferson Building, Room LJG42, (202) 707-5537
    Open Monday-Friday, 8:30 a.m. to 9:30 p.m., Saturday, 8:30 a.m. to 5:00 p.m. Internet at:
      http://lcweb.loc.gov/rr/genealogy/
  Manuscripts - Madison Building, Room LM101, (202) 707-5387
    Open Monday-Saturday, 8:30 a.m. to 5:00 p.m.
  Newspapers and Current Periodicals - Madison Building, (202) 707-5690
    Open Monday-Friday 8:30 a.m. to 9:00 p.m.; Saturday, 8:30 a.m. to 5:00 p.m.; and Sunday 1:00 to 5:00 p.m.
  Rare Book and Special Collections - Jefferson Building, (202) 707-5435
    Open Monday-Friday, 8:30 a.m. to 5:00 p.m., closed Saturday

---

Martin Luther King Memorial Library
Washingtoniana Division
3rd Floor
901 G Street, N.W.
Washington, D.C. 20001
(202) 717-1213
Open Monday-Thursday, 9:00 a.m. to 9:00 p.m.; Friday-Saturday, 9:00 a.m. to 5:30 p.m.; and Sunday 1:00 to 5:00 p.m.

Maryland Historical Society Library
201 West Monument Street
Baltimore, Maryland 21201
(410) 685-3750
http://www.mdhs.org/library/5ptform.html
Open Tuesday-Friday, 10:00 a.m. to 4:30 p.m. and Saturday 9:00 a.m. to 4:30 p.m.
Closed 2 weeks in January for inventory

Maryland State Archives
Hall of Records
350 Rowe Boulevard
Annapolis, Maryland 21401
(410) 260-6400
http://www.mdarchives.state.md.us
Open Monday-Saturday, 8:30 a.m. to 4:30 p.m., except closed Saturdays, 12:00 noon to 1:00 p.m.

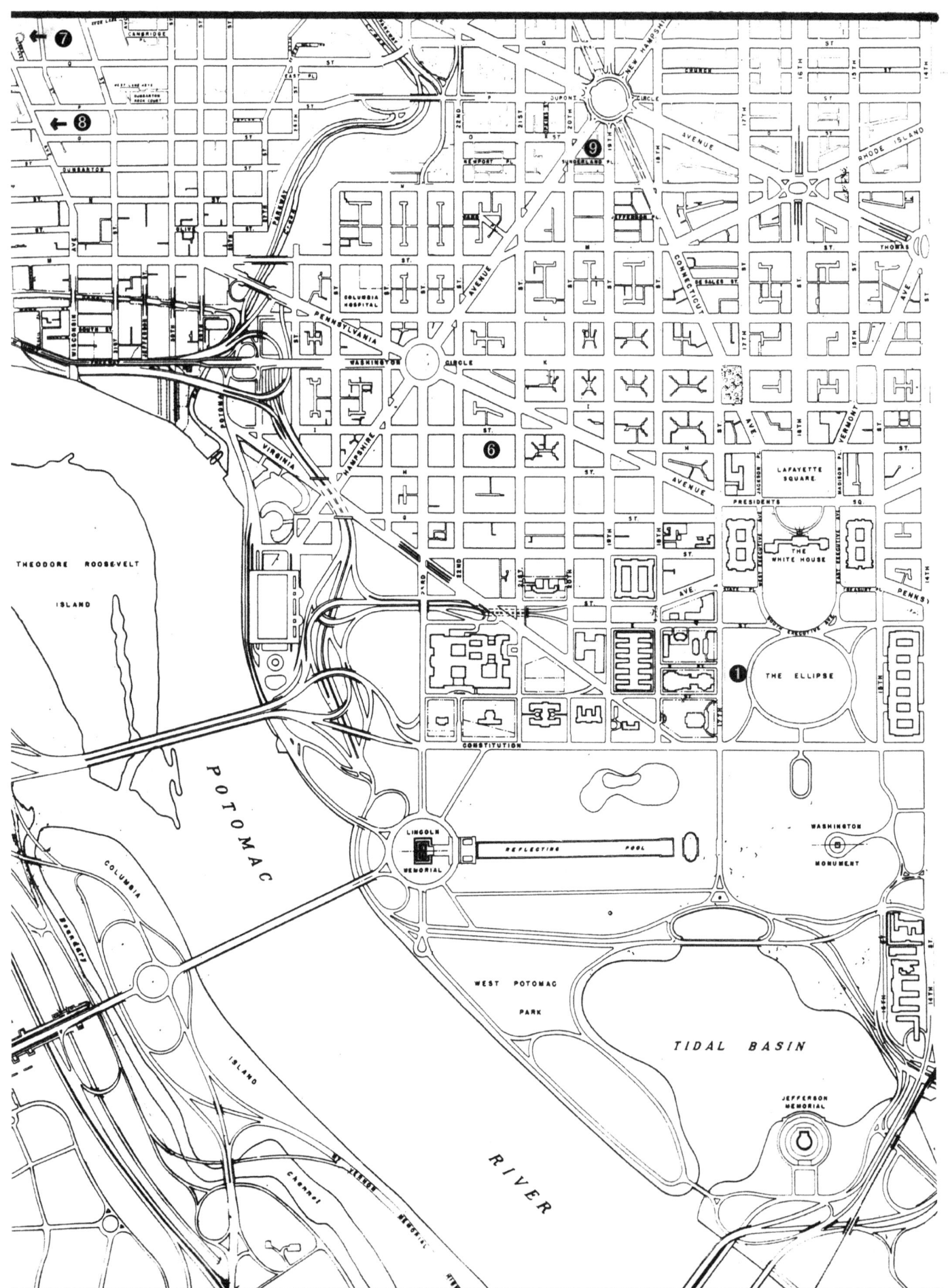

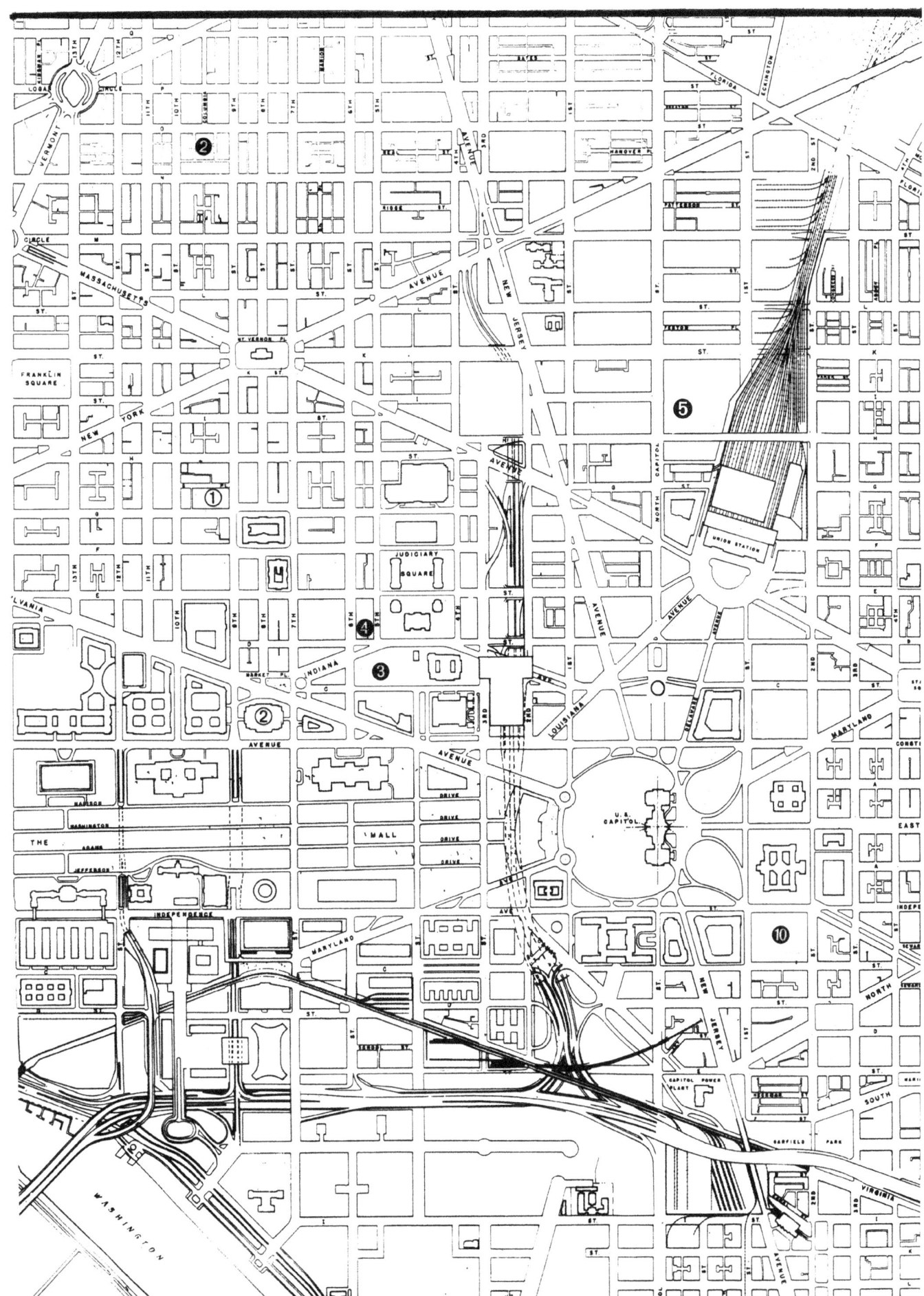

A Guide to Records of the District of Columbia

Montgomery County Historical Society Library
103 West Montgomery Avenue
Rockville, Maryland 20850
(301) 340-2974
Open Tuesday-Saturday, 12:00 noon to 4:00 p.m., and first Sunday of month, 2:00 p.m. to 5:00 p.m. Fee required.

Montgomery County Regional Library
Maryland Room
99 Maryland Avenue
Rockville, Maryland 20850
(301) 217-3800
Open Monday-Thursday, 9:00 a.m. to 9:00 p.m., Friday and Saturday 9:00 a.m. to 5:00 p.m.; and Sunday, 1:00 p.m. to 5:00 p.m.

National Archives and Records Administration
Archives II
8601 Adelphi Road
College Park, Maryland 20740
(301) 713-6800
Open Monday and Wednesday, 8:45 a.m. to 5:00 p.m.; Tuesday, Thursday and Friday, 8:45 a.m. to 9:00 p.m.; Saturday, 8:45 a.m. to 4:45 p.m. Shuttle bus service between Archives II and the downtown facility (Pennsylvania Avenue) runs Monday through Friday.

National Archives and Records Administration ②
Pennsylvania Avenue and 8th Street, N.W.
Washington, D.C. 20408
(202) 501-5400
Research Room hours are Monday and Wednesday, 8:45 a.m. to 5:00 p.m.; Tuesday, Thursday and Friday, 8:45 a.m. to 9:00 p.m.; and Saturday, 8:45 a.m. to 4:45 p.m.

National Archives and Records Administration
Washington National Records Center
Room 105
4205 Suitland Road
Suitland, Maryland 20746
(301) 457-7000
Mailing address:
National Archives, Washington, D.C. 20409

Open for Research on Monday through Friday, 8:00 a.m. to 4:00 p.m.

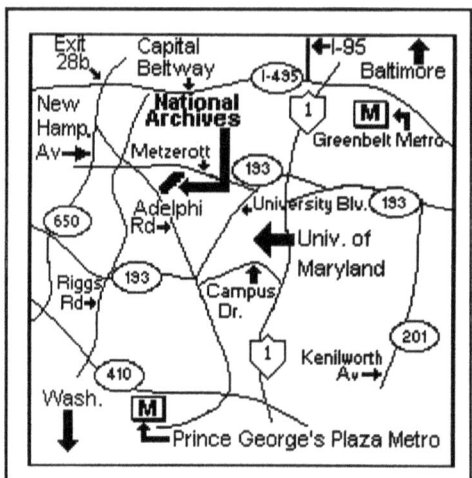

Location of Archives II

Research Locations

National Genealogical Society Library
Glebe House
4527 17th Street North
Arlington, Virginia 22207
(703) 525-0050
http://www.ngsgenealogy.org/library/
Open Monday, 10:00 a.m. to 5:00 p.m.;
  Wednesday, 10:00 a.m. to 9:00 p.m.;
  Friday and Saturday 10:00 a.m. to 4:00 p.m.

Prince George's County Genealogical Society Library
12219 Tulip Grove Drive
Bowie, Maryland 20715
(301) 262-2063
Open First Wednesday, 10:00 a.m. to 1:00 p.m., other Wednesdays 10:00 a.m. to 7:00 p.m.; last Saturday, 1:00 p.m. to 5:00 p.m.

ON-LINE CARD CATALOG

Using Library of Congress On-Line Card Catalog Via Computer. The Library of Congress card catalog was closed in the early 1980's after which no new acquisitions were manually indexed. Books acquired after 1968, and in some cases earlier, are electronically indexed in the automated data systems. In the early 1990's, the online catalog was accessible over the Internet by using TelNet. More recently, a searchable, self-explanatory version of the combined Library of Congress catalogues is found at Internet URL:

http://catalog.loc.gov

The searchable catalog performs basic searches based on title, subject, author or notes. More advanced searches allow users to select items by language, dates, publisher, category, LC Call Number, ISBN, ISSN, Dewey, or LCCN. The data is typically displayed in call number sequence. One of the more interesting types of searches that can be done is to browse the shelf list. This presents items in call number sequence and shows similar items in the collection for a particular topic.

Map of Research Centers

On the preceding pages is a map of the central area of Washington showing the location of research centers. Some research centers are within a few blocks of one another and visits to two or three places can be combined in one trip.

Index

A

ABAJIAN
    Albert 50
ABBATICCHIO
    Ada R. Alexander 48
ABBEY
    John Rowan 46
ABBOTT
    Daniel A. 49
Abby Manor 80
ABEL
    Chr. 49
Accounts 7, 8, 54
    Abstracts 79
Adas Israel Cemetery 43
Administration Bonds 8
Administration Docket Books 7
Administration Docket Books, O.S. 7
Administrations 62
Administrative Bonds 7
Administrative Case Files, O.S. 7
Admiralty Case Files 56
Admiralty Cases 59
Admiralty Docket 56
Admiralty Records 56
Adoption Case Files 59
Adoption Dockets 59
Agriculture Census Schedules 3
Aldersgate Methodist Church 38
Alexander's Island 80
Alexandria . . . ix, xii, 3-5, 8, 41, 49, 53, 56, 57
Alexandria City Courthouse ix
Alexandria County . . . . ix, xii, 8, 53
All Souls' Church 41
American Auditor Newspaper 63
American Jewish Archives 51
Anacostia Methodist Episcopal Church . . . 34
Anacostia River . . . . xi, xii
Annapolis 14, 41
Appeals Case Files 62
Appearance Docket 58
Appellate Jurisdiction 62
Applications for Naturalization 62
Appointments 60, 65
Apprenticeship Indentures 6, 8
    Homer A. 8
Arbitrators 54
Architectural Drawings 65
Archives II 14
Arlington 24
Arlington County ix
Arlington County Courthouse ix
Army Corps of Engineers xv
Arrest Books 67
Articles of Incorporation 65
Asbury Methodist Episcopal Church 34
Asbury United Methodist Church 34
Ascension and St. Agnes Church 31
Assessment Records 11, 13
Associate Methodist Church 38
Associate Reformed Presbyterian Church
    39
Association of Relief for Destitute Colored
    Women and Children 3
Atlantic World Newspaper 63
Atlases 77
Attachments 58
Auction Licenses 66

B

BAIST
    G. William 78
BALCH
    Stephen B., Rev. 40
Baltimore 13, 34
Baltimore County xi
Bankruptcy Bonds 60
Bankruptcy Case Files 60
Bankruptcy Case Papers 55
Bankruptcy Docket 55
Bankruptcy Dockets 60
Bankruptcy Minutes 60
Bankruptcy Records 53, 54, 60
Baptism Records 31-41
Baptist Cemetery 43
Baptist Church Records 29, 30
BATSON
    William 46
Battleground National Cemetery 43
Bawdy Houses 65
BEALL
    Brooke 76

    George 76
    Mr. 12
    Ninian xi
    Thomas 76
Beall's Levels Tract 80
BECKETT
    William 43
Beckett's Burial Ground 43
Beethoven ix
Belts [Family] Burial Ground 44
Benedict 69
Bennings Station 47, 48
Berean Baptist Church 42
Berlin ix
BERRET
    James G. xvi
BIRCH
    Joseph F. 48
Birth Records 23, 32, 33, 39
Bladensburg 69
BLAKE
    James H. xvi
BLOW
    Henry T. xiii
Board of Architects 65
Board of Assessors xiv
Board of Commissioners xv
Board of Common Council xiv
Board of Health .... xiv-xvi, 65
Board of Public Works .... xiv, xv
Bonds for Appeals 58
Bonds in Equity Cases 59
Bonds of Justices of Peace and Constables
    60
Bonds of Notaries Public 60
BOSCHKE
    A. 77
Bounty Land Warrants 69
BOWEN
    Sayles J. xvi
BOYD
    William H. 43
BOYDEN
    John 29
Bradbury Heights 38
BRADLEY
    William A. xvi
BRENT
    Robert xvi
Bridge Street Presbyterian Church 40

BRIGHAM
    Clarence Saunders 64
Brightwood 35
Brightwood Cemetery 44
BRISCOE
    Alice I. 50
BROADHEAD
    John M. 73
BROWN
    Solomon G. 46
Building and Land Regulations Administration
    14
Building Permits 14
Burial Records 31-33
BURNES
    David xvi
    James 80
Business Directories 75

C

Cabinet Newspaper 63
Calvert County xi
CAMP
    Nany J. 46
    Virginia B. 46
Capitol Hill United Methodist Church 36
CARBERRY
    Thomas xvi
CARROLL
    Bishop 31
    Charles xi
    Daniel .... xii, xvi, 80
    Dudley 35
    Family 30
Carroll Prison 66
Carrollsburg .... xi, xvi, 12
    Plan of xviii
Case Files . 6-8, 53, 54, 56, 58-60, 62, 70, 84
Catholic Church Records 30, 31
CATLETT
    David C. 42
Cemeteries 7, 31, 43-52
Cemetery Records 43-52
Census Enumeration Districts 2
Census Schedules 1-3
Centinel of Liberty or Georgetown and
    Washington Advertiser 63, 64
Central Guard House 66
Central Methodist Protestant Church 38

Index

Central Presbyterian Church 38
CEPHAS
    John 44
Cephas [Family] Burial Ground 44
Chancery Records 54
Chancery Rules Cases 54
CHAPEL
    J.E. 44
Chapel's [Private] Burial Ground 44
CHAPMAN
    John ix
Charles County . . . . xi, 69
Cheltenham 49
Children 65
Christ Church Capitol Hill 32
Christ Episcopal Church, Georgetown 32
Christ Protestant Episcopal Church 32
Church of the Ascension 31
Church of the Covenant 39
Church of the Epiphany 31
Church of the Pilgrims 40
Church Records 29-42
Churches 6, 11, 17, 18, 22, 29-51, 74, 84
Cincinnati 51
Circuit Court 53-58, 60-62, 73
City Directories 4, 5
City Hall 34
Civil Appearances 54
Civil War xiv, 30, 35, 43, 44, 50-52, 59, 68-72,
                                          74, 76
Civil War Pension Application Files 69
CLARK
    Isaac 22
CLARKE
    Nina H. 37
CLEARY
    Mary A. 19
CLEVELAND
    Grover 71
    H.A. 21
COLE
    Charles C. 19
College Burial Ground 44
College Park 14, 30
Columbian Centinel Newspaper 63
Columbian Chronicle Newspaper 63, 64
Columbian College 47, 74
Columbian Gazette (Union) Newspaper . . 63
Columbian Harmony Cemetery 44
Columbian Observer Newspaper 63

Columbian Register Newspaper 63
Columbian Star Newspaper 64
Commerce Department Building
    Fire in 2
Commissioner of Public Buildings 15
Commissioners xi-xiii, xv, xvi, 15, 51, 65, 72, 73
Commissioners and Public Buildings 15
Communicant Records 33, 40
Compiled Records Showing Service of Military
        Units in Volunteer 68
Comunicant Records 31
Concordia Lutheran Church 34
Concordia Lutheran Evangelical Church . . 37
Confirmation Records 31, 32
Congress Ground 44
Congress Street Methodist Protestant Church
    38
Congressional Cemetery 44, 45, 47
Connogocheque xii
Consumer and Regulatory Affairs 14
Convent Burial Ground 45
Convictions Obtained by the Court, ... 57
CONWAY
    Moncure Daniel 41
COOK
    Eleanor M.V. ix
Copyright Records 57
CORCORAN
    William W. 33, 48, 76
Corcoran Gallery of Art 76
Corporation Ordinances . . . . xiii, 16
COSENTINO
    Andrew J. 78
Courier Newspaper 63
Court Records, Record Group 21 53-62
Covenant-First Presbyterian Church 39
COYLE
    John F. 64
CREW
    Harvey W. 29
Criminal Appearances 54, 57
Criminal Case Files 59
Criminal Court 53, 57, 62
Criminal Court Dockets 57
Criminal Court Minutes 57
Criminal Dockets 59
Criminal Minutes 59
Criminal Proceedings 57
Criminal Records 59
Cumberland 76

A Guide to Records of the District of Columbia

CUTTER
    Arthur B. 80
CUTTS
    Richard D. 48

D

D.A.R. Library . 1, 6, 18, 29, 30, 33, 39, 44, 45,
                       48, 49, 76, 77, 84
    Genealogical Records Committee (G.R.C.)
    6
D.C. Archives 6-8, 14, 17, 18, 23, 24, 52,
                               65-67, 84
D.C. Courthouse 6
DAHLGREN
    Hildreth 48
Daily Federal Republican Newspaper 63
Daily Globe Newspaper 63
Daily Morning Chronicle Newspaper 63
Daily National Intelligencer 64
Daily National Journal Newspaper 64
Danforth Chapel 34
DANGERFIELD
    Henry 45
Dangerfield [Family] Burial Ground 45
Daughters of the American Revolution 29
DAVIDSON
    John 80
    Samuel . . . . xvi, 76
DEAKINS
    William 32
Dean's [Private] Burial Ground 45
Death Records . 23, 24, 32, 34, 35, 37-41, 70
Death Records, Foreign 24
Declaration of Intention 61
Declaration of Intention to Become Citizens
    62
Deeds, Recording of xii
Defectives, Dependents and Delinquents . . 3
Delayed Births 24
DELZELL
    James 50
DEMAREE
    Fannie Lander 50
DENNISON
    William xiii
Depositions 62
DICKINS
    Francis Asbury 71

DIGGES
    Family 30
DILTS
    Bryan Lee 1, 4
Discharges 54
Disinterment Permits 52
District Court 1, 6, 18, 56, 57, 59-61
District Court Case Files 59
District Court Cases 59
District of Columbia
    Name First Used xii
District of Columbia Militia 71
Divorce Records 18, 54
DIXON
    Benjamin Franklin 41
    Joan Marie 64
Docket 7, 53-56, 58, 62, 66, 73
Docket Book 66
Docket Books 53
Docket of Appeals 62
Dockets of Chancery 54
DONOVAN
    Jane 35
DOWD
    Mary-Jane 13
Drovers' Rest 43, 44
Duddington Pasture 80
Dumbarton Avenue Methodist Church . 34-36
Dumbarton Avenue United Methodist Church
    47

E

E Street Baptist Church 30
East Point 71
East Washington Station 35, 38
Eastern Branch . . . . xi, xii, 80
Eastern Methodist Cemetery 45
Eastern Presbyterian Church 38
Ebenezer Cemetery 45
Ebenezer Church 35, 36
Ebenezer Station 36, 45
Ebenezer United Methodist Church 36
Eckington Presbyterian Church 39
EDGINGTON
    Frank E. 40
Education Institutions 74
Education Records 74, 75
1812 Bounty Land Warrants 69
1812 Pension Application Files 69
1812 War Militia 69

Index

Ejectment Suits at Law 58
Eldbrooke Methodist Cemetery 52
Eldbrooke Methodist Church 47
ELIOT
    William P. 77
ELLIOTT
    John Habersham 31
Emancipation and Manumission Records 72-74
Emancipation Papers 55
Emancipation Records 55, 72
EMERY
    Matthew G. xvi
EMORY
    John 35
Emory Chapel 35
Emory Methodist Church 35
Employment 66
Employment Records 16
Engineer Department 66
ENGLES
    Minnie A. 27
ENNIS
    Robert Brooks 32
Enumeration Districts 1, 2
Epiphany Lutheran Church 34
Episcopal Church Records 31-34
Equity Case Files 59
Equity Cases Auditors Reports 59
Equity Dockets 58
Equity Index 58
Equity Injunction Undertakings 59
Equity Minutes 58
Equity Papers 54
Equity Records 54, 58
Estate Accounts 8
Estate Administration Records 7
Estate Inventories 8
Evening Star Newspaper 63, 64
EXTON
    Peter 52
Extradition 59

F

F Street Presbyterian Church 39
FAEHTZ
    E.F.M. . . . . xvi, xix
Fairfax County xii
FARLEY
    Lawrence M. 46
    Martha E. 46
Federal Assessment of 1798 for the District of
    Columbia 13
Federal Republican and Commercial Gazette
    Newspaper 63
Federal Republican Newspaper 63
Female Union Band Society 47
Female Union Band Society Burying Ground
    47
FENWICK
    Family 30
Fifteenth Street Presbyterian Church 39
Final Disposition of Case 58
First Baptist Church 29, 30
First Methodist Protestant Church 38
First Presbyterian Church 39
First Trinity Lutheran Church 34
First Unitarian Church 41
First Wesley Chapel 38
FISHBURN
    M. Ross 22
FISHER
    Margaret 35
FLETCHER
    Sarah A. 10
Florida Avenue xii
Foggy Bottom xi
FORCE
    Peter xvi
Foreign Death Records 24
Foreign Guardian & Lunatics Estate Records 7
Fort Stanton 66
Fort Stevens 35, 43
Foundry Methodist Episcopal Church . 34, 35
Fourth Baptist Church 29
Fourth Methodist Episcopal Church 38
Fourth Presbyterian Church 39
Fourth Street Methodist Church 45
Fourth Street Methodist Episcopal Church
    35-37
FOXALL
    Henry 35
Francis DeSales Cemetery 45
Franciscan Monastery Cemetery 52
Frederick County xi
Frederick, Lord Baltimore xi
Free Schedules 1
Freedman's Savings and Trust Company . 75
Freedmen's Bureau 75
Freedmen's Hospital 74

A Guide to Records of the District of Columbia

Freedmen's Records 74
Freedom Registers 55
French and Indian War 33
Friends Burying Ground 49
Friends Meeting House 41
Friends Religious Society of the National Capital
      Area Association 41
Fugitive Slave Cases 55
Funeral Records 33
Funerals Records 39
FUNK
      Jacob xi
Funkstown xi

G

GAHN
      Bessie Wilmarth 13
GALES
      Joseph xvi
GANTT
      Mr. 12
GARDEN
      Alexander 45
Garden's [Private] Burial Ground 45
GARFIELD
      General 41
GARLET
      Charles B. 2
GATTI
      Lawrence P. 41
Gelman Library 5, 29, 70, 71, 74, 78, 84
Genealogical Records Committee 29
Genealogies, Published 77
General Government Records 65
General List of Slaves 13
Geographic History xi
George Town Academy 74
George Washington University . . 5, 29, 70, 71,
      74, 78, 84
Georgetown . xi-xvi, xx, 1, 4, 5, 11, 13-16, 29,
      31-36, 38, 40, 43-49, 52, 63, 64,
      74-77, 85
      Charter of 15
      Plan of . . . . xx, xxi
Georgetown Advocate Newspaper 63
Georgetown College 74
Georgetown College Burial Ground 44
Georgetown Columbian & District Advertiser
      63

Georgetown Courier Newspaper 63
Georgetown D.C. Weekly Ledger Newspaper
      64
Georgetown Daily Advertiser Newspaper . 63
Georgetown Officials 16
Georgetown Ordinances 16
Georgetown Presbyterian Church 40
Georgetown Records . . . . xiii, 15, 16
Georgetown Regional Library . . 13, 15, 63, 85
Georgetown Tax Assessments, 1800-1879
      14
Georgetown Tax Records 16
Georgetown Times and Potowmack Packet
      Newspaper 64
Georgetown University 31, 44-46, 74
Georgetown Visitation Convent 31, 52
Georgetown Weekly Ledger Newspaper . . 63
Georgia 71
German Evangelical Lutheran Church 34
Glenwood Cemetery 45, 46
Good Hope Burial Ground 46
GOODLOE
      Daniel R. 73
Goose Creek xi
GORDON
      George xi
GOTT
      Mary K. 49
Government History xiii
Government Hospital for the Insane 50
Grace Church 32
Grace Episcopal Church 32
Grace Protestant Episcopal Church 32
Grace Reformed Church 42
Graceland Cemetery 46, 51
Grand Jury Case Papers 59
Grand Jury Dockets 59
Grand Jury Lists 54
GREEN
      Constance McLaughlin 33
GREENLEAF
      James 12
Greenleaf's Point 35
GRIM
      Medora E. 50
GRISSETT
      James H. 20, 21
Guardian Dockets 7
Guardians 65
Guardianship Bonds 7

Index

Transcripts 7
Guardianship Records 6-8
Guardianships 62

H

Habeas Corpus 66
Habeas Corpus and Extradition Records . 59
Habeas Corpus Case Files 59
Habeas Corpus Dockets 59
Habeas Corpus Minutes 59
Habeas Corpus Records 55
Hackney Carriage Licenses 66
HAGNER
    Alexander Burton 33
HALL
    Charles Henry 32
Hall of Records 41
Hamburgh . . . . xi, xvi, 12
    Plan of xvii
Harmony Cemetery 44
Harmony Memorial Park 44
HARRIS
    Wanda 42
HARRISON
    Louisa 31
HASLUP
    Alice Emma 41
Hawkins & Beatty's Addition to Georgetown
    48
HAWLEY
    William, Rev. 32
HEBBON
    Eliza 46
Hebbon's [Family] Burial Ground 46
HENSON
    William 47
HERNDON
    Herman W. 16
HEWITT
    John 8
HILL
    Edward E. 43
Hillsdale 46, 47
Hillsdale Burial Ground 46
HINES
    Christian 43, 69
Historical Society of Pennsylvania 71
Historical Society of Washington, D.C. . xiii, 5,
               11, 32, 72, 77, 78, 85

HOAGLAND
    Kim 14
HOLMEAD
    Anthony 46, 80
Holmead's Burial Ground 46, 51
Holmead's Cemetery 46
Holy Rood Cemetery 46
    Burial Records 31
Holy Trinity Catholic Church 31
HOMANS
    Benjamin 5
Hop Yard 80
HOPKINS
    Griffith M. 77
HOSKINS
    Helen 46
    Henry M. 46
House Index by Quadrant 15
House Records 15
HOWARD
    Oliver Otis 75
    Robert 47
Howard University 51, 75
Howard's [Private] Burial Ground 47
Human Services 23
HURLEY
    Malvina R. 48
Hyattsville 77
HYNSON
    Jerry M. 75

I

Immigration and Naturalization Service . . . 61
Impartial Observer and Washington Advertiser
    64
Impartial Observer and Washington Advertiser
    Newspaper 64
Independent American Newspaper 63
Index to Compiled Service Records of Volunteer
    Soldiers 68
Index to Dockets 59
Index to Mechanics Liens 60
Index to Rendezvous Reports 68
Indexes to Deposit Ledgers in Branches of the
    Freedman's Savings 75
Indiana ix
Industrial Census Schedules 3
Injunctions 54
Insane Asylum 47

A Guide to Records of the District of Columbia

Insolvency Minutes 55
Insolvents Case Papers 55
Institutional Burying Ground 52
Interment Register 24
Internal Revenue Assessments 14
Inventories 8
Isherwood Tract 80
Israel Bethel African Methodist Episcopal Church 36
Israel Metropolitan Christian Methodist Episcopal Church 36
Italy ix

J
JACKSON
    Ronald Vern 1, 3, 4
JACOBSEN
    Phebe R. 41
Jail Records 66
Jamaica Tract 80
JANNEY
    Family 49
JEFFERSON
    Thomas . . . . ix, 76
JENKINS
    Thomas 47
Jenkins Hill xii
Jenkins' [Private] Burial Ground 47
Jesuit Community Cemetery 52
Jew's Burial Ground 51
John Wesley African Methodist Episcopal (A.M.E.) Zion Church 36
John Wesley Church 36
JOHNSON
    Charles H. 50
    Lorenzo Dow 37
    Thomas xii
Jones' Chapel Burial Ground 47
Journals of Expenditures . . . . xiii, 16
Journals of Proceedings 16
Journals of Proceedings of the Corporation of Georgetown xiii
Journals of the Proceedings of the Board of Aldermen . . . . xiii, 15
Journals of the Proceedings of the Common Council . . . . xiii, 16
Judgment Records 54
Judgments 58
Judgments in Cases at Law 58
Judgments of Municipal Court 58
Justice of the Peace Records 62
Justices of Peace and Constables 60

K
KEENE
    Gerald E. 35
KELLY
    Laurence J. 31
KETCHAM
    John H. xiii
KING
    Horatio 73
    Nicholas 77, 78
    Vincent 10
KLEINTZ
    Dorsey 52
KOHLER
    Sue A. 37
KURTZ
    Grace W. 39

L
L'ENFANT
    Pierre xii
Lafayette Square 33
LaFONTANE
    Joseph 10
Land Records 11-13
LATROBE
    Benjamin 33
Lauinger Library 31, 74, 85
Law Case Files 58
Law Dockets 58
Law Minutes 58
Law Records 58
Law, Appellate and Criminal Records 53
LDS Microfilm 2, 11, 14, 16, 17, 23, 24, 29-42, 44, 45, 48, 49, 51, 53, 55, 64, 66, 70-73, 75, 78
LEACH
    Frank Willing 64
Leases 11
Legitimations 24
LEIDY
    Susan H. 50
LEIGH
    Alexandra L. 50

Index

LENOX
    Walter xvi
LEONARD
    William Andrew 42
Levy Court xii
LEWIS
    John, Rev. 32
Library of Congress xiii, xxi, 5, 16, 30, 43, 63, 76-78, 80, 85, 89
Library of Congress On-Line Card Catalog
    89
Library of Virginia .... ix, 70
Licenses 60, 66
Lien Law Records 55, 60
Lien Record 60
Liens 58
LINCOLN
    Abraham 68
LINGAN
    James M. xvi
Liquor Licenses .... xii, 66
Little Ebenezer Church 36
Lorton 66
Lovely Lane Museum 34
LOWE
    Jessamin R. 27
LUKENS
    Hannah 49
Lunatics Estate Records 7
Lutheran Church Records 34
LYNN
    Judge 29

M

Macedonia Burial Ground 47
MACKIN
    James F. 19
MADISON
    James 39
MAGRUDER
    William B. xvi
Maine 72
MANDANYOHL
    Nicholas 46
MANDAS
    Peter 46
Manufactured Goods 66
Manumission and Emancipation Record .. 55
Manumission Papers 55

Manumission Records 72
Manuscript Collections 76
Map xii, xvi, xx-xxiv, 14, 37, 44, 46, 51, 77, 78, 80, 82-84, 86, 89
Maps 77
Maritime Law 54
Marriage Bureau 17, 84
Marriage Licenses 16, 56
Marriage Licenses, Cancelled 17
Marriage Records 17-19, 31-41, 54, 56
Marriage Registers 17
Marriage Returns 17
MARTIN
    George H. 64
    Joseph 78
Martin Luther King Memorial Library 5, 14, 15, 63, 64, 78, 85
Maryland 2, ix, xi, xii, 1, 4, 6, 7, 11-15, 18, 30, 33, 34, 37, 39, 41, 44, 45, 52, 63, 68, 69, 72, 74, 76, 77, 84, 85, 88
Maryland Historical Society 13, 77, 85
Maryland State Archives 77, 85
MAURY
    John W. xvi
MAYO
    Charles J.S. 19
McKendree Chapel of the Methodist Episcopal
    Church 36
McKINLEY
    William 71
McMillan Commission 13
McPhearson's [Private] Burial Ground 47
McPHERSON
    Family 49
Mechanics Lien Case Files 60
Meeting House, The 36
MEIGS
    R. 19
MERRILL
    Samuel Hill 72
METCALF
    Frank J. 64
Methodist Burial Ground 47
Methodist Cemetery 47
Methodist Episcopal Church Records .. 34-38
Methodist Protestant Church Records 38
Metropolitan African Methodist Episcopal
    Church 37
Metropolitan Newspaper 63
Metropolitan Police 65, 67

Metropolitan Presbyterian Church 40
METZLER
    Edward 49
Mexican War 68, 72
Mexico Tract 80
Midwife License Registers 60
Military Naturalization 62
Military Petitions 62
Military Records 67-72
Militia of the District of Columbia 1828-1832
    71
Mill Tract 80
MILLER
    William Alexander 42
Minister Applications 18
Minister Licenses 18
Minute Books 53, 54
Minutes . 34, 36, 37, 39, 40, 42, 53-61, 65, 73
Miscellaneous Records 65-75
MITCHELL
    Millard F. 20
    Rose Trexler 32
Monitor Newspaper 64
Monocacy River xi
Montgomery County .. ix, xi, xii, 1, 13, 63, 72,
                            76, 77, 88
Montgomery County Historical Society ... 88
Montgomery Street Church 47
MOORE
    Jacob 47
    Richard Allen 4
Moore's Cemetery 50
Moore's [Family] Burial Ground 47
MORRIS
    Robert 12
Mortality Schedules 2
Mortgages 11
Mount Olivet Cemetery 45, 47, 49-51
Mount Pleasant Plain Cemetery 47
Mount Tabor Methodist Church 38
Mount Vernon Place Church 42
Mount Zion Cemetery 47
Mount Zion Church 36
Mount Zion Methodist Episcopal Church .. 36
Mount Zion United Methodist Church 47
Mrs. Colvin's Weekly Messenger 64
Mt. Zion Cemetery 48
MUDD
    T.D. 26

Museum and Washington and George-town
    Advertiser 63
MYSHENCOFF
    Nicholas 50

N
NADIN
    Catherine 50
Napoleon ix
National Archives .. xii, xiii, 1-8, 11-18, 29, 43,
    52, 53, 55, 61, 63, 65, 66, 68-75, 77, 88
National Era Newspaper 63
National Genealogical Society 64, 77, 88
National Intelligencer Newspaper 64
National Journal Newspaper 64
National Messenger Newspaper 63
National Observer Newspaper 64
National Office of Vital Statistics 2
National Palladium Newspaper 64
National Presbyterian Church 39
National Zoo 47
Naturalization Index 61
Naturalization Papers 61
Naturalization Record, Old Circuit Court .. 62
Naturalization Record, Supreme Court ... 62
Naturalization Records 56, 60
Navy Yard 30, 32
Navy Yard Baptist Church 30
NEIMEYER
    David E. 75
NEVITT
    James 46
    James C. 46
New National Era Newspaper 63
New York xii
New York Avenue Church 40
New York Avenue Presbyterian Church ... 40
New York Harbor ix
Newspapers 63, 64
NICHOLS
    Lucy A. 20
NICHOLSON
    John 12
Nineteenth Street Baptist Church 29
Non-Population Schedules 3
North Capitol Presbyterian Church 39
Northumberland County, Pennsylvania ... 49
Notaries 60

Index

O

O'CALLAGHN
    Matthew 19
Oak Hill Cemetery 48
Oaths of Office 67
ODEN
    Benjamin 80
Office of Public Buildings and Grounds ... 13
Office of Public Records .... ix, 84
Ohio .... ix, 51
Ohio Valley ix
Old Capitol Prison 66
Old Divorce Docket 54
Old Divorces 54
Old Ebenezer Cemetery 45
Old Methodist Burying Ground 47, 48
Old Presbyterian Cemetery 48, 49
Old Presbyterian Church Cemetery 48
Olio Newspaper 63
Order Book 58
Orders of the Court 59
Ordinances .... xii, 16
Original Proprietors 12
Orphans Court 8, 57
Orphans Real Estate 7
ORR
    Benjamin G. xvi

P

PARKS
    Gary W. 4
Parrott's Woods 48
Patents 62
Patuxent River xi
Pawnbroker Licenses 66
PAYNE
    John 48
Payne's Burial Ground 42, 48
Payne's Cemetery 44
Peabody Room 13, 15, 63, 77, 85
PEALE
    Peale ix
PECKHAM
    George Lewis 48
Pennsylvania 49
Pension and Bounty Land 68
Pension Application Files 69
PETER
    Grace Dunlop xvi

    Robert .... xvi, 80
Petition Docket 54
Petitions for Partition 54
Pew Rent Accounts 31
Philadelphia .... xii, 39, 49, 71
PHILIBERT
    Helene 30
PHILIP
    Louis 49
Physicians and Midwives 67
Physicians' License Registers 60
PIERCE
    Abner C. 35
    Alycon Trubey 72
Pierce's Mill 35, 51
PINNEY
    William 47
PIPPENGER
    Wesley E. 8, 13, 18, 24, 43, 52
Piscataway Parish 33
Plan .... xii, xiii, xvi-xviii, 79
Plat Books 77
Pleasant Grove 77
Police Court 62
Police Records 67
POLK
    R.L. 5
POMPEY
    Sherman Lee 72
POPE
    Francis xi
Port Royal 76
Port Royal Tract 80
Potowmack River .... xi, xii
Potters Field 48
PRATT
    F.W. .... xvi, xix
Presbyterian Burying Ground 49
    Tombstone Inscriptions 40
Presbyterian Cemetery 48, 49
Presbyterian Church Records 38-41
Presidential Reorganization Plan No. 3 xiii, xvi
Prince George's County .... xii, 1
Prince George's County Genealogical Society
.... 88
Prince George's County Memorial Library . 77
Prince George's Parish 33
Prince George's County xi
Prison Bounds Bonds 54
Prison Records 66

Probate Records 6-8, 62
PROCTOR
    John Claggett 64
Proprietors 12
Prospect Hill Cemetery 49
PROVINE
    Dorothy S. . . . . ix, xiii, 8, 18, 55, 65
Public Buildings 15
PYNE
    Smith, Rev. 32

Q

Quaker Burial Ground 49
Quaker Burying Ground 41
Quakers 41
Queen Farm Burying Ground 52
Queens Chapel Cemetery 45

R

RAPINE
    Daniel xvi
RAY
    Laura Collison 35
Real and Personal Property Assessments
    13
Real and Personal Property Records 11
Recognizances 57
Recorder of Deeds 11, 13, 65, 84
Records History xiii
Records of the Assistant Commissioner for the
    District of Columbia 74
Records of the Superintendent of Education for
    the District of Columbia 74
Register of Commissions of the District of
    Columbia Militia 71
Register of Licensed Physicians and Midwives
    67
Register of Officers of the Militia of the District of
    Columbia 71
Register of Wills 6-8, 84
Registers of Cadet Admissions, 1800-1953
    71
Registers of Enlistments in the United States
    Army, 1798-1914 68
Release of Debtors 54
Research Locations 84
Return of a Birth 23
Return of a Still Birth 23

Returns from U.S. Military Posts 1800-1916
    68
Revolutionary War 69
Rhode Island Avenue Methodist Protestant
    Church 38
RICHARD
    Frank Monnier 26, 27
    Justin E. 26, 27
    Minnie A. 26
    Minnie A. Engles 27
Richmond 38, 40, 70, 75
RIDGELY
    Helen West 52
Rock Creek xi
Rock Creek Cemetery 46, 49, 50
Rock Creek Church 33
Rock Creek Parish 33
Rock of Dumbarton xi
Rockville 32, 77
Rome xi
ROOSEVELT
    Theodore 71
Rosedale Methodist Church 41
Rosemont Cemetery 47, 50
Rule Book 58
Rules Case Files 54
Runaway Slaves Ledger 66
Russell Barracks 66
Ryan Chapel 34
Ryland Chapel of the Methodist Episcopal
    Church 37
Ryland Epworth United Methodist Church . 37
RYON
    Norman E. 50

S

SABIN
    Abigail Cooper 50
SCAGGS
    Sarah 51
Scaggs' [Family] Burial Ground 51
SCHAFFTER
    Dorothy 40
SCHOLFIELD
    Family 49
SEATON
    William W. xvi
SEAVER
    Family 49

Index

Second Baptist Church 30
Second Colored Church 37
Second Colored Wesleyan Church 37
Second Presbyterian Church 39, 40
Sedgwick Barracks 66
Senator Newspaper 63
Seventh Street Presbyterian Church 40
SHANNON
    J. Harry 64
SHEPHERD
    Infant 28
    Nancy 28
    William 28
Sheriff Farm Burying Ground 52
SHIVES
    Vallora L. 46
SHOEMAKER
    Family 49
    George 49
    Jonathan 49
    Pierce 51
Shoemaker's Farm [Family] Burial Ground
    51
SHOVAR
    David A. 46
Sibley Farm Burying Ground 52
Simm's Rope-Walk 36
Sixth Street Presbyterian Church 41
Slave Schedules 1
Slave Trade Records 53
Slavery Records 55
SLUBY
    Paul Edward 18, 34, 39, 42-52, 64
SMALLWOOD
    Samuel N. xvi
SMITH
    Richard 51
Smith's [Family] Burial Ground 51
SNOWDEN
    D.W. 25
Soldiers' Home 49, 70
Soldiers' Home Cemetery 51
South Carolina 75
Spain ix
Spanish-American War 68
SPINNER
    F.E. 73
Spirit of Seventy-Six Newspaper 64
St. Agnes Church 31
St. Alban's Protestant Episcopal Church .. 32

St. Elizabeth's Hospital 47
St. Elizabeth's Hospital Cemeteries 50
St. Francis DeSales Catholic Church 30
St. James Creek xi
St. John the Baptist Russian Orthodox Church
    50
St. John's Church 32
St. John's Protestant Episcopal Church 32, 33
St. Luke's United Methodist Church 38
St. Mary's Catholic Church 30
St. Mary's Chapel for Colored People 42
St. Mary's [German] Catholic Cemetery .. 50
St. Matthew's Catholic Cemetery 50
St. Matthew's Catholic Church 30
St. Patrick's Catholic Cemetery 51
St. Patrick's Catholic Church 30
St. Patrick's Church 39, 51
St. Paul's English Lutheran Church 34
St. Paul's Episcopal Church 33, 49
St. Peter's Catholic Cemetery 51
St. Peter's Roman Catholic Church 30
St. Stephens Church 41
St. Thomas Bay xi
States and Union Newspaper 63
STEIGER
    William Tell 25
STEPHENSON
    Richard W. 78
STERN
    Alfred W., Collection 5
Stet Calendar 58
STOTT
    Charles 40
STUART
    David xii
Subpoenas 54
Superior Court 17
Supersedeas Bonds 54
Supreme Court 17, 53, 55-62
SUTPHIN
    Eugene A. 9
    James T. 9
    Lucy R. 9
    Susan T. 9
    William A. 9
    William L. 9
    Winfred V. 9
SYLVESTER
    Richard 67

T

Tabernacle, The 38
TAPP
    Norman W. 50
    William A. 50
Tax Assessments 13, 67
Tax Lists . . . . xiii, 16
Tax Records 11, 14, 16
TAYLOR
    James Henry 38
TEBBS
    Moses 28
TEEPLES
    Gary Ronald 4
Temple Baptist Church 30
TEN EYCK
    Dorothy Lauder 33
Tennallytown 44, 77
THOMAS
    Milton P. 13
THOMPSON
    George 50
Tiber Creek . . . . xi, xii
Times and Patowmack Packet Newspaper
    63
TORBERT
    Alice C. 15
TOWERS
    John T. xvi
Trinity Catholic Church 46
Trinity German Evangelical Lutheran Church
    34
Trinity Methodist Church 35-37
Trinity Protestant Episcopal Church 33
TYLER
    Frederick Stansbury 31

U

Union Baptist Cemetery 52
Union Bethel African Methodist Episcopal
    Church 37
Union Chapel Methodist Episcopal Church
    37
Union Methodist Episcopal Church 37
Union Theological Seminary 38, 40
Union United Methodist Church 34
Union Wesley African Methodist Episcopal Zion
    Church 37
Union Wesley Chapel 37

Uniontown 34
United Church of Christ 37
United Methodist Church of Bradbury Heights
    38
United States Military Academy 52
United States Telegraph Newspaper 64
Universal Gazette Newspaper 64
University Baptist Church 30

V

VAN GENDER
    Sarah F. 16
VAN NESS
    General 30
    John P. xvi
    Marcia Burnes 31
Veitch Farm Burying Ground 52
Veterans' Census Schedules 70
VILAS
    Martin Samuel 51
VINTON
    Samue F. 73
Virginia . 2, ix, xii, 8, 24, 30, 38, 40, 41, 45, 46,
    49, 53, 64, 66, 69, 70, 74, 76-78, 82,
    83, 88
Vital Records Division 23, 84

W

WADDY
    Henry 47
WAESCHE
    H.T. 35
WALKER
    George 80
    Homer A. 8, 18
WALLACH
    Richard xvi
War of 1812 . . . . 35, 68, 69, 72
WASHINGTON
    George . . . . xii, 15
Washington Asylum 48, 51, 66
Washington Asylum Burial Ground . . . 48, 51
Washington Bee Newspaper 63
Washington Cathedral 32-34
Washington Cemetery 44
Washington City
    Charter . . . . xiii, xiv
    Incorporated xiii

Index

Plan of, Buildings in xxiv
Plan of, Lots in xxii
Washington City Chronicle Newspaper . . . 64
Washington City Weekly Gazette 64
Washington County . . . . xii, xiv, 8, 53, 63, 67
Washington Federalist Newspaper 63
Washington Gazette Newspaper 64
Washington Hebrew Congregation Cemetery
. . . . 51
Washington Light Infantry Battalion of Volunteers 70
Washington National Records Center 6, 7, 18
Washington Parish Burial Ground 44
Washington Republican & Congressional Examiner 64
Washington Star Newspaper 63, 64
Washington Times Herald Newspaper . . . 63
Washington Times Newspaper 63
WATERS
    Helen H. 48
    Helen R. 48
We the People Newspaper 64
WEIGHTMAN
    Roger C. xvi
WEINERT
    Janet 53
WELLS
    Charles J. 72
WELSH
    Sallie K. 46
    Welda A. 46
WENTZ
    Charles H. 30
Wesley Chapel of the Methodist Episcopal Church 38
Wesley Methodist Church 49
West Street Presbyterian Church 40
Western Burial Ground 46, 51
Westminster Presbyterian Church 40
Westminster United Presbyterian Church . 41
WHARTON
    C.H.W. 10
Widow's Mite Tract 80
Will Records 6
WILLIAMS
    Brooke 71
Wills 6, 8
    Abstracts 6
    Mary Alice 72
    Typescripts 6

WILSON
    Keziah 6
    Woodrow 38
    Zadoc 6
WINMILL
    Wylma 1
WINSLOW
    James H. 42
Woodlawn Cemetery 44, 46, 51
Works Projects Administration 33
World War I 71
WORMLEY
    Stanton Lawrence . 44, 46, 47, 49, 50, 52
WRIGHT
    F. Edward 18, 64, 72

Y

Yellow fever epidemic ix
YOUNG
    Abraham 80
    Notley . . . . xvi, 80
    Widow 80
    William 80
Young Men's Cemetery 28
Young Mens Burial (Colored) Ground 47

Z

ZACHRISON
    Shirley P. 1
ZOLLINGER
    Mary E. 48
ZUSCHNITT
    Katie 46
ZYPRECHT
    Mrs. 49
ZYTKOSKEE
    Laura T. 50

Other Heritage Books by Wesley E. Pippenger:

Alexandria (Arlington) County, Virginia Death Records, 1853-1896

Alexandria City and Arlington County, Virginia Records Index: Vol. 1

Alexandria City and Arlington County, Virginia Records Index: Vol. 2

Alexandria County, Virginia Marriage Records, 1853-1895

Alexandria Virginia Marriage Index, January 10, 1893 to August 31, 1905

Alexandria, Virginia Marriages, 1870-1892

Alexandria, Virginia Town Lots, 1749-1801, Together with the Proceedings of the Board of Trustees, 1749-1780

Alexandria, Virginia Wills, Administrations and Guardianships, 1786-1800

Alexandria, Virginia 1808 Census (Wards 1, 2, 3, and 4)

Alexandria, Virginia Death Records, 1863-1896

Alexandria, Virginia Hustings Court Orders, Volume 1, 1780-1787

Connections and Separations: Divorce, Name Change and Other Genealogical Tidbits from the Acts of the Virginia General Assembly

Daily National Intelligencer *Index to Deaths, 1855-1870*

Daily National Intelligencer, *Washington, District of Columbia Marriages and Deaths Notices (January 1, 1851 to December 30, 1854)*

Dead People on the Move: Reconstruction of the Georgetown Presbyterian Burying Ground, Holmead's (Western) Burying Ground, and other Removals in the District of Columbia

Death Notices from Richmond, Virginia Newspapers, 1841-1853

District of Columbia Ancestors, A Guide to Records of the District of Columbia

District of Columbia Death Records: August 1, 1874-July 31, 1879

District of Columbia Foreign Deaths, 1888-1923

District of Columbia Guardianship Index, 1802-1928

District of Columbia Interments (Index to Deaths), January 1, 1855 to July 31, 1874

District of Columbia Marriage Licenses, Register 1: 1811-1858

District of Columbia Marriage Licenses, Register 2: 1858-1870

District of Columbia Marriage Records Index, 1877-1885

District of Columbia Marriage Records Index, October 20, 1885 to January 20, 1892: Marriage Record Books 21 to 30

District of Columbia Probate Records, 1801-1852

District of Columbia: Original Land Owners, 1791-1800

Early Church Records of Alexandria City and Fairfax County, Virginia

Georgetown, District of Columbia 1850 Federal Population Census (Schedule I) and 1853 Directory of Residents of Georgetown

Georgetown, District of Columbia Marriage and Death Notices, 1801-1838

Husbands and Wives Associated with Early Alexandria, Virginia (and the Surrounding Area), 3rd Edition, Revised

Index to District of Columbia Estates, 1801-1929

Index to Virginia Estates, 1800-1865 Volumes 4, 5 and 6

John Alexander, a Northern Neck Proprietor, His Family, Friends and Kin

Legislative Petitions of Alexandria, 1778-1861

Pippenger and Pittenger Families

Proceedings of the Orphan's Court, Washington County, District of Columbia, 1801-1808

The Georgetown Courier *Marriage and Death Notices: Georgetown, District of Columbia, November 18, 1865 to May 6, 1876*

The Georgetown Directory for the Year 1830: to which is appended, a Short Description of the Churches, Public Institutions, and the Original Charter of Georgetown, and Extracts of the Laws Pertaining to the Chesapeake and Ohio Canal Company

The Virginia Gazette and Alexandria Advertiser: *Volume 1, September 3, 1789 to November 11, 1790*

The Virginia Journal and Alexandria Advertiser: *Volume I (February 5, 1784 to January 27, 1785)*

Volume II (February 3, 1785 to January 26, 1786)

Volume III (March 2, 1786 to January 25, 1787)

Volume IV (February 8, 1787 to May 21, 1789)

The Washington and Georgetown Directory of 1853

Tombstone Inscriptions of Alexandria, Volumes 1-4

www.ingramcontent.com/pod-product-compliance
Lightning Source LLC
Chambersburg PA
CBHW080550170426
43195CB00016B/2734